Defining America's
Social Problems

Defining America's Social Problems

Jack D. Douglas
University of California, San Diego

PRENTICE-HALL, INC.
Englewood, New Jersey

0-13-197624-9

Library of Congress Catalog Card Number 73-17263
PRINTED IN THE UNITED STATES OF AMERICA

10   9   8   7   6   5   4   3   2   1

PRENTICE-HALL INTERNATIONAL, INC., *London*
PRENTICE-HALL OF AUSTRALIA, PTY. LTD., *Sydney*
PRENTICE-HALL OF CANADA, LTD., *Toronto*
PRENTICE-HALL OF INDIA PRIVATE LIMITED, *New Delhi*
PRENTICE-HALL OF JAPAN, INC., *Tokyo*

Contents

Preface

Social problems has been a basic field of sociology since its beginnings in the nineteenth century. Indeed, without the desire to do something about social problems, and the consequent desire to use the scientific method to study those problems, most people probably would not be willing to put up with the "subversive ideas" of sociology and there would probably be no such intellectual discipline.

Regardless of its basic importance to sociology, the field of social problems has traditionally been a stagnant one with little effect on the rest of sociology and all too little effect on the rest of our society. The reason for this seems all too obvious. The traditional approach to social problems was really little more than a branch of social welfare and welfare political economics. The whole field was dominated by an overwhelmingly uncreative ethos. Rather than trying to provide basic insights into the nature of social problems, ideas that would illuminate our whole society and our whole social approach (or lack of approach) to social problems, the sociologists in this field insisted on restricting their work to testing out (and generally "unmasking") commonsense ideas about race, proverty, mental illness, divorce, and other *big* social problems. These sociologists followed in the van of commonsense ideas about social problems, provided what they believed to be "facts" about those problems which most people did not know or preferred not to face, and then provided some hints about social policies that might be adopted to deal with them.

This uncreative and even stereotyped approach to social problems was most apparent in the ideas about "social pathology" that dominated this field for decades. This entire approach assumed that there was a list of criminals, deviants, sick people, and evil conditions which constituted problems for the society. There was something *wrong* with them and the sociologists were going to help eradicate them. "Eliminate the pathology and the socially pathological" was the implicit slogan of this whole approach. Only rarely did they raise any questions about how or why some things or some people came to be seen as pathological, what it meant to be defined as pathological, whether they really fit the category of pathological, what the implications of such a labeling were, and so on.

This uncreative approach was also apparent in the "text-booky" cataloging of our social problems. Even when the federal government was setting up commissions to investigate what our social problems were, sociologists were still commonly assuming they knew what they were and that everybody would agree with them. They simply laid them out in a list. In fact, they laid them out in the table of contents of their text books. Any student who went through one of those social problems courses can well remember that assumption of sociological omniscience: "America's social problems are the following . . ."

As for our society more generally, our age of sociological innocence is past. Few sociologists today would make bland assertions about what our social problems are or about what should be done about them. Beginning with Robert K. Merton's analysis of the definitions of social problems and the inter-actionist analysis of social problems by Herbert Blumer and Howard Becker, we have come increasingly to see the social definition of social problems as a matter of great importance in itself and a highly problematic matter. Indeed, we have come to recognize that the social definition of social problems is crucial to determining whether anything will be done politically to deal with things we may personally consider to be problems. And we have come to recognize that these social definitions of what are and are not social problems are the outcomes of political processes that may be largely independent of the social conditions, the "things out there." Millions of people may waste away in poverty unless some individuals or some groups in our society succeed in convincing the government or other masses of citizens that they are indeed wasting away and that they do indeed constitute a social problem about which we should do something.

The sociology of social problems has suddenly become a creative and exciting field of study. No longer is the field dominated by sterotypes of common sense. Suddenly the discipline is able to offer fundamental insights into the whole nature of social problems in our society, rather than merely filling in the details of "evil things." While we have certainly not achieved any utopian state of insight, and are not likely to do so, I thing we can now make far greater contributions to our society's entire approach to social problems.

This book is primarily an attempt to present the basic developments that have produced this state of affairs in the sociology of social problems and then to add my own contribution to those developments. It is intended to be a creative analysis of the social definitions or social meanings of social problems, but it is built from the ground up in as clear a manner as possible so that any student at the introductory level can participate in the analysis. As such, it is aimed at being the beginning of the courses on social problems, regardless of the particular nature of one's later approach to the subject.

This book is also an attempt to show how it is that the social definition of social problems has become such an important activity in our society. I have tried to show that there are certain aspects of our technological society, especially certain aspects of our politics, which have made our social ideas about social problems crucial determinants of what gets done and doesn't get done in our society, especially by government.

Both professors and students have come increasingly to believe that understanding is the one crucial contribution education can make to students' lives. After the facts of how many poor there are have disappeared from memory or been made irrelevant by new facts, the understanding of the different meanings of "poverty" and how "poverty" is measured will remain and enable one to better deal with any problems of poverty in our society. Understanding is the goal of this book. If it contributes to our general social understanding of the nature of social problems, there is some hope that it will contribute more to our efforts to solve our social problems than a vastly greater amount of "fact-mongering" would ever do. Certainly it is my fondest hope that it will do so.

But every reader of this book will quickly discover that I have no hope of finding any easy or certain solutions to any of our social problems. The very nature of our social definitions of social problems and social solutions makes that impossible. I hope, then, that this book will foster caution, pessimism, and even suspicion about optimistic or simple ideas about solving our problems. They are the beginnings of sociological wisdom, of the kind of understanding we must have to provide any realistic, necessarily partial solutions to our problems. But neither the difficulties nor the necessary uncertainties should lead us to despair. Certainly I believe there are realistic grounds to hope that our greater sociological understanding can help us find better solutions to our problems. Without that hope, neither this book nor sociology would be worthwhile. I hope this book will foster a wiser approach to all social problems, not a desperate flight from them.

J.D.D.

Defining America's Social Problems

A great part of both the strength and the weakness of our national existence lies in the fact that Americans do not abide very quietly the evils of life. We are forever restlessly pitting ourselves against them, demanding changes, improvements, remedies, but not often with sufficient sense of the limits that the human condition will in the end insistently impose upon us. . . .

So we go off on periodical psychic sprees that purport to be moral crusades: liberate the people once and for all from the gold bugs, restore absolute popular democracy or completely honest competition in business, wipe out the saloon and liquor forever from the nation's life, destroy the political machines and put an end to corruption, or achieve absolute, total, and final security against war, espionage, and the affairs of the external world. The people who attach themselves to these several absolutions are not always the same people, but they do create for each other a common climate of absolutist enthusiasm. . . . It is its limitation that it often wanders over the border between reality and impossibility. This was, I believe, pre-eminently true of the Progressive generation. It is hardly an accident that the generation that wanted to bring about direct popular rule, break up the political machines, and circumvent representative government was the same generation that imposed Prohibition on the country and proposed to make the world safe for democracy.

Richard Hofstadter,
The Age of Reform.

Introduction

Man's experience of the problematic relationships between his needs and his world is so basic to his life that John Dewey and many others have seen all human thought as an attempt to cope with these problems. In the same way, man's experience of the problems he shares with his fellow men leads him to develop complex ideas and theories about social problems. An important part of all organized social action is determined by these ideas and aimed at solving these problems.

American society has always suffered from many things Americans defined as social problems, and much of our national effort has been directed towards solving such problems. Indeed, our federal government was formed in large part to solve certain social problems, especially economic ones, believed to be caused by the lack of a strong central government. But, until recently, we have generally felt confident that, however great, our social problems were fewer than those suffered by other societies and could be solved by reason and cooperation.

The traditional stereotype of Americans pictured us as inspired by soaring optimism. However great the obstacles of nature or man, however grim our immediate prospects, we were supposed to face the future with a firm conviction that something would turn up to transform these grim prospects into a happy fulfilment of our most urgent needs. At the least, we were supposed to believe that hard work, informed by the wisdom of man's inventive mind and guided by the invisible hand of God or fortune, would ultimately lead us to triumph over all adversities.

Like all stereotypes, this picture of soaring optimism was a distortion. American history shows us many famous figures who had dark forebodings of our national fate: Washington feared all "foreign entanglements" and sometimes saw the new American government as a perilous "experiment"; John Adams feared the anarchy of the democratic spirit; Jefferson feared the destruction of democracy in a nation of expanding cities; few historical figures show us a picture of more unrelenting sadness than that of Lincoln; and Henry Adams provided Western man with one of the most foreboding pictures of the industrial revolution. But, unlike many stereotypes, this one probably had some grain of truth. The almost unprecedented territorial expansion and economic growth of the United States in the nineteenth century was both the product and the reinforcer of a national spirit of soaring optimism. Few figures have been more typical of America than the public booster, the businessman proclaiming the "glorious future" of his city and of all those fortunate enough to invest their sweat or wealth in that future.

However true it may have seemed for an earlier age, this picture of the optimistic American has been shattered by the developments of the past quarter century. While there are still plenty of boosters and some unrelenting optimists, most Americans seem more doubtful, worried, even gloomy and foreboding, about the future. So deep has this sense of doubt become in recent years that soaring optimism has given way in some cases to an apocalyptic pessimism comparable in scope to Renaissance fears of impending universal chaos. The dread of an impending nuclear holocaust and of ecological doom has proven irresistible to many and at times has generated mass movements characterized by anxiety, anguish, bitter recriminations, and demands for an immediate end to all optimistic expansion. The vivid portrayals of our impending doom at times have approached the ghoulish delights of a medieval dance of death. We have entered a second era of progressivism which will surpass the first such era in its anxious concern with social problems.

In the last decade American society has been torn by bitter civil strife. Many of our cities have been struck by riots; most of our elite universities have been plagued by strikes, marches, sit-ins, rock-throwing, fires, and bombs. The call for revolution has been more insistent and widespread than it has been for fifty years or more. Millions who have not heeded the call to revolution nonetheless agree that something must be fundamentally wrong with American society. As men of common sense and practical wisdom see it, a time of unprecedented wealth and power is a time when there should be least unrest and self-doubt. If the United States has achieved what almost all people strive for and what Americans had looked forward to with such optimistic anticipation, why should there be so much doubt, anxiety, and danger? Worst of all, most of us had desired such prosperity and power in part precisely because we believed it would eliminate such anxieties and angers. The administrations in the 1960s sought to eliminate the social problems of poverty and ignorance by inducing rapid economic growth and by allocating great and growing sums of federal taxes to poor areas and to educational institutions—precisely where the greatest doubt and anger erupted *after* these programs has been launched.

These events have demonstrated once again the uncertainty and fragility of social order. They have shown us that no society, no matter how wealthy and powerful, is immune to deep anxieties and serious revolt. They have suggested that no society

can be immune to civil strife and even chaos, least of all one
as complex and constructed of as many disparate parts as
American society. As Arthur Schlesinger, Jr. has so vividly
described it, these events aroused the spectre of violence and
chaos in the mind of John F. Kennedy:

> To the President I would cite the Roosevelts, Wilson, Jack-
> son and so on in arguing the inevitability and superiority of
> the politics of combat as against the politics of consensus.
> But, while he did not dispute the historical points, he plainly
> saw no reason for rushing prematurely into battle.
>
> I think now he had deeper reasons for this than I
> understood at the time—that his cast of mind had a pro-
> founder source than a pragmatist's preference for a law over
> an issue, than a rationalist's distaste for give-'em-hell par-
> tisanship, or even than a statesman's need to hoard national
> confidence against the possibility that foreign crisis might
> require swift and unpopular presidential decisions. I believe
> today that its basic source may have been an acute and
> anguished sense of the fragility of the membranes of
> civilization, stretched so thin over a nation so disparate in
> its composition, so tense in its interior relationships, so
> cunningly enmeshed in underground fears and antagonisms,
> so entrapped by history in the ethos of violence.[1]

These events of the last decade and their attendant fears
have helped to convince an increasing number of Americans
that our conventional wisdom about social order and disorder,
and the relationship of social problems to this order and disorder,
is no longer adequate to deal with the situations we face in our
complex technological society. Though we shall always find it
necessary to rely upon the deeper wisdom of our common
humanity and our cultural tradition in setting our goals and
solving our problems, something more than conventional wisdom

[1] Arthur M. Schlesinger, Jr., *A Thousand Days* (Greenwich, Conn.:
Fawcett Publications, 1965), 664-665.

is needed to deal with social problems which are themselves partly the result of the destruction of conventions. We cannot revive dead conventions, or wait futilely for a new and more effective conventional wisdom to arise in a world that kills convention.

What is demanded is the objective knowledge of our social problems that can be provided only by the social sciences. We must forge an ever closer alliance between the deeper wisdom of our practical thought and this growing body of objective knowledge of our social problems, and we must do so with a sense of urgency born of a realization that many of the problems we face today could destroy us if we do not.

It is my purpose in this work to present and, hopefully, push forward the sociological understanding of social problems that we need. We shall find, however, that this central task of the sociology of social problems is not as simple as sociologists long thought. We shall find that the sociological enterprise itself poses some problems for society which we must manage effectively before we can completely fulfil the promise of sociological understanding. Moreover, rather than providing any simple categories of social problems, outlining the facts about them, and proposing what seem to me to be the solutions to them, we shall find it necessary to consider a vastly more complex realm of phenomena—*the social meanings of social problems.* Rather than imposing our own categories and thoughts about social problems upon society, we shall find it necessary to study social problems as defined by the many different groups in our pluralistic society. By doing so, however, we shall reveal a realm of social reality that few of us have ever considered and that I believe we shall find indispensable in understanding and finding practical solutions to the problems of our ever more complex technological society.

chapter 1

Man in Crisis:
The Relevance of Sociology

We are moving rapidly and irrevocably into a new world. Many of the ancient assumptions underlying human social existence are being transformed by the scientific-technological revolution. Science and technology have been growing steadily in the Western societies for several centuries, but only in our own century has all of mankind been swept up in their advance; and only with the advent of nuclear power and the computer since World War II has it become obvious that science and technology are producing the first man-made revolution that will unalterably transform the fates of all men.

Although this revolution is already worldwide, American society, the world center of science and technology today, is both the prime source of the revolution and the society being most rapidly transformed by it. Because we are at the center of this transformation and are already so intimately involved in it, it is often more difficult for us to see how revolutionary it is than for those who have not been so profoundly affected by it. The changes resulting from science and technology have become so much a part of our lives that we do not normally see them or

7

the ways in which they are affecting us personally as well as the foundations of our society. Even the beginnings of the space age have been so rapidly assimiliated that landings on the moon have relatively little emotional impact on Americans, though people around the world have been stirred. The mass media have had to resort to dramatizations of events to overcome the emotional discounting of change we have adopted to screen-out the constant barrage of emotional stimuli to which we are subjected.

Much of this screening-out is a result of the intense competition by mass medias for our limited attention—and our patronage. Even news of international crises has become so commonplace that it elicits little sense of alarm. With our vast communication networks webbing the earth, ready to send instant messages of urgency and distress from every electronically rigged corner of earth—or outer space—many of us have become jaded by the seemingly endless social convulsions and human suffering.

The young, who are rarely tuned in to this vast news network until they reach college age, often recoil in horror when they do become aware of the cruel deaths of a million human beings in the distant jungles of Biafra, or the years of carnage in the rice paddies of Vietnam, or any of the hundreds of other "hot news items" that agitate the electronic web. In their new-found anguish some of them would destroy the infamy that they believe has allowed such enormities to become facts of life. They lash out at all established powers, believing that those powers must have caused it all. This young minority lacks perspective because they do not yet know the immense history of human suffering, the frightful intricacies of any society, and the intractability of many of the problems even when attacked with the concerted good will of all involved. But the relative lack of perspective of some of the young is more than counterbalanced by the lack of perspective on the part of many of the older members of our society. They have become so jaded over the

years by the many news flashes about these crises and so pessimistic about the possibilities of doing anything about them that
they have lost the proper sense of their enormity. Worst of all,
having become inured through overexposure to such instant
crises and to the immense changes produced by science and
technology, most members of our society seem to have become
inured as well to the more profound and longlasting crises that
confront us. They have become blind to the many growing
threats to their most cherished values and their own lives. Even
the public outcries against the more immediate crises, such as
the pollution of our natural environment, often serve to focus
attention away from the underlying, prolonged social crises we
face. The preoccupation with symptoms and their treatment
becomes an escape from the more frightening causes of those
symptoms and from the pain we shall have to endure to prevent
even worse problems in the future.

The Prolonged Crisis and Sociology

There are serious disagreements among the analysts of social
problems concerning what are underlying causes and what are
merely symptoms of social problems. To deny the validity of
these disagreements would be both wrong and presumptuous.
But at the same time there seems to be basic agreement among
social analysts and social critics on two major points concerning
our present situation. First, it is generally agreed that science
and technology are fundamental causes of the great changes that
are taking place in our world today. Second, it is generally
agreed that times of great social change involve great social
dislocations, conflicts, and suffering. Unfortunately, the relationship between these two points, and their implications for our
society, are rarely noted: if we accept these two ideas, then it

seems clear that *we must expect the accelerating pace of scientifically and technologically induced social change to produce an accelerating rate of social dislocation, conflict, and suffering, at least for some parts of our society.*

The industrial revolution that took place over several centuries in Western societies was an important source of revolutions, wars, and increased suffering for millions of people. Ancient institutions, beliefs, and values were destroyed or transformed; old elites were cast down and new ones uplifted; some classes were impoverished, while others were enriched; many people were enslaved by colonization, while a few were made free; and weapons of war were made vastly more destructive without any compensating increases in the arts of peace. It would be a mistake to look only at the costs of the industrial revolution without seeing the vast enrichment of everyday lives that eventually grew out of it, or to conclude that all of these developments were simple and inevitable outcomes of that revolution. Industrialization was only one crucial process among many complex ones, all involving free choices by individuals, that brought about these developments. Most of us would probably agree that, on balance, the industrial revolution has produced more good than harm. But how many of us, understanding the terrible costs in broken lives and destroyed values, would so willingly commit ourselves and other men to such a centuries-long path of development? Even more, had they understood the costs, how many men of the sixteenth or seventeenth centuries would have willingly committed themselves and their successors to such a historical path?

There is a surface similarity between this kind of "if-we-had-only-known" exercise and the choices facing us today. Since we have every reason to expect that the scientific and technological revolution, being so much more sweeping than the earlier industrial revolution, has the potential of producing far greater dislocations, conflicts, and suffering, do we not face a situation in which the choice of allowing science and technology to develop further necessarily entails the decision to accept or promote these far greater dislocations, conflicts, and suffering? And, therefore, do we not face a situation in which all humane, if not all sane, men must choose the opposite path of trying to progressively limit, or even destroy, the "evil forces" of science and technology? Those who are already captives of the revolutionary forces, and who, therefore, can no longer stand back to critically evaluate them, may scoff; but this view of science and technology as evil forces that must be returned to their Pandora's box is one that has gained increasing credibility among educated men as one doomsday machine has followed another in the atomic age, as each new missile system has become more totally destructive than the one before, and as each new pollutant has made our environment more dangerous. In recent years some of the young who share this belief have even become modern Luddites who seek to destroy the "evil machines" and stop the builders from devising new ones.

Some have tried to defend the scientific-technological revolution with the old argument about the *competition trap.* They rightly point out that, even if we tried to reverse the revolution, our competitors and enemies would not have to follow suit. Indeed, our dropping-out might well be an incentive for them to speed up to get an ever greater advantage over us, perhaps eventually to conquer or destroy us. But this argument, however valid, is relevant only to the question of tactics. The counter-revolutionists need only argue that we must seek international agreements to stop or reverse the development of science and technology in exactly the same way we have sought agreements to limit the development of germ warfare, nuclear weapons, and missile delivery systems.

Another argument used against the counterrevolutionaries is that of "impracticality": it is supposed to be impractical to oppose the unfettered development of science and technology because the vast majority of people, having forgotten their erstwhile fears of the "mad scientist," are now firmly committed to the revolution. But if we must actually anticipate a few centuries of social upheavals and conflicts in which some of the antagonists are armed with doomsday machines produced by the technologists, how practical would we be to go along with the current vicissitudes of public opinion? If we have no real hope of better anticipating and solving the social problems resulting from great social changes than did the men of the industrial age, then surely the only *practical* choice of educated men would be to try desperately to change public opinion before we are all destroyed by the "blind march of progress."

At this point the supporters of the revolution might remind us that in spite of the suffering induced by the industrial revolution, the practical wisdom of common sense, as used by politicians in making crucial social policies, did in the end prove sufficient to produce an outcome that most of us would accept as better than where we started. Using this as a precedent, one might then argue that we have reason to hope for the same outcome from the scientific-technological revolution. But the industrial revolution, while more closely related to our present social revolution than any other, cannot really serve as a precedent for what is happening today. The scientific and technological revolution is far too sweeping, and some of its products far too destructive, for us to place any hope in the same common sense decision-making processes that enabled us to muddle through the industrial revolution. That common sense, which by the first half of the twentieth century had produced the industrial slums, the fascist tyrannies, a worldwide depression, the strategic bombings of many of the great centers of civilization, and the progressive pollution of our natural environment, would give us little hope of avoiding far greater devastation and far worse technological tyrannies if it were armed with the ultimate weapons of the technological age and faced with immensely more complicated social problems.

As I shall argue below, we must inevitably rely upon the practical understanding of politicians and diplomats to produce concrete solutions to our problems, but in the complex and dangerous era of science and technology such political action, however great the practical wisdom involved, will not be sufficient to solve problems and prevent crises. Because science and technology add a new level of complexity to the problems of our society, we shall have to move to a new level of complexity in producing the knowledge necessary to deal with those problems. We shall have to rely increasingly on the knowledge made available by the social sciences to guide our practical political actions aimed at solving and averting social problems.

There is, of course, a seeming paradox involved in relying increasingly on the sciences of society to solve the problems caused by the effects of science and technology on society. And certainly there are good grounds to fear that any simpleminded use of such a policy of *social homeopathy* (that is, of applying more of the same science to solve the problems created by science) will in fact only produce more problems. But there are better grounds for believing that we can avoid the seeming paradox and its dangers, as long as we take them seriously and deal with them realistically. At the most general level, as Gerald Holton has argued, there is plenty of precedent for hoping that this homeopathic remedy can work:

> The dire state of affairs is supposed to be remedied by an injection of a larger scientific and technological component into our culture, yet the recent advances in science and technology are themselves identified as the forces responsible for the state of affairs in the first place. These are the agencies that have been contributing to the enormous increase in the rate of innovation and social change, and that have helped to perfect new weapons that make the possibility of instantaneous destruction of Western civilization a real and continued threat. Thus, it would seem that we are asked to seek safety by delivering ourselves more

fully to the very forces that appear to be responsible for the crisis.

While we may intuitively feel that the choice is unpleasant, it is perhaps not necessarily so paradoxical as it seems. A number of social or physical systems offer models in which stability, when disrupted by the introduction of a new factor, can be re-established at some level only by increasing the role of the new factor even further. Examples that come readily to mind are the introduction of literacy or industrialization or political emancipation into a traditional primitive society. Or, again, when an ionized atom begins to capture an electron, energy in the form of photons will in general continue inexorably to be radiated from the system until the electron has passed through the various energy levels to the ground state, at which point the quantum numbers symbolizing the system have the smallest values and the system is again stable.[1]

At the more concrete level there are many problems created by the very science created to deal with the increasingly complex problems of an increasingly technological society. But we can only deal with the problems created by sociology once we have discussed how sociology is potentially of crucial importance in solving the problems of increasing technology.

The Unique Commitment of Sociology: Solving Social Problems

Social scientists know that the social sciences developed much later and more slowly than the natural sciences, yet they

[1] Gerald Holton, *Science and Culture* (Boston: Beacon Press, 1967), p. X.

have commonly treated this fact as a historical accident, or worse, simply as the justification for the less developed state of the social sciences. But there are good reasons for believing that this obvious historical fact was no accident and is more important than an excuse.

The relatively slow development of the social sciences in the Western world is especially remarkable because one of the basic motives of the early natural scientists was their desire to understand God better by studying what God had created—the *natural* world. Yet, if this were so, why would they not first direct their scientific work toward that one creature, man, who they believed was created in God's image and the study of whom would, therefore, seem to reveal the most about the Creator? Why would so deeply religious a man as Isaac Newton seek his God in the paths of the moon or the trajectories of natural bodies rather than in the works of man? Why did it not seem strange to him that God should be revealed better in the forces of gravity than in the meaningful forces that move men to act? Why did this question not seem to warrant any serious consideration?

Some historians of science might argue that Newton and hundreds of other scientists were committed to studying the paths of the moon and the trajectories of bodies because they believed that these alone were subject to description and analysis in terms of the "magick of number," which they believed was an embodiment of the holy. But Spinoza had already tried to analyze human morality in terms of geometry, and in Newton's day John Graunt had shown how one could quantitatively analyze mortality statistics of London to try to reveal truths about man similar to those learned long before about natural bodies. Moreover, at least one of them saw a direct connection between the quantitative analysis of social phenomena and the study of the divine order of God, as we can see in the title of Johann Peter Süssmilch's important work on demography in the middle of the eighteenth century—*Die Göttliche Ordnung in den*

Veränderungen des menschlichen Geschlechts (The Divine Order in the Variations in Human Affairs). Yet this approach was not picked up by others and developed further.

This failure of the great majority of scientists and non-scientists to see the early developments in the social sciences as a great opportunity to pursue their religious motivations through the scientific study of man may seem less strange if we remember that a large percentage of men in our own day, a time when men are deeply committed to the scientific mode of thought, still strongly resist any idea of applying science to the study of man. This present resistance would suggest that there was a similar resistance in the seventeenth and eighteenth centuries, which was so powerful that men hardly had to express it and which is related to some lasting aspects of Western culture.

There seems to be a basic conflict between Western man's traditional common sense view of the nature of man and the scientific standpoint. The *natural stance* of common sense regards as *absolute* the values, motives, feelings, and ideas of the self as actor: they are largely unquestioned and unexamined, their validity taken for granted.[2] Values are seen as the most absolute of these and, indeed, as imposed by God from outside the individual. Consequently, the man of common sense who took this absolutist view would never question or examine his values, never ask himself, "Should I have this value or some other value?" Though he was less absolutist about his feelings, motives, and ideas, recognizing them as influenced by the world of objects and therefore as more subject to examination and questioning, he commonly took them for granted as well and saw them as a necessary part of being. Just as it was believed that God had imposed on man the values or morals by which he was to live, it was also originally believed that God had "revealed" the

---

[2] I have previously analyzed the absolutism of values in *American Social Order: Social Rules in a Pluralistic Society* (New York: The Free Press, 1971).

truth about such things as the structure of the universe, though the latter was examined and questioned in an object-like, or objective, manner long before a nonabsolutist view of values could be entertained.

Science examined and studied nature. To turn this form of thought upon oneself not only threatened to treat the self, the subject, as an object, but also brought into dispute the un-questioned bases of action—the feelings, motives, ideas, and values of the actor. The scientific approach to the study of man seemed to threaten Western man's whole concept of himself and the foundation of practical action. It is little wonder that he steadfastly resisted taking the scientific view of himself.[3] Yet the truth is that this resistance was eventually overcome; by the nineteenth century a large and growing proportion of educated people in the Western societies were accepting this scientific view of man. Why?

It is important to note first that the dominant forms of early social sciences were precisely those that challenged least of all the traditional absolutist view of man. Much of early social science, in fact, consisted of analyses of non-Western societies, especially primitive societies, whose members could be treated as objects and whose values could be objectively analyzed without directly threatening Western man's universe of meanings. Very importantly, as we shall see at the beginning of Chapter 2, the early social science studies of Western society shared the absolutist views of the natural stance of common sense: the early social sciences merely substituted a scientific absolutism for the absolutism of common sense. Yet even this form of social science threatened the common sense bases of action to some degree, so there must have been good reason for accepting it.

While some men may be moved by lofty commitments to

[3] For a detailed treatment of these issues see Jack D. Douglas, *The Impact of Sociology* (New York: Appleton-Century-Crofts, 1970), pp. 250-280.

the search for truth, even to the extent of accepting a soul-rending change in their natural perspective on the world, most men are bound by the practical considerations of their everyday lives and, in fact, are convinced that the very nature of truth is tied up with the practical constraints of that everyday life. *The great majority of men could only be convinced to accept the scientific view of man (and therefore of themselves) because it seemed necessary for practical reasons to do so.*

As the Western societies became more complex, in good part because of the rapid development of natural science and technology, the absolutist stance of common sense was no longer able to provide the information and explanations of society that people felt they needed to adequately solve their practical problems in everyday life. The officials responsible for solving social problems were the first to feel this need, and as we shall see below, part of their need was for the rhetorical power that scientific forms gave their pronouncements rather than for "hard" scientific information and theories. But the sincere feeling of need has spread as our societies have become more complex.

Since its origins as an independent discipline in the nineteenth century, sociology has been dedicated to developing a science of man that would be specifically oriented toward solving the increasingly complex social problems of Western societies.[4] All of the other social sciences are either committed to studying other societies or earlier periods of our own society, as is the case with anthropology and history, or are committed to studying some narrow aspect of our societies, as is the case with political science and economics. Because of this, sociology has a *unique* commitment to providing us with the knowledge we feel we need to find practical solutions to our social problems. But what is

[4] Durkheim put this commitment very strikingly in *The Rules of Sociological Method* when he said, "Why strive for knowledge of reality if this knowledge cannot serve us in life?"

there about sociology that would lead a reasonable man to expect it to provide the kind of knowledge he needs to deal with our social problems today?

The Need for Scientific Knowledge in a Complex Society

Commonsense attitudes are determined primarily by the practical interests facing an individual at a particular time in a concrete situation. The man of commonsense wants to know how to get a job in order to provide his family with food and shelter— right now and in the situation he faces, not next year and not in the situation someone else faces. His thinking about economic problems, then, is largely restricted to solving his own problems in getting a job or succeeding at a job, rather than aimed at understanding the general problems society has in ensuring employment and success for its members.

In a reasonably simple society, such as the American agricultural society up through the nineteenth century, this practical man needed to understand little more about society than what he could see in his immediate surroundings. He needed to know about land and farming, about weather and building; if he wished to work for someone else, he needed to know his neighbors and how to present himself as a good worker; if he planned to sell some part of his crop to others, he needed to know the local market to decide what kinds of crops he should plant. But as the social realm of what is relevant to his practical situation expanded, becoming more complex, more inter-dependent, and more rapidly changing, he needed to know more and more about larger segments of society if he were to make a living at farming. As his market became more interdependent with the market of the state, the nation, or the world, he needed increasingly to be able to anticipate and control what would happen far from home if he were to avoid disastrous swings in his crop prices; yet the growing complexity and change made the acquiring of this knowledge ever more difficult for the man bound to his immediate situation.

In an increasingly complex and changing society, as all Western societies have been for several centuries, the knowledge needed to solve practical problems must steadily expand in scope beyond the immediate situation, must increasingly consider complex interdependencies, and must increasingly be able to anticipate future situations. The only kind of knowledge that meets these requirements is scientific knowledge, for this is the only knowledge that is specifically *transituational* or *objective,* that is, going beyond and largely independent of the goals and situations of those creating the knowledge. It is precisely knowledge of this sort about social problems that sociology is uniquely committed to providing for society, and it is for this reason that sociology and the more specialized social sciences have become increasingly important in solving our social problems.

Sociology's simplest contribution to practical attempts to solve our social problems is objective knowledge of many different parts of our massive and complex society. We can see how important this contribution is when we consider the situation of the decision maker at the federal level. Any man responsible for solving national social problems almost inevitably lacks first-hand knowledge of the problem as experienced throughout the many parts of this vast society. He may know what unemployment is like in Washington or Los Angeles, and he may even have direct experience of the problem in several places; but he will almost inevitably be ignorant of the details of the problem throughout most of the society. Moreover, he can be sure that unemployment in West Virginia will be different from unemployment in Los Angeles. How is he to find out what is going on in the many parts of the society?

There are several possible sources of this knowledge, a few

of which have been used for centuries by government leaders faced with such ignorance. One obvious possibility is to ask the man involved, for surely he will know the truth of what is going on in his own realm of everyday life. But, even granting that he does know the truth, which may not be the case in such a complex technological world as ours, it is apparent to any decision maker that he might not tell the truth, since he generally has an important stake in the decision being made. The same would hold true of any elected representatives of the people directly involved. Mayors or governors, for example, would not be the best people to ask how money for urban renewal should be spent throughout the country, for they are generally even more involved in financial dealings at the local level than the average citizen. Alternatively, one might send out one's own emissaries to find out what is going on. Since they are not directly involved in the local situation, they could normally be expected to be more objective—and more honest—in their reports. But while this method of getting information on local situations is far better than the first, it has the disadvantage of relying on individuals who are wholly outsiders, who may well have their own axes to grind in their reports to the central administrations, and who may not be at all adept in objectively determining what is going on.

The next step in trying to get reliable and valid information about what is going on throughout a complex society is to make use of men who do not have local commitments that would lead to dishonest reports, who have no axes to grind with the central administration, who have developed methods of getting objective information on social situations, and who have invested the time and effort necessary to get systematic, objective information on many parts of the society. While this is too idealized a version of contemporary sociologists, sociologists generally fit this picture better than any other significant group creating information about our society.

As we shall see in Chapter 2, the difficulty of getting valid

36422

and reliable information on social problems is especially great in American society because it is so pluralistic.[5] The pluralism of our society helps to produce great disagreements over what is happening in its different parts, *even among those who are observing the same situation.* This is so because the people observing the same situation may be members of different groups that share different meanings relevant to that situation. We can easily see this from two examples of differences in interpretation that have had great importance in producing and maintaining some commonly defined social problems.

It has long been common knowledge that there exists great conflicts between the police and various minority groups in urban America, conflicts that align whole communities against the police, even when these communities are deeply concerned about controlling crime in their areas. For example, it has been recognized that many of the urban riots in the 1960s, such as the Watts riot, were directed at the police by a wide spectrum of the black communities. What has not been commonly recognized is that a large part of these conflicts is a direct result of different meanings imputed to everyday situations in which the police and the minority groups encounter each other. Some of these differences in interpretation have been vividly described by Irving Piliavin and Carl Werthmann in their sociological study of the police in such a community:

> From the front seat of a moving patrol car, street life in a typical Negro ghetto is perceived as an uninterrupted sequence of suspicious scenes. Every well dressed man or woman standing aimlessly on the street during hours when most people are at work is carefully scrutinized for signs of an illegal source of income; every boy wearing boots, black pants, long hair, and a club jacket is viewed as potentially responsible for some item on the list of muggings,

---

[5] For a consideration of the evidence and arguments about this pluralism see *American Social Order, op. cit.*

broken windows, and petty thefts that still remain to be cleared; and every hostile glance directed at the passing patrolman is read as a sign of possible guilt.

The residents of the neighborhoods regard this kind of surveillance as the deepest of insults. As soon as a patrolman begins to interrogate, the suspect can easily see that his moral identity is being challenged because of his dress, his hair style, his skin color, and his presence in the ghetto itself.

Negro gang members are constantly singled out for interrogation by the police, and the boys develop their own techniques of retaliation. They taunt the police with jibes and threaten their authority with gestures of insolence, as if daring the police to become bigots and bullies in order to defend their honor. Moreover, these techniques of retaliation often do succeed in provoking this response. When suspect after suspect becomes hostile and surly, the police begin to see themselves as representing the law among a people that lack proper respect for it. They too begin to feel maligned, and they soon become defensively cynical and aggressively moralistic. From the point of view of a patrolman, night sticks are only used upon sufficient provocation, and arrests are only made with just cause.[6]

Jerome Skolnick has shown the same kind of conflict over the meanings imputed to commonly observed situations in his analysis of the *social meanings of social order* between the police on the one hand and minority communities on the other. In this particular example he tries to show the different and frequently conflicting meanings of "social order":

Not only are the police in a democracy the product of a series of compromises between conflicting principles or ideas, but the ideas themselves are not as clear as they (and we)

[6] Carl Werthman and Irving Piliavin, "Gang Members and the Police," in David Bardua, *The Police* (New York: John Wiley, 1957), pp. 56-57.

have so far suggested. If "law and order" is a misleading cliche, then a gross conception of order may be even more misleading. Depending on the institution or community, there may be quite different conceptions of order, some more permissive, others less. A traditional martial conception of order, for example, abhors individual differences. The soldier whose bearing or uniform sets him off from his comrades in arms is an abomination to his commanding officer. Even the slightest deviation, such as wearing gloves on a cold day, is forbidden as an expression of differences in individual feelings. In any given military unit, either all the soldiers wear gloves, or none do. The hands of some soldiers will perspire, others will be numb with cold, but all soldiers *will* act alike.

Other institutions or portions of society are traditionally more yielding. The area surrounding the University of Paris is noted for its emphasis upon individuality. Students, artists, writers may be dressed elegantly or poorly, raffishly or provocatively, the mode being considered an extension of the ego, an expression of personality, or perhaps merely an attempt to experiment with novelty. The idea of order in this setting is surely a more permissive conception than the standard military notion. Our conclusion is that conceptions of order seem to be variable and tend to correspond to the requirements of different communities or institutions.[7]

Urban police are normally outsiders in the poorer areas they patrol and large segments of these poorer communities distrust or even hate the police.[8] Given a situation of mutual distrust and suspicion, the police departments have found it extremely difficult to recruit qualified patrolmen from these areas. This helps to ensure that patrolmen will be outsiders to the communities

---

[7] Jerome Skolnick, *Justice without Trial* (New York: John Wiley, 1967), p. 10.

[8] I have discussed the reasons for this in *Crime and Justice in American Society* (New York: Bobbs-Merrill, 1971), pp. 3-44.

they patrol and ensure that they will remain outsiders, unable to get close enough to the people to find out how they see things. Yet to do efficient patrol work, the police must have an understanding of the meanings of things to the people. Otherwise, they will not know what to make of the things they see. What happens is that the police are forced to give to situations *ad hoc meanings* that seem plausible to them, without being able to know if this is how the people see it. Consequently, the police all too frequently misinterpret what the people are doing and wind up causing further distrust and suspicion. Instead of acting in such a way as to solve problems, they commonly exacerbate them, and their very attempts to solve problems can create new ones. (Social problems caused by attempts to solve earlier social problems are increasingly common and are important enough to be given the special name of *iatrogenic social problems—* iatrogenic because they are analogous to the iatrogenic diseases caused by medical treatment of other illnesses.)

In such situations the police are not able to get the information they need. The sociologist, who has developed the *methods of participant observation* precisely for the purpose of getting reliable and valid information on the meanings shared by a group, is able to do so better than anyone else.[9] Such information then becomes available to anyone who wishes to understand how such groups see things so that they can at least avoid the absurd conflicts based on misunderstandings.

The second example of the importance of the sociologist in providing information on the disparate parts of our society has great bearing on all policy decisions dealing with our urban problems, which affect the expenditure of billions of dollars. In the early part of this century the progressive movement led a great crusade against the slums. The reformers and social

---

[9] For analyses of the problems involved in participant-observer studies involving potential distrust see the essays in Jack D. Douglas, ed., *Observing Deviance* (New York: Random House, 1971).

workers who were prominent in this social movement were convinced that the slums bred social disorder (or social disorganization) and thereby produced every kind of vice and depravity. They concluded that only a massive destruction of the old slums, and their complete replacement by new (clean) housing, would end this social disorder and thereby all of the vice and depravity. The working-class and lower-class people who live in the slums would be turned into "clean, virtuous, middle-class citizens" by putting them into the "clean, virtuous environments" of middle-class people. These beliefs led them to propose sweeping, vastly expensive social programs to replace the slums with government housing projects. As these ideas and the belief in the program spread, they became basic justifications for the extensive urban renewal programs of the federal and local governments.

After scores of sociological studies and many years of failure of the urban renewal programs to eliminate crime, it is now clear that this whole analysis was based on a terrible misunderstanding of the nature of social life in slums, resulting from outsiders imposing their own meanings of "filth," "street life," and "dilapidated housing" on the social groups who lived in the slums. The sociologists found that there are many different kinds of social life in slums, many different reasons why people live in the slums, and that slums are no more the "disorganized progenitors" of the vice to be found in them than suburban homes and spacious lawns are progenitors of the false advertising, fraudulent business practices, embezzlement, and wife swapping practiced by some of their inhabitants. Indeed, many slums were found by sociologists to have a social life quite the opposite of that conceived by the slum-haters. John Seeley has provided one of the most striking descriptions of this contrast:

> Slums differ, of course, and I have lived intensively only in one, Back-of-the-Yards, Chicago, in the early 'forties, and, together with others, have studied another, "Relocation Area A" in Indianapolis. I do not intend to give in detail

any account of the former, especially as the main features of a somewhat similar area were sketched in William Foote Whyte's *Street Corner Society*. Something of the intensity, excitement, rewardingness, and color of the slum that I experienced is missing from his account of his slum, either because his *was* different or because sociological reporting militates against vibrancy of description (or, perhaps, because we cut into the material of our participant-observer experience in different ways). In any case, I would have to say, for what it is worth, that no society I have lived in before or since, seemed to me to present to so many of its members so many possibilities and actualities of fulfillment of a number at least of basic human demands: for an outlet for aggressiveness, for adventure, for a sense of effectiveness, for deep feelings of belonging without undue sacrifice of uniqueness or identity, for sex satisfaction, for strong if not fierce loyalties, for a sense of independence from the pervasive, omnicompetent, omniscient authority-in-general, which at that time still overwhelmed the middle-class child to a greater degree than it now does. These things had their prices, of course—not all values can be simultaneously maximized. But few of the inhabitants whom I reciprocally took "slumming" into middle-class life understood it, or, where they did, were at all envious of it. And, be it asserted, this was not a matter of "ignorance" or incapacity to "appreciate finer things." It was merely an inability to see one moderately coherent and sense-making satisfaction-system which they didn't know, as preferable to the quite coherent and sense-making satisfaction system they did know. This is not analogous to Beethoven versus boogie-woogie, but more nearly to the choice between English and French as a vehicle of expression. (I will not even say which is which.) [10]

[10] John R. Seeley, "The Slum: Its Nature, Use, and Users," *Journal of The American Institute of Planners*, Volume XXV (February, 1959), pp. 7-14.

Insofar as this misunderstanding led to the planned destruction of old slum communities, it contributed to the misdirected expenditure of billions of dollars by federal and local agencies. Insofar as the destruction of old slum communities actually contributed to further crime, unhappiness, and so on, the conventional ideas about slums produced iatrogenic social problems.

This second example offers us a fine illustration not only of the need for social scientists who can provide valid information on the different segments of our society, but also of the dangers of providing invalid information when social scientists unquestioningly take the standpoint of commonsense understandings. For several decades sociologists, almost all of whom came from "clean middle-class backgrounds," and almost all of whom wanted to "do something for the poor to reduce their suffering," took the same view of the slums as the social workers and the progressives. Having made the same basic assumptions that slum life was disorganized and produced crime and vice, the sociologists then unconsciously oriented their research in such a way that they "proved" what they had assumed all along. Instead of getting inside the slum communities to see how the people of the slums understood their world, the sociologists stood outside and imposed the old commonsense (middle-class) meanings on the slums, until William Foote Whyte took the revolutionary step of living part-time in a Boston slum for three years and learned how to understand what things meant to the Italian-Americans who lived there.[11]

While there are problems involved in providing objective, factual information on the many segments of our society, the task of providing such information is the easiest part to fulfill of sociology's unique commitment.. The far more difficult and potentially more important part of our task is providing valid

---

[11] William Foote Whyte, *Street Corner Society* (Chicago: University of Chicago Press, 1955).

scientific explanations of social events which will allow us both to explain the interdependencies of present events and eventually to predict future events.

By comparing the commonsense and sociological theories of crime, we can see the great importance of theoretical explanations of the relations among social factors in any attempt to solve social problems. To most middle- or upper-class Americans the causes of crime and the ways of preventing crime are largely taken for granted. Those who take this natural stance toward crime see crime as a violation of social rules that are absolute because some things are "always wrong and always will be." They also see crime as the result of highly individual factors, such as "evil or sick personalities," and believe that strict enforcement of the laws and harsh prison sentences that represent the criminal's "debt to society" are the way to end crime for all time. These commonsense, theoretical ideas lie behind most police work and behind much of the social policy for dealing with crime passed at the national and local levels over the years, including the crime control bills passed in the 1960s.

Sociological studies of crime have revealed that almost all of the basic assumptions of this commonsense view are wrong. First, anthropologists and sociologists found that violations of social rules are found in all societies and among all groups of people. As Durkheim argued, the existence of rule violations seems to be related to something basic about societies:

> Crime is present not only in the majority of societies of one particular species but in all societies of all types. There is no society that is not confronted with the problem of criminality. Its form changes; the acts thus characterized are not the same everywhere; but, everywhere and always, there have been men who have behaved in such a way as to draw upon themselves penal repression. . . .
>
> Here we are, then, in the presence of a conclusion in appearance quite paradoxical. Let us make no mistake. To

classify crime among the phenomena of normal sociology is not to say merely that it is an inevitable, although regrettable phenomenon, due to the incorrigible wickedness of men; it is to affirm that it is a factor in public health, an integral part of all healthy societies. This result is, at first glance, surprising enough to have puzzled even ourselves for a long time. Once this first surprise has been overcome, however, it is not difficult to find reasons explaining this normality and at the same time confirming it.

In the first place crime is normal because a society exempt from it is utterly impossible. Crime, we have shown elsewhere, consists of an act that offends certain very strong collective sentiments. In a society in which criminal acts are no longer committed, the sentiments they offend would have to be found without exception in all individual consciousnesses, and they must be found to exist with the same degree as sentiments contrary to them. Assuming that this condition could actually be realized, crime would not thereby disappear; it would only change its form, for the very cause which would thus dry up the sources of criminality would immediately open up new ones.[12]

This not only challenges the whole idea of "ending crime for all time," but also raises serious questions about the relationship between rule violations and other aspects of society. Sociologists first tried to show the ways in which other aspects of society are important in leading individuals to commit crimes. But they eventually came to see the nature of the rules themselves as important elements in the social processes producing crimes. They recognized this partly because it became so obvious that different societies have different laws specifying different kinds of actions as crimes. But they recognized it also because it was clear from any study of the history of laws in Western societies

[12] Emile Durkheim, *The Rules of Sociological Method* (Glencoe: The Free Press, 1950), pp. 65-66.

that criminal laws against certain activities are even relativistic within *one* society. This was revealed, for example, by Howard Becker's study of the marihuana laws in American society, in which he showed that a legal, if not wholly respectable, form of behavior was made a very serious crime by the passage of the Marihuana Stamp Tax law in 1937, which was passed largely as a result of public relations work by the Federal Bureau of Narcotics:

> The Treasury Department's Bureau of Narcotics furnished most of the enterprise that produced the Marihuana Tax Act. While it is, of course, difficult to know what the motives of Bureau officials were, we need assume no more than that they perceived an area of wrongdoing that properly belonged in their jurisdiction and moved to put it there. The personal interest they satisfied in pressing for marihuana legislation was one common to many officials: the interest in successfully accomplishing the task one has been assigned and in acquiring the best tools with which to accomplish it. The Bureau's efforts took two forms: cooperating in the development of state legislation affecting the use of marihuana, and providing facts and figures for journalistic accounts of the problem. These are two important modes of action available to all entrepreneurs seeking the adoption of rules: they can enlist the support of other interested organizations and develop, through the use of the press and other communications media, a favorable public attitude toward the proposed rule. If the efforts are successful, the public becomes aware of a definite problem and the appropriate organizations act in concert to produce the desired rule.[13]

Factual findings of this sort led sociologists to examine the basic relationship between rules and rule violations, and they

[13] Howard Becker, *Outsiders* (New York: Free Press, 1963), pp. 138-139.

came to see what was not at all obvious to the man of common-sense who looked at the laws as absolute: without the social rules, such as the laws, there would be no violations, so the enactment of the rules must be looked at as an important cause of the violations and of the existence of violators:

> . . . *social groups create deviance by making the rules whose infraction constitutes deviance,* and by applying those rules to particular people and labeling them as outsiders. From this point of view, deviance is *not* a quality of the act the person commits, but rather a consequence of the application by others of rules and sanctions to an "offender." The deviant is one to whom that label has successfully been applied; deviant behavior is behavior that people so label.[14]

This line of thought, then, raises the basic question of whether it might not be preferable to the members of society to consider ending some kinds of crimes by simply eliminating the laws against them and thereby ending at the same time the vast costs involved in enforcing laws for which there are no victims when they are violated, such as smoking marihuana, abortion, and gambling.

As this research was pursued further, sociologists began to investigate what led to the enactment of criminal laws which subsequently produced crimes and criminals. These investigations lead us to see the partial class bias in criminal law that goes back hundreds of years to a time when criminal laws were explicitly based on a desire to protect the rights of the noble classes.[15] We find that the basic distinction in law between criminal law and civil law is closely related to differences in class behavior. There are certain kinds of activities which for many different reasons are more likely to be committed by lower-class individuals, such

---

[14] Ibid., p. 9.

[15] See my essay in *Crime and Justice in American Society, op. cit.,* pp. 3-44.

as robbery and acts of violence. There are others which are far more likely to be committed by middle- and upper-class individuals, such as monopolistic pricing, restricting trade, and fraud. The lower-class types of rule violations are far more likely to be defined by law as crimes, while the rule violations of middle- and upper-class groups are far more likely to be defined as civil violations or else to be defined as crimes but, as in the case of fraud, in such a way that it is almost impossible to prove them against the violators. (To prove fraud it is necessary to prove "intent to defraud" and such proof is normally possible only when the violator has been extremely careless.)

This whole sociological perspective on crime is almost completely outside the perspective of the commonsense man today. The policeman or the middle-class citizen who supports his local police sees only the fact that it is the duty of the police to closely survey the lower-class individuals, since they are the ones who most commonly commit the kinds of violations the police are entrusted with controlling. He does not see the history of class-bred criminal laws or the class composition of the state legislative bodies. He knows only that the "bad guys," the "criminal types," are the lower-class types. They become his enemies. To lower-class people it becomes a fact of life that the police will survey and harass them far more than they will middle- and upper-class people and that the violations by businessmen and professionals against the lower-class people will generally go unnoticed by the police. The police become "bad guys" to them and each side develops highly moralistic attitudes toward the other. They become the captives of their own immediate situations, cannot see things from the standpoint of the other side, cannot understand how things got the way they are except in terms of the "evil" of the "bad guys," and cannot see any way out of the situation except by eliminating them. The sociologist who stands outside of both conflicting groups and succeeds in seeing the conflict from both their standpoints and from a historical and comparative perspective is far more able to see how they got into this deadly situation, and consequently, what can be done to get them out of it short of "eliminating the bad guys."

In the same way, the man of commonsense takes the present methods of prosecution, adjudication, and punishment for granted; they necessarily constitute "justice," the criminal's "debt to society," and the "solution to the crime problem." Most Americans are not even aware that what goes on behind the palatial fronts of our "Halls of Justice" is a complex, highly discriminatory system of "bargain justice," a bureaucratic system created to process the lower-class people accused of crimes, a system more in accord with the principles of mass production than with those of justice set forth by our constitution.[16] To those who do not know what goes on, it is a mystery that people processed by this system should feel so much anger and rage against what they see as injustice. The anger and the rage only go to prove that there really is something "evil" about such people. It is no mystery to the sociologists who have studied our police, our prosecutors, and our courts.

To the man of common sense, imprisonment is the solution to crime: the more imprisonment, the less crime. If crime goes up, we need harsher criminal laws and "swifter justice" to put more of the criminals in prison for longer periods. Then there will be less crime; the problem will be solved. Sociological research has shown over and over again that this relationship does not hold. In fact, the relationship between harsh sentences and future crime seems to be the opposite: those punished most harshly are most likely to return to prison for more punishment. Even worse, sociologists have found repeatedly that the new common sense about crime and imprisonment, as embodied in the idea that we can rehabilitate criminals through therapy and training while they are imprisoned, is also completely unsub-

[16] See Abraham S. Blumberg, "Criminal Justice in America," in *Crime And Justice In American Society, ibid.,* pp. 45-78.

stantiated by any valid evidence.[17] Though the reasons for this failure are still unclear, there is growing evidence that it is a result of two factors; one is the existence of very strong "contra-cultures" in prison, that is, subcultures among the inmates that are directed against the law: the other is the "prisonization" of prisoners, or acculturation into these contracultures. It has also become increasingly clear that imprisonment and rehabilitation fail because the sense of injustice and distrust created by the legal process supports the contracultures and because crime is more related to normal life situations in some segments of society than it is to any "evil intentions" of the criminals. All of this has led sociologists increasingly to question attempts to use imprisonment as a means of solving the crime problem and to argue that imprisonment may be making the problem worse, instead of solving it. Many sociologists have begun to argue that we must reconstruct our system of law and law enforcement to eliminate the class biases, to "decriminalize" those acts which do not harm other people, and to eliminate imprisonment in favor of enforced civil claims against those who steal or damage property or persons. They propose a system of *restitutive justice* in which the violator would be found guilty by civil procedures and would have to pay for his violation by continuing at a normal job and paying the victims for all damages. If such proposals were followed, we might find that imprisonment for most acts would disappear just as it disappeared for debt in the nineteenth century, and we might find the problem of crime solved far better than it had been by relying on ideas highly bound to the narrow situations of men of common sense.

It is easy to see that these sociological explanations of the relationship between various social factors and crime have vast significance for any attempts to solve the social problems of crime. It is also easy to see that if these explanations are right,

[17] See Leroy C. Gould and J. Zvi Namenwirth, "Contrary Objectives: Crime Control," *ibid.*, pp. 237-268.

then our present commonsense attempts to solve the problems are highly counterproductive. It is more difficult, but potentially far more important, to see the implications of such theoretical arguments for the future of our society.

As the complexity and the rate of social change have grown inexorably, the potential importance of sociology has also grown. The more complex a society and the more rapidly it changes, the less adequate will its members find attempts to solve their problems by a *wait-and-see strategy*. If they simply wait until social problems arise before they try to do anything about them, they will find that the problems become more complexly inter-woven with other aspects of the society, and consequently, more intractable. If one waits for riots and revolutions and the counterrevolutionary social movements that consistently develop before dealing with the problems that give rise to them, those problems will be more difficult to solve than if they had been dealt with in their early stages. Moreover, as our technological society becomes more interdependent, we will find that problems that reach a crisis stage tend to precipitate crises throughout a much wider part of society than they would have done at a less complex stage of society.

In order to predict the future with any degree of reliability we must have valid social theories. In our commonsense, prac-tical activities we base our actions to a great extent on predic-tions about the future. Some of these predictions are wise ones that produce policies that meet growing problems very well, but others are disastrous. Homesteader acts and land-grant colleges would probably be seen by most people as excellent policies based on sure anticipations of future problems and the ways to deal with them, while refusals to take a strong stand against fascism because policy makers believed "they don't really mean it" and refusals to change government policies to deal with a growing depression because policy makers believed "prosperity is just around the corner" would be seen as disasters. No matter how well-intentioned a man's policies, they may prove disastrous if they are based on wrong predictions about future events. Yet all the evidence indicates that commonsense predictions are at best highly unreliable, and we can expect them to become even more so.

Sociology is already able to make important contributions to our attempts to anticipate social problems and to plan how to meet them before they become intractable, but most of these present contributions are based on short-run extrapolations, or simple extensions, from current trends. The most obvious examples of this come from the field of demography, in which short-run extrapolations are pretty reliable because most trends in population continue for a number of years. By making some relatively simple assumptions about birth rates and death rates, it is possible to project alternative population growth patterns for a few decades that will be generally reliable unless drastic social changes should occur, such as major wars or break-throughs in medicine. Such projections are very useful for social planning of education, social investment in various occupations, land investments, and so on. They can be even more useful by allowing us to predict basic social effects of population changes. For example, because we have a rather reliable idea of how the age distribution of our population will change over the next twenty years or more, we can anticipate that the recent down-ward trend in the average age will be strongly reversed in the years ahead, as we get a smaller percentage of very young people and a larger percentage of very old people. We can even anticipate that, unless something happens to change all the present trends in population development, by the end of this century the American population will be strikingly shifted away from the younger age groups toward the older age groups. Moreover, since it is clear that older people have reliably different interests, voting patterns, and so on, we can expect these population changes to have a great effect on politics and social policies in American society. Since the old are more likely to vote for their own interests than are the young, we can expect this to have a far greater influence on government policies than did the coming of age of the "war babies," with the resultant drop in the average age, in the late 1950s and the 1960s. Moreover, we can expect these effects of an increasingly older population to be more drastic, if current attempts to limit the birth rate are successful.

Sociological analyses of the official agencies of control, such as the police, provide us with another example of the ways in which the sociological theory can help us to anticipate important social changes with profound implications for social problems. Sociological research has found repeatedly that bureaucracies almost inevitably become largely autonomous and that the nature of the organizations become a basic determinant of what the members of the organizations will do, independent of the goals for which the organizations were established. These findings have been dealt with and explained in many different ways, ranging from the "iron law of oligarchy," to the "displacement of goals," and "informal organization." But all of these approaches emphasize the self-determining nature of bureaucracies and the ways in which they create their own problems in the very areas in which they were supposed to be solving them. In fact, these findings are so consistent that we have every reason to expect that in many cases the iatrogenic social problems generated by bureaucracies will be worse than the social problems they were set up to control. The most obvious implication of this for any strategies aimed at solving social problems is that we must always weigh the importance of solving the original social problem against the importance of the iatrogenic social problems that might be byproducts of our solution.

One special kind of iatrogenic social problem that has been receiving increased consideration by sociologists shows the importance of simple extrapolations from complex trends. This is the problem of restrictions on individual freedoms, especially tyrannical restrictions, which are inevitably produced to some degree by any bureaucracy trying to control social events. As our society has become more complex and pluralistic over the last century, hundreds of new kinds of official agencies of control have been created at every level of government to try to control the effects of these complexities and these pluralistic differences. Police, agriculture inspectors, FDA, IRS, court psychiatrists, school psychologists, FAB, FTC, FCC, FBI, treasury agents, air pollution control agencies, planning commissions, zoning boards, rent control boards, NLRB, BNDD, CIA, and all the hundreds of other official agencies of control that honeycomb our complex society and impinge on almost every aspect of our everyday lives were generally created for purposes which the vast majority of us would see as worthwhile. But every bureaucracy of control produces, directly and indirectly, restrictions on our everyday lives; some of these are created intentionally while others are the inevitable result of the bureaucracies using their discretionary powers to extend their controls and to create new ones. Their effects on our freedoms are mixed: in so far as they prevent others from destroying our freedoms, as the police do when they prevent gangsters from forcing us to make payoffs, they protect our freedoms; but in so far as they necessarily have power to survey and control us, even for the purpose of preserving such freedoms, they thereby destroy those and other freedoms in the *normal* course of their work.

Once we note the history of these developments, and once we are aware of the ways in which such bureaucracies of social control become partially autonomous constraints on our individual freedoms, we recognize that there is a seemingly inexorable trend in modern American society toward ever greater control of our lives, and ever greater restrictions on our individual freedoms. We also see that the iatrogenic social problems created by this trend are increasing. Once we have recognized these trends, a simple extrapolation (which seems justified because the trend is so long and so relatively unchecked by counter-balancing factors) leads us to anticipate increasing social controls, decreasing individual freedoms, and in general, increasing iatrogenic social problems. We have every reason to expect, then, that the small but growing outcry against invasions of privacy by government agencies, against police power, and so on, will become greater. By anticipating these developments, and by making quick changes in our social policies, we may be able to prevent the development of a subtle but terribly efficient form of modern tyranny, a *technological tyranny* springing from the most humane intentions and buttressed by the most idealistic rhetoric of the experts manning the bureaucracies of control.[18]

[18] This analysis of "Future Problems" is partially based on the analysis of "Potential Social Problems" in Chapter 6.

SUGGESTED READINGS

There are many scholarly works that try to unravel the complex background of our current social crisis, but few have stood the scrutiny of scholarly critiques as well as Karl Polanyi's classic work *The Great Transformation: The Political and Economic Origins of Our Time* (Boston: Beacon Press, 1957). Still fewer have proven so readable. Polanyi traces the progressive "breakdown" of nineteenth-century Western civilization to the uncontrolled market economy that subsumed all of society to the unrationalized forces of the industrial economy, but steadfastly avoids becoming ideological and insists that we need a recommitment to humanity, including human freedom in the widest sense, rather than a submersion of man in any of the new forms of economic collectivism. The critical reader will see too great a tendency in the book to trace all of our critical problems to the uncontrolled market (industrial) economy, but he will also find a wealth of scholarly insight into our current crisis.

While scholars such as Polanyi and Mannheim have concentrated on the historical sources of our problems and on the sense of personal alienation so often associated with the mass industrialized society, many social thinkers have increasingly turned their attention to the problems posed by the very nature of our postindustrial society—the technological society, as Jacques Ellul has christened it in his book of that title (New York: Knopf, 1967). Ellul has accepted the arguments of Mannheim and others about the alienating effects of mass, industrialized society but has tried to go beyond them to show that this sense of alienation is due to the very nature of the technological society and the social environment produced by it, regardless of whether the technological society is a planned society or a "free market" society. Moreover, he has tried to show that the increasingly single-minded commitment of modern man to technology has become a growing form of modern tyranny: the technological tyranny has replaced man's ancient domination by physical necessities.

Whereas Jacques Ellul's work concentrates on what he believes is a strong trend towards technological tyranny, and seems to leave open some hope that the trend can be reversed by conscious recognition of the problems and by quick action, Herbert Marcuse's famous work, *One-Dimensional Man* (Boston: Beacon Press, 1964), argues that we have already arrived at an ironclad technological tyranny and offers no hope of escape. Marcuse extends the argument of Ellul and others by trying to show that our one-dimensional existence, dominated by technology, is made to look like freedom itself and the source of "the good life" by an unremitting din of mass propaganda. Though Marcuse's work does not draw on the mass of empirical social science work that lies behind the works of Polanyi, Mannheim, and Ellul and suffers both from a lack of balanced argument and a turgid style, it serves as a fine warning of "what might happen" (in the tradition of Orwell's classic *1984*), if we don't succeed in understanding and reversing the current trends towards technological tyranny.

Sociologists, since the beginning of their discipline, have been deeply concerned with the relevance of sociology to the solution of pressing social problems. It is not surprising, then, that so many of them have directed some of their finest efforts at answering questions concerning the relevance of sociology. *The Relevance of Sociology,* edited by Jack D. Douglas (New York: Appleton-Century-Crofts, 1970), is a collection of the classic statements on these questions, beginning with Max Weber and continuing into the present. The reader will find that most of these statements, besides being highly eloquent in defense of applied sociology, also examine in detail all of the basic problems involved in applying sociological knowledge, which we shall consider further in Chapter 2.

In spite of sociologists' continued commitment to studying social problems and trying to solve them, from the 1930s to the early 1960s the discipline was dominated by a public façade of abstract theory and meticulous statistical studies. *The Sociological Imagination* by C. Wright Mills (New York: Oxford University Press, 1959) signalled the revival of sociologists's concern with the larger problems of society. It shows the basic commitment of all the great sociologists to understanding the social bases of these problems and to helping solve those problems. While the work does not give sufficient emphasis to the value of careful sociological studies of the facts of social problems, it is still a valuable corrective to irrelevance in sociological work.

While most readers will find Alvin Gouldner's *The Coming Crisis of Western Sociology* (New York: Basic Books, 1970) marred by excessive personal attacks on other sociologists, it is an important recent addition to Mills's critique of irrelevant sociology. Gouldner argues that the traditional abstract theories of sociology are no longer felt to be adequate to understand and deal with our urgent social problems. The reader will find Gouldner's advocacy of a more activist sociology an interesting alternative to the positions proposed in this book.

chapter 2

Applied Sociology: Problems and Prospects

Even if sociologists were able to determine the facts about our present social situation with great precision, to theoretically explain the relationships between these facts, to chart the trends of events, and to predict the kinds of situations that would arise if these trends continued, they still would not be able to tell us in any scientific way what should be done in the present situation or exactly what social situations might arise in the future. Scientific facts are not the only realities and generally are not the most crucial ones. Scientific explanation does not constitute the whole of human understanding and is of little value until put in the context of that more global, more humanistic understanding. A social trend is not human destiny, and any predictability of human events is constrained by the necessity of human choice.

While sociology is of great and growing importance to any efforts to solve our complex social problems, the days of sanguine optimism about the unbounded values of sociological knowledge are past. Unlike some of the French positivists of the early part of this century, we have no reason to believe that science can provide us with the scientific moral decisions and the certain knowledge that will save us from ourselves. Twenty-five years ago George Lundberg pleaded for faith in the ability of a science of society and showed unbounded optimism in the possibility that this science could indeed save us: "When we give our undivided faith to science, we shall possess a faith more worthy of allegiance than many we vainly have followed in the past, and we also shall accelerate the translation of our faith into actuality." [1] But few sociologists today share this unbounded optimism, and in the nuclear age of intercontinental ballistic missiles, fewer still would plead for an unbounded faith in the ability of science to save us. We now know both from more reasoned analyses and, more importantly, from experience how great are the problems of applying any scientific knowledge to the practical solutions of social problems and how much greater are the constraints upon deriving any value implications from our science. Indeed, we have good reason to fear the possible effects of some aspects of sociology and the other social sciences on our most cherished human freedoms. In fact, these problems and these fears have loomed so large for some sociologists in recent years that they have all but despaired of gaining anything of practical value from sociology.

How Practical Is Sociological Knowledge?

I have argued in Chapter 1 that sociology is of great and growing importance in our practical efforts to solve social problems, and I have given examples of the three major ways in which I believe it serves this purpose. In doing so I have purposefully chosen examples which bear out my argument, because I believe that on balance these positive conclusions are

[1] George Lundberg, *Can Science Save Us?* (New York: Longmans, 1947), p. 104.

justified. But these positive examples must not obscure the great problems involved in applying sociological knowledge to social problems.

Probably the most telling criticism of the application of sociology to social problems is that raised by critics such as Derek Phillips. As Phillips has argued, there are many examples in recent sociological works of ways in which even the supposedly hard facts of sociological research, especially the statistical facts, have been shown not to be facts at all, but rather, to be biased misinformation. For example, detailed studies of even the simplest kinds of information, such as census data, reveal errors as high as 10 to 15 percent. Checks on the validity of self-report data, such as self-reports on whom one voted for in a recent election, have been found to be wrong by as much as 30 percent. Studies of such commonly used statistical data as the official statistics of juvenile delinquency have revealed them to be so biased in many different ways that they are directly comparable to gossip or hearsay, as Aaron Cicourel has argued.[2] Indeed, my own research on such once unquestioned forms of official data as the official statistics on suicide has demonstrated that there is no reliable relationship between real frequencies of such socially meaningful acts as suicide and the official statistics on suicide. In my more recent work I have tried as well to show how and why this is true, though to greatly varying degrees, of all forms of official information on morally meaningful phenomena and to a lesser degree of all statistical studies of such phenomena, whether done by officials or by sociologists.[3]

On the negative side, these findings show that there have been hundreds of sociological studies and explanations of such

[2] See Derek Phillips, "Sociologists and Their Knowledge," *The American Behavioral Scientist* (May, 1971) and Aaron V. Cicourel, *The Social Organization of Juvenile Justice* (New York: John Wiley, 1968).

[3] See Jack D. Douglas, *The Social Meanings of Suicide* (Princeton: Princeton University Press, 1967) and *American Social Order, op. cit.*

social problems that were quite invalid and that supported policies incapable of solving the problems. But there is a very important positive aspect to these findings as well. They immediately lead us to a new estimate of all official policies based on official statistics of this sort. For example, once we understand how unreliable the official statistics on crime are and how easily they are corrupted and manipulated by the officials themselves, we know we cannot take seriously such official proclamations as: "The statistics prove that the spiraling wave of crime is destroying the moral fibre of American society and will destroy the very foundations of our nation—unless we immediately give more power and money to the police." Simply knowing the unreliable nature of this official information is an important form of protection against being manipulated by officials. But this new knowledge of our own ignorance is also important in leading us to greater progress in gathering and using social information in all future official and sociological work. In sociology, for example, it has led us to rely almost exclusively upon various forms of participant observation to gain knowledge about the social lives of deviant groups.

This same kind of criticism of supposed facts and their implications for social policy can be levelled at many of the questionnaire and interview survey techniques used to study certain problems, such as the study of mental illness in midtown Manhattan by Srole, *et al.* The Srole study purports to reveal that nearly 50 percent of Manhattanites need some kind of psychiatric help for everything from outright psychoses not previously discovered to simple behavior disorders.[4] Almost all of the recent studies of psychiatric work by Anselm Strauss, Thomas Sheff, Erving Goffman, and many others make it clear that these studies impose *ad hoc* professional criteria of mental

---

[4] Leo Srole *et al., Mental Health in the Metropolis* (New York: McGraw-Hill, 1962).

health in very abnormal situations upon people who have very different standards of mental health. Rather than giving us a more precise picture of culturally defined mental health conditions in our society, these studies give us a distorted picture presented as reality, one that, because of the prestige of medical experts, could be used to create worse iatrogenic problems of "medical tyranny" than the original problems of mental illness. (We shall return below to the problem of "expert tyranny.") However, it would be wrong to see this as merely a negative contribution of sociology. Not only do we have here an important example of learning what we don't know, but all of these findings also involve important discoveries about the social world that few men have conceived of before. The necessity of having to undo so much earlier work of other social scientists must give us a deep sense of humility in asserting the value of our own facts in planning social policies, but it certainly gives us no more reason for concluding that earlier mistakes show the absurdity of all social scientific thought than the discovery by the child that matches burn justifies his concluding that all fire is evil. On the contrary, our very conclusion that the earlier works were wrong and dangerous is itself an implicit recognition of the high degree of creative and sophisticated advances we have made in our understanding of the basic methods of achieving factual information about social action.

A second general criticism of the practical value of sociology is that leveled by Howard Waitzkin. As he argues: "Traditionally, social philosophers and social scientists have offered the hope that society some day could be ordered according to rational scientific principles . . . each generation of sociologists has advocated a sociology actively involved in social problems . . . These hopes notwithstanding, the world still awaits the scientific solution of social problems."[5] Waitzkin then proceeds to give

[5] Howard Waitzkin, "Truth's Search for Power," *Social Problems,* Volume 15, pp. 408-19.

very good evidence of the ways in which social science evidence is sought out by officials and businessmen only to be shoved aside when the practical decision is to be made or, perhaps more commonly, to be used as a *front of expert knowledge* to gain acceptance of what they want to do for unscientific reasons. He then argues that there are some basic reasons for this continuing irrelevance of social science knowledge, including the fundamental difficulties of achieving objective knowledge in the social sciences, the practical professional problems sociologists face in doing detailed studies relevant to solving social problems, and the failure of American policy makers to develop the kind of centralized social planning that would make social science evidence really applicable to our problems. Though we shall be considering below the difficult problems of objectivity in sociological work and the dangers entailed in allowing our work to be used as a front of respectability by others, the question of the *practical application gap* between sociological knowledge and its actual use in solving social problems must be considered here.

Waitzkin's argument is correct in two respects. First, it is true that regardless of the exhortations to apply their knowledge to solving social problems, sociologists have paid little attention to applied sociology and much of what has been done has been relegated to graduate students' theses and incomplete reports written for agencies who then file the work away without using it. This negligence of the practical aspects of sociology has been largely due to the fact that sociologists are predominantly academic and are more oriented toward pure science and intellectualism than are most of the natural science disciplines, which have a much greater commitment to the applied branches of their sciences. However, this fact must not obscure the ways in which sociology and the other social sciences have been used in formulating policies aimed at solving problems, and it must in itself be reason to expect that sociology could contribute far more of practical value to solving these problems if sociologists became more committed to applied sociology. Rather than indicating that the past lack of application justifies despair and renunciation, this part of the argument demonstrates the need for renewed efforts in applying sociology.

Besides being remiss in not devoting sufficient attention to research on the concrete details of social problems, sociologists also have generally failed to give enough attention to anticipating social problems. While sociologists have commonly talked a great deal about the importance of predicting social events, they have rarely put their theoretical commitments to the test by trying to predict what will happen over the short run, and fewer still have risked the gross uncertainties involved in speculating beyond the next decade, perhaps because they have been burned too often in the past by premature optimism over the predictability of social events. For example, the neopositivistic proponents of the population curve in the 1920s and 1930s were convinced that the American birth rate would soon level off and even begin to decline in the 1940s, a theory which was unfortunately quickly proven to be diametrically opposed to the actual trend. Whatever the reason, this part of the sociological promise can never be fulfilled until we make enough attempts at predicting events to be able to learn from our mistakes just what the possibilities of such predictions are.

Until sociologists become more concerned with predicting future social problems and speculating about such problems where our knowledge does not allow more definite predictions, we shall continually be presented with the disconcerting picture of the sociological expert on social problems following in the wake of the journalists. Again and again we have seen sociologists loudly proclaiming impending doom from growing social problems—*after* journalists have begun to beat the drums of public opinion. The recent upsurge in sociologists' concern over the supposedly impending ecological crisis produced by the many forms of pollution is an excellent example: while the expert evidence has been there for many years and has led many scientists to proclaim pollution a grave threat to mankind, sociologists did almost no work on the social phenomena involved until *after* the public had been so aroused that ecology became a major political concern uniting all segments of the society behind pollution control. As in so many other instances, the sociologists' failure to think "futuristically" has left them with little more purpose than that of doing the postmortems to determine how the popular definition of pollution as a social problem occurred. While looking backward is very important to the development of our science, we must use sociology more in the service of anticipating future problems.

In general, we can only close the gap between the promise of sociology and the practical application of sociological ideas and knowledge by paying far greater attention to the *application process* itself, that is, to the actual processes involved in applying sociology to practical activities.[6] Today this means that we must place greater emphasis not only on the development of applied knowledge (including predictability) but also on the ways in which sociology is used or not used.

Specifically, this means that we must not only create knowledge, but also be advocates and critical analysts of its use. Regardless of past failures to achieve the promise of sociological contributions to solving social problems, there is plenty of reason to believe that the men of practical affairs often would have been far more successful in trying to deal with social problems if they had relied more on the available sociological knowledge about social problems. Melvin Tumin, for example, has argued persuasively that our problems of race, especially the open conflicts such as the urban riots of the 1960s, would have been less serious if officials had paid more attention to the long line of sociological research showing the rising discontent in these urban areas:

[6] I have analyzed the application processes in greater detail in *The Relevance of Sociology* (New York: Appleton-Century-Crofts, 1970).

Quite contrary to ordinary and widespread belief about scientific "ivory towers", there has been a serious and despairing lag between the time that scientists have published crucial research findings and the time, if at all, that public and private policy have moved toward any implementation of these findings. This, of course, renders preposterous the common allegations of ivory-tower escapism by academic scientists.

For there can be no doubt in the minds of anyone familiar with the social science research on race relations that today we would not have a history of recurring riots and civil disorders, nor a menacing threat of continued and unending riots and disorders, participated in by Negroes of all classes and educational levels, if starting with the 1942 publication of the Myrdal volume on the situation of the American Negro, government and other agencies at federal, state and local levels had been at all responsive in any significant degree to the obvious warnings and danger signs that social science research posted with much vigor and prominence.

One may say, in effect, that a major cause of the enormous foment of hate, anger, and despair in the Negro community today, and of the capacity of a small group of extreme militants to take legitimate leadership away (even if only temporarily) from the most serious, thoughtful, and concerned traditional leadership of the Negro community, has been the failure of the American government and public to respond to Negro needs in precisely the ways in which social science research since the 1940s, and even before, has indicated that these could and should be responded to, if we did not want to have what we have today by way of extraordinary intergroup conflict and hostility.[7]

If sociologists become stronger and better advocates for using

[7] Melvin Tumin, "Some Social Consequences of Research on Racial Relations," originally published in *The American Sociologist*, republished in *The Impact of Sociology, op. cit.*

our sociological knowledge, we may be able to avoid many problems of this sort in the future.

Unfortunately, there is also hard evidence of problems created by the application processes, especially at the level of *interaction between scientists and practical men.* Because the scientists and practical men usually live in distinct subcultures, with different assumptions about the nature and uses of truth, not only do they commonly not understand and approach concrete problems in the same way, but they also do not understand the nature of and reasons for their differences. Many of the basic problems of the practical application process grow out of these misunderstood differences. Some of the worst examples of this were revealed by the confused development of the policies of the Johnson Administration's famous "War on Poverty", especially those administered by the Office of Economic Opportunity (OEO).

Poverty came to be seen as a great and pressing social problem in American society in the 1960s, at the very time the dimensions of the problem had shrunk so that they encompassed only a distinct minority of the population. Since the social scientists, especially the sociologists and the economists, had done a large number of studies of the poor, government planners turned to them for advice on solving the problems of poverty.

As we shall see in Chapter 3, commonsense ideas about the causes of poverty are often in conflict. A large number of Americans still consider the individuals involved to be responsible for their poverty, while another large number, taking the more recent view of social causality, tend to see social factors as the dominant causes. The traditional view, then, sees poverty as the result of something different and bad about the individuals, whereas the more recent view sees poverty as the result of something in the social situation of those individuals. The sociologists who had done work on poverty were divided in their fundamental assumptions about poverty along the same lines, for the simple reason that they shared this commonsense background. But, since most of the sociologists assumed social causality, their differences centered on the question of whether it was something about the external social situation faced by the poor or something about society which they had incorporated into their personality structures which had produced their poverty.

The sociological theory of poverty that concentrated on the immediate situation of the individual was commonly derived from Robert K. Merton's famous theory of anomie and social structure and saw the socially determined "structure of legitimate opportunities" as the basic determinant of economic success or failure.[8] Opposed to this *opportunity theory of poverty* was the *subculture theory of poverty,* which argued that the poor are different from those who are not poor in specific ways that lead to their continued poverty.[9] Both theories assumed that the social structure or social system operated in such a way as to produce the poverty, but the opportunity theory led to the conclusion that one could solve the problem of poverty by simply changing the structure of legitimate economic opportunities available to the poor, whereas the subculture theory led to the conclusion that the problem of poverty could only be solved if the basic beliefs, values and feelings transmitted by one generation of the poor to the next were somehow changed.

The opportunity theory became the assumption underlying and justifying the federal War on Poverty of the 1960s and led to the general policies of the OEO, which was primarily responsible for expending the billions of dollars in this project. The reasons why this particular theory was adopted are vague, but it was probably because its emphasis on the immediate social

[8] Robert K. Merton, "Social Structure and Anomie," *American Sociological Review,* 3 (October, 1938), pp. 672–682.

[9] The subculture theory of poverty is probably best represented by Edward Banfield, *The Unheavenly City* (Boston: Little, Brown, 1970). The opposition to this theory has probably been best represented by Charles Valentine, *Culture and Poverty* (Chicago: University of Chicago Press, 1967).

situation and on opportunity fit the American ideal of individual action and complemented the modern ideal of equal opportunity for all; furthermore it offered immediate returns, which seemed necessary both because of the rising clamor of the poor and because of the quadrennial presidential elections. While the actual effectiveness of this war was probably mixed and was difficult to estimate, the general conclusion of most people was that we suffered a defeat in our attack on the problem of poverty, and this conclusion led to a gradual, general retreat from such efforts.

The application process used by the government officials planning the program, and encouraged by some of the social scientists, completely overlooked this conflict among the social scientists over the causes of poverty. As Daniel Moynihan has argued,[10] the administration became committed to the opportunity theory largely for unknown reasons and in unknown ways. In addition, the program became committed to the community involvement principle of the famous Title One for largely unknown reasons.[11] This principle created tremendous conflicts at all levels of government across the country and eventually proved very important in strangling the whole program.

The conflicts among social scientists, which are probably a direct result of both the highly complex nature of the phenomenon of poverty and of the relative lack of good research in this area, were almost completely overlooked in the application process. Then, unplanned and unexpected, items were added to the program by unknown bureaucrats and politicians.[12] The problems lay largely in failures at the application stage and the result was an immensely costly failure that has already produced a quiet policy of "benign neglect" of the problems of poverty.

[10] See Daniel P. Moynihan, *Maximum Feasible Misunderstanding* (New York: Free Press, 1969).
    [11] *Ibid.*
    [12] *Ibid.*

Rather than being a source of despair and a reason for denying the practical value of sociological knowledge, these problems of applying our knowledge should be a subject of intensive study by sociologists. We must try to deal with these problems as well as learn the causes of social problems. But even if we succeed in doing this there will still be difficulties to be faced in fulfilling the promise of sociology.

Value Commitments and Objectivity in the Sociology of Social Problems

Men of practical affairs sometimes reject sociological analyses of social problems or proposals for solving social problems as "just so much ideology," by which they mean that the sociologist is merely imposing under the guise of science his own values and politics on social problems. Sometimes this assertion is merely an insincere attempt to defeat a proposal that would involve some undesired costs for the person making the assertion, though there are times when this assertion is true and, more importantly, times when it is false yet indicative of a fundamental truth about social science in general.

There are some so-called sociologists who purposefully use sociology as a respectable mask for political activity. This is especially true in an age of conflicts and rampant "politicization" of so many aspects of American life, an age in which many people have come to see God as a politically useful opiate, while many others have come to see opiates as a politically useful god. There are some New Left sociologists who do not believe in any form of objectivity in any kind of thinking; science to them is merely another political tool, no better than any other form of bourgeois politics, though some of them seem to think it may be worse than most other forms. Statements by such New Left theorists about social problems are intended to be political, ideological statements. Most of these theorists are probably honest in their intentions and prepared to admit that they are merely making political statements, though it is possible that some dishonestly use the mantle of science so that their statements will have more influence with the public.

Regardless of the honesty or dishonesty of its proponents, this kind of ideological sociology is no sociology at all and will be treated by any truly practical man as just another kind of ideology. As we have already seen, the most distinguishing characteristic of sociology is its commitment to the creation of objective knowledge about man and society, that is, knowledge that transcends the person and situation of the knower. This necessarily involves freeing that knowledge from the values and political desires of the individual knower. Consequently, one may deny the possibility of creating such objective knowledge and thereby deny the possibility of sociology; but one cannot both deny the possibility of objective knowledge of man and society and insist that one is engaged in sociology without making a travesty of the one necessary meaning of sociology. The serious question then is whether we can in fact have objective knowledge about society.

Until the early twentieth century, almost all scientists thought of objectivity as *absolute objectivity*.[13] They believed it was possible to make scientific knowledge a form of absolute truth, a truth that would be "object-like" or "thing-like," as Durkheim described objectivity in his famous work on sociological methods. Such absolute objective knowledge would be completely independent of the nature of the knowing human

[13] See "The Relevance of Sociology," *op. cit.,* and my essay, "Understanding Everyday Life," in Jack D. Douglas, ed., *Understanding Everyday Life* (Chicago: Aldine, 1970).

mind and of the concrete individuals and situations in which the knowledge was created. It was thought to be a form of knowledge that had to be described or presented in terms of rationalized mathematical forms on a set of eternal, universal coordinates. Such objectivity was believed to share all the properties of any absolute meanings, so scientific truths or laws were believed to be "discovered," not created, to be "necessary" rather than simply alternative formulations, and to be so much a part of reality that any other form of intelligence, such as minds from other worlds, would have to share the same way of seeing them.

This concept of the absolute objectivity of scientific knowledge is still held by most members of Western culture. Because it became such a powerful part of the positivistic tradition of the social sciences, in which "positive science" was merely a French phrase for absolute objective science, and because the social scientists have been struggling until recent decades to justify themselves to men of common sense, objectivity has continued to mean absolute objectivity to a great many social scientists. This is a basic reason for the near obsession of many social scientists (especially economists, but also many sociologists) with mathematical forms of presentation. The mathematical forms present the image of rationalized and objectified knowledge and constitute a very powerful form of rhetoric that can convince many men of commonsense that what is being said must indeed be the truth. It is also this idea of absolute objectivity that lies behind "verification" theory in sociology, which holds that any idea can be subjected to the same test to determine its validity (or its non-validity).

While many natural scientists still use this idea of absolute objectivity in their everyday work, most of them now recognize that absolute objectivity can only be a matter of faith and a goal which few can ever realistically hope to reach. Some of the most thoughtful and philosophical of these scientists have even become so pessimistic about the possibilities of any objectivity in their own work that they would agree with Max Born's famous expression of despair in his autobiography, *Physics in My Generation*:

> In 1921 I believed—and I shared this belief with most of my contemporary physicists—that science produced an objective knowledge of the world, which is governed by deterministic laws. The scientific method seemed to me superior to other, more subjective ways of forming a picture of the world—philosophy, poetry and religion; and I even thought the unambiguous language of science to be a step towards a better understanding between human beings.
>
> In 1951 I believed in none of these things. The border between object and subject had been blurred, deterministic laws had been replaced by statistical ones, and although physicists understood one another well enough across all national frontiers they had contributed nothing to a better understanding of nations, but had helped in inventing and applying the most horrible weapons of destruction.[14]

While the problems of constructing knowledge are much greater than any positivist would have dared to summon up in his nightmares, there seems to be no justification for such pessimism as that expressed by Born and others who have come close to embracing solipsism. Most scientists now recognize that both their individual and group values are important determinants of their work in important ways. There is little doubt that values and private interests are important in determining the subjects scientists will study. In sociology this is clear in choices such as those that have led to thousands of sociological articles on juvenile delinquency and almost none on consumer fraud. Few would doubt that consumer fraud affects far more people and involves billions of dollars more than juvenile delinquency, but our values and our private interests (fed by research funds) led to an intensive concentration on delinquency and an almost total neglect of consumer fraud. It is also obvious that values deter-

[14] Max Born, *Physics in My Generation* (London: Pergamon Press, 1956).

mine many of the ways in which we do social research: for example, we are generally reluctant to do "secret research" or to spend much time "hanging out" with deviants in order to get the best possible evidence on their everyday lives.

While it is not immediately obvious, it has become increasingly clear that the very idea of science either is partially constituted by values, such as the commitment to seek the truth, or cannot be fulfilled without commitment to certain values, such as honesty and free inquiry. Moreover, almost any scientist knows that he finds some ideas about reality either unthinkable or unacceptable because of certain personal values he holds. While this occurs in natural sciences (for example, Albert Einstein refused to look at the idea that there is a deterministic world "out there" as merely some kind of hypothesis and this made him hostile to the development of quantum mechanics), it is more common and more important in the social sciences where we are dealing with problems that involve our own identities and those of our friends and loved ones. Just as doctors generally will not treat themselves or members of their families because of their close personal involvements, there are also sociologists of great honesty who will not try to study or sociologically analyze certain subjects dear to their hearts. Most of us, for example, will not try to study our children and some of us will not try to study race relations.

Scientists, historians of science, and philosophers of science have also increasingly come to recognize that science is generally *grounded in commonsense assumptions and ideas about reality.* Most of the ideas first arrived at in any science come directly out of common sense simply because men of common sense have always understood for practical purposes many of the basic relationships between phenomena in the world. For example, both pool players and builders understand without knowing any physics, that angles of incidence are equal to angles of reflection and that topheavy bodies are unstable. Scientists merely systematize such ideas and make them more theoretical and precise. More importantly, ideas basic to all of science, such as objectivity itself, are based on our commonsense ideas about truth. Indeed, since Gödel's work, mathematicians and logicians have generally believed that even mathematics cannot be totally rationalized, so that it always remains partially grounded in our commonsense experience of the world or in our way of thinking. Historians of science deal with ideas such as the metaphysical foundations of science and the extrascientific and extraempirical determinants of the structure of revolutions in scientific thought.

The social sciences are profoundly grounded in such commonsense ideas. Most of the basic ideas of any sociological theories thus far constructed can be found rather clearly stated in many commonsense, nonscientific forms, probably for the simple reason that this discipline is still relatively young and close to its commonsense foundations. Again, most sociological ideas depend heavily on our commonsense understandings for their applications in the everyday world, and most sociological data is based on the presumption of a thorough understanding of how to communicate adequately in ordinary language with men of common sense who are to be studied.

Those sociologists who still believe in the possibility and necessity of the positivistic conception of absolute objectivity and its derivative ideas about verification theories commonly believe that any such grounding of sociology in common sense would reduce it all to the vulgarities of common sense and would make all scientific objectivity impossible. It is this attitude that led the positivistic sociologists, such as Emile Durkheim, to reject and even deride commonsense ideas about suicide and everything else, even though they unknowingly based all of their work on ideas derived from common sense. It is this attitude that led so many sociologists to insist upon the need for "value-free" sociology in order to make their work objective.

These fears that grounding our work in common sense would

make objectivity impossible or would even make solipsism necessary are all groundless. Truth and objectivity are not the exclusive property of science. All competent members of society understand the rudimentary ideas of truth and objectivity in the same way the scientists do; it was from those members of society the scientists got their ideas. The fundamental idea of objective knowledge is that the phenomena known are knowable to other minds in the same way and, therefore, not dependent upon anything peculiar about the person doing the knowing or about his personal situation. *Objective knowledge is transpersonal and transituational.* (Normally we shall simply say that it is transituational, understanding that we include transpersonal in that term.) In our everyday lives we take it for granted that knowing can be transituational or objective, though we commonly talk about it in terms of truth and falsehood, and we have a vast number of ideas about how transituational knowing is done and what prevents it from being done. Ideas such as "bias," "illusion," "delusion," and "proof" do not make any adequate sense unless they are regarded in the context of these basic ideas about truth and falsehood.

One of the most basic ideas is that *independent evidence or testimony is the fundamental test or proof of truth.* Independent evidence shows that the knowing is transituational. We are applying this test when we ask people: "Did you hear what I heard?" "Don't you agree that's what happened?" "Do you see that plane or are my eyes deceiving me?" This test is being used when children ask their siblings to "tell her you saw him do it too," and when judicial laws of evidence require eyewitness evidence. The more independent sources, the more objective the evidence.

It is this *test of independent evidence* or witness that scientists have made the crucial test of objectivity in science. Specifically, the scientific test consists of investigators using the same methods but working independently of each other to see if they can reproduce observations or experimental results. Other concepts of objectivity are largely derived from this basic idea. The requirement that scientific methods and results be made public, for example, is directly aimed at making sure that the observations can be subjected to independent retests.

Since the social sciences are more grounded in commonsense experience than the natural sciences, social scientists face greater problems in making their methods of observation explicit enough for such retests, but this very fact makes it all the more important that they do so. One of the crucial failures of the social sciences thus far has been the tendency to provide very little information on how research was actually conducted (as opposed to the presentation of ideal methods) so that others can use the same methods to see if they get approximately the same results, and the concomitant tendency to shy away from retests and try to do only new research.

The greater grounding of the social sciences in common sense also makes it more vital for us to try to control our personal involvements so that our findings will not be determined so greatly by them. This problem is especially formidable in the study of social problems because social problems are apt to engage the passions of most of those involved in the arguments that rage over them. Some sociologists, such as Alvin Gouldner, have concluded that since we cannot eliminate all the influences on our research we might as well accept them and let them have freer play:

> When Weber condemned the lecture hall as a forum for value-affirmation he had in mind most particularly the expression of *political* values. The point of Weber's polemic is not directed against all values with equal sharpness. It was not the expression of aesthetic or even religious values that Weber sees as most objectionable in the university, but, primarily, those of politics. His promotion of the value-free doctrine may, then, be seen not so much as an effort to

amoralize as to depoliticize the university and to remove it from the political struggle. The political conflicts then echoing in the German university did not entail comparatively trivial differences, such as those now between Democrats and Republicans in the United States. Weber's proposal of the value-free doctrine was, in part, an effort to establish a *modus vivendi* among academicians whose political commitments were often intensely felt and in violent opposition.

Under these historical conditions, the value-free doctrine was a proposal for an academic truce. It said, in effect, if we all keep quiet about our political views then we may all be able to get on with our work. But if the value-free principle was suitable in Weber's Germany because it served to restrain political passions, it is equally useful in America today where, not only is there pitiably little difference in politics but men often have no politics at all. Perhaps the need of the American university today, as of American society more generally, is for more commitment to politics and for more diversity of political views. It would seem that now the national need is to take the lid off, not to screw it on more tightly.[15]

Rather than recognizing the greater problem we have and insisting that we must more carefully control the possible determinations of our observations of the political and problem realms of life, this position would encourage each sociologist to let his own political views become more important determinants of his findings. The result would be to push us further away from objectivity.

Since we rely on direct experience of the social world for our crucial understanding of it, we must participate to understand it. Moreover, since we need more direct and concrete understanding of the application processes in dealing with social problems, which are predominantly in the political arena, we

---

[15] Alvin Gouldner, "Anti-Minotaur: The Myth of Value-Free Sociology," *Social Problems*, 9 (1962), pp. 199-213.

are in need of more direct participation in this area. But as sociologists we need experience from all the different, conflicting viewpoints on problem situations since this is necessary for creative transsituational knowledge of social problems. For sociologists to become directly involved from the standpoint of their own political views in those areas they are trying to be objective about would restrict their understanding to the perspective they hold as political actors and to the political situations in which they are involved. If we do that, we are doing it from the standpoint of commonsense actors, which means that though we may have the objectivity about our involvements that commonsense actors can have, we are not transcending this level of understanding to create more objective knowledge.

Rather than despairing of objectivity and casting ourselves into solipsism or partisanship, we should recognize that we can create *progressively objective knowledge* about social problems if we carefully control our own involvements in the research process and if we subject our research to systematic, independent retests. But we cannot realistically hope to escape from common sense entirely, especially not by simply banning common sense from our considerations. We must make use of common sense, but we can only become more objective if we subject common sense to study. As we shall see throughout this book, one of the great contributions of sociology to the objective understanding of problems and their solutions comes from the systematic analysis of the common sense, social meanings of social problems and solutions. Men of common sense are just as capable of being involved in partisan political activity as sociologists, so the sociologist is only doing what anyone else does when he becomes a partisan political actor; but the sociologist makes a unique contribution to solving our problems when he contributes progressively objective understandings to our commonsense treatments of problems. It is this that the members of society need and want from sociologists as scientists of society.

Overcoming the Dangers of Expert Tyranny in the Technological Society

This view of objectivity does not mean that social scientists can return to an era of unconcern over the uses of their research and theory, an era of "free enterprise science" when research and related theorizing were open to those who could and would "buy" it. Research and theory done this way almost inevitably becomes situation-bound because it is based from the beginning on the value premises of those who finance it. This, as we pointed out, was one reason why sociologists did such a massive amount of work on juvenile delinquency and none on the other phenomena seen by many groups as social problems. This dependancy on their sponsors was also a reason why the sociologists doing the official research on delinquency were content to use the statistics on it provided them by the officials: when one is studying delinquency from the perspective of the officials and for the purposes pursued by the officials, it may make good sense to use the official statistics. But such research and resulting theories wind up being very situation bound, very unobjective, and of use primarily to justify official programs or to impose official controls on the delinquents. The sociologist winds up being highly partisan rather than objective.

In a technological society any kind of knowledge seen as expert knowledge comes to have great prestige and to affect the way people think about things and the way they choose to act. Insofar as it is seen by the public as expert knowledge, sociological knowledge can become a crucial determinant of how people define social problems and what they think should be done about them. Because of this, sociology can be used to determine the social definitions of social problems and solutions, rather than to provide objective knowledge about the problems. To do this, however, is to use sociology as a mask of scientific knowledge to control or manipulate people, rather than honestly to fulfil its promise of providing transsituational, scientific knowledge about society's problems and their solutions. If sociologists allow their work to be determined by those with the "buying power" to provide money for their research, they create the possibility of sociology being used as a front to manipulate the public. Sociology would thereby become an important contributor to expert or *technological tyranny,* which itself could soon come to be seen as one of our greatest social problems in the techno-logical society. If that should happen, sociology itself might come to be seen by many as constituting a fundamental social problem rather than a science.[16]

Sociologists can prevent this usurpation of their discipline for political purposes only by maintaining their independence from partisan political points of view and by retaining their commitment to provide progressively objective knowledge about society's problems. Regardless of where the financing for their work comes from and regardless of their own personal values and political preferences, sociologists can prevent the use of sociology to help build technological tyranny by insisting that they themselves must decide which problems should be studied, and that all research must be done so as to reveal the multi-dimensional social perspective on the problems.

The world is not in need of sociological kings or technocrats, any more than it has ever been in need of philosopher kings. It is not in need of a pseudoscience of society that only supports the development of technological tyrannies. It is very much in need of the *sociological understanding* of society's problems and their possible solutions that comes from a combination of commonsense wisdom and progressively objective knowledge.

---

[16] I have discussed the dangers of expert tyranny in our technological society in *Freedom and Tyranny: Social Problems in the Technological Society* (New York: Random House, 1970).

SUGGESTED READINGS

Robert Lynd's *Knowledge for What?* (Princeton, N.J.: Princeton University Press, 1939) is the single most comprehensive work on the relevance of sociology and the other social sciences to the solution of our social problems. Though he saw many of the problems involved in the practical application of sociology to society (which we shall consider in the next chapter) Lynd was uncomprising in his insistence that sociological knowledge has practical applications and that part of the basic purpose of sociology is to apply that knowledge to solving social problems. To demonstrate his major point, Lynd gives concrete examples of the practical advantages of sociological knowledge over the common sense of the 1930s. Written in the heat of concern in the later years of the depression, this work is still very relevant to sociologists' attempts to solve our social problems.

The Impact of Sociology (New York: Appleton-Century-Crofts, 1970), a collection of essays edited by Jack D. Douglas, shows how the social sciences have affected social thought in general and social policies in particular in Western societies over the last few centuries. Some of the first chapters, especially those by R. H. Tawney and Ernst Cassirer, show how the new scientific understanding of society helped to change ancient patterns of thought. Later essays, such as Herbert Garfinkel's "Social Science Evidence and the School Segregation Cases," show how the social sciences today affect policy decisions that have fundamental implications for our whole society. Most of the essays are also concerned with the problems posed by this growing influence of the social sciences.

Probably the best collection of essays on the complex and problematic relationships existing today between all of the sciences and the rest of society is *Science and Culture* (Boston: Beacon Press, 1965), a book of essays edited by Gerald Holton. Many of these, including the excellent introduction by Gerald

Holton, examine the changing nature of the sciences, especially the changes in the basic ideas about objectivity. Other essays examine the effects of science on basic forms of cultural thinking and on our most important institutions. While the work could have benefited from more consideration of the growing influence of the social sciences, it forms an excellent complement to *The Impact of Sociology.*

Maximum Feasible Misunderstanding by Daniel P. Moynihan (New York: Free Press, 1969) offers probably the best available account of the kinds of problems that have arisen in an actual attempt to apply sociological knowledge to social problems. Moynihan, relying primarily upon his own involvement in government programs, tries to show how sociologists and other social scientists helped to turn the massive OEO program in a direction that proved ineffective in solving the problems of poverty. Their failures were due partly to their own unwillingness to consider the weaknesses of their theories and partly to their failure to understand and control the complex political processes that determined what program would actually be implemented. While the work suffers from being too much a personal statement, with little consideration of how others involved might have seen it and with too much justification of Moynihan's own position, it is an invaluable corrective to overoptimism about the present practical values of sociological attempts to solve social problems.

Like Moynihan, Loren Baritz in his book *The Servants of Power* (Wesleyan, Conn.: Wesleyan University Press, 1960) also questions the benign influence of social scientists' involvement in practical activities. Using the long history of industrial social science, Baritz shows how social scientists have sold their services, at times unquestioningly, to the highest bidders. Specifically, he shows how social scientists tried to help management win in their conflicts with the workers, even going so far as to try to find ways to make the workers feel that they were free in choosing policies already determined by management. As with most works, this one does not adequately look at the argument from the other side. (For example, what defense of their actions would those industrial sociologists offer today?) But it will help to prevent any simpleminded assumption of the benevolence of experts.

An even more chilling account of the mindless commitment of many "scientific experts" to policies that attack our basic freedoms to know and choose our government's policies is Sidney Slomich's *The American Nightmare* (New York: Macmillan, 1971). Having spent sixteen years as an expert (political scientist) working for the Pentagon and other government agencies, Slomich is able to report of the scientific experts from the inside. He has concluded that the attempts to change society from the inside by using expert knowledge were a failure and that these attempts actually became a façade of scientific expertise to justify whatever the men in power had decided to do. While the work suffers from the same weaknesses as Moynihan's, his contention that "we see in Vietnam, as at Auschwitz, the result of technical solutions to political problems" is a vital reminder that expert knowledge must always be used by men with common-sense wisdom and must be controlled by free men, or the social sciences can become a grave danger to us all.

Since his earlier works, *Science and Human Behavior* and *Walden Two*, B. F. Skinner has rightly been recognized as the foremost proponent of technocracy, or the rule of society by scientific experts. In *Beyond Freedom and Dignity* (New York: Knopf, 1971), he steadfastly maintains that we can only solve our growing social problems by allowing social scientists (that is, behaviorist social scientists using his own theories of operant conditioning derived from studies of pigeons) to plan our whole society. He recognizes, and now insists, that this can only be done by eliminating freedoms and the search for personal dignity. Indeed, he sees this move away from freedom as inevitable: "It is in the nature of scientific progress that the functions of autonomous man be taken over by one as the role of the environment is better understood." The reader will find Skinner's book in opposition to all of the ideas of necessary freedom and sociological understanding proposed in this book.

chapter 3

Early Theories of
Social Problems

To almost all men of common sense, the supposed problem of defining social problems is no problem at all: social problems are those things that are wrong with society, that cause suffering to a significant portion of the members of society, and that should be eliminated. Moreover, practical men see no difficulty in defining specific problems, or even in specifying what are the most important and least important problems facing us at any one time. As a famous newspaper columnist recently wrote: "Without doubt, race is the greatest problem in the United States. . . . It is so big and pervasive that generally we don't talk about it much." [1] Other members of our society assert with equal lack of doubt that crime is our one great social problem, poverty is our one overriding problem, irreligion and immorality are the only big social problems and cause all the rest, the military-industrial complex is the greatest problem America has ever faced, the internal threat of Communism is America's great peril, the problem with America today is that everyone wants

---

[1] T. R. B., "Hello-Goodbye," *The New Republic* (Dec. 26, 1970), p. 4.

everything for nothing and no one wants to work. . . . We have all heard innumerable statements of this sort throughout our lives. All of them reveal the *absolutist perspective on social problems* which still characterizes most commonsense discourse about social problems and much sociological work as well.

The absolutist perspective on social problems is generally grounded in the *absolutist perspective on social meanings,* so we would do well to first consider the properties of this general perspective of common sense on social meanings.[2] Let us consider a typical example of an absolutist attempt to specify what things mean to men, in this case an attempt to specify the motives of five different groups of men in three different cultures:

> "This is what separated us from you; we made demands. You were satisfied to serve the power of your nation and we dreamed of giving ours her truth." So wrote Albert Camus to a German friend in 1943, striving to explain what possessed those Frenchmen who chose to resist the Nazi occupation following the fall of France. In Spain, thousands have sat in and struck for Basque autonomy in open defiance of the Franco regime. In Russia, Alexander Solzhenitsyn joins a band of dissident intellectuals pressing for human rights, a cause which other Soviet artists, scientists and even generals have been severely punished for advocating; a plane is hijacked and two Jews sentenced to death in Leningrad. In Poland, workers rebel against prolonged deprivations, and are shot.
>
> The risks these rebels run are infinite, their chances of success infinitesimal (though Polish workers did secure some gains). The apparatus of the state surrounds them; watches, frightens, harasses. It can imprison, torture, banish its victims to insane asylums.
>
> What motivates men to dare so much for conviction with so little hope for gain? Partly it must be a faith in the

[2] I have dealt with the general absolutist perspective on social meanings in *The Social Meanings of Suicide, op. cit.*

future—not their own, or even their children's, but a distant day when history will vindicate them. Partly, too, it must be a need to affirm the humanity of man through immediate acts. Beyond this, there doubtlessly derives from rebellion a sense of self-respect, of camaraderie, sometimes even of exhilaration, that compensates for anticipated suffering, and gives individual meaning to life within a society subservient to statedefined policies and myths.[3]

In general, the absolutist perspective on meanings sees the meanings of things to human beings as: (1) *invariant* or unchanging, regardless of time, place, and situation; (2) *unproblematic* for any ordinary or normal individual; and (3) in some way *imposed* on individuals from outside, rather than created by them. We see each of these properties in the example above. The authors have briefly described situations in five very different cultures and have then proceeded to provide the "obvious" motives of all of these individuals *without any direct evidence at all on what they themselves might think or say about their motives* and without considering possible alternative meanings. All one has to do is observe the simple properties of the situations and persons and the meanings are provided automatically

This example is slightly atypical in its failure to see the relativity of meanings in different cultures. Moreover, it is not the case that all members of society, or any one member in all situations, see social meanings as absolute. Common sense is more complex than this and there has been a growing recognition over the last few centuries of the problems of meanings in our society. Relativity of meanings in different cultures has now become a common belief among educated members of our

---

[3] Editors, "Courage," *The New Republic* (Jan. 9, 1971), p. 14. I have used popular journals of a variety of political persuasions to exemplify my major points. I have tried to use examples across the political spectrum to show there are no important basic differences in their commonsense constructions of the meanings of social problems and to avoid any biases in my analyses.

society. (These same authors quoted above would insist on such crosscultural relativity in many other things, such as in their considerations of the meanings of American participation in the Vietnamese war; but in this case the traditional assumptions of absolutism fit their purposes better.) But, despite the trend to regard things from a relativistic point of view, the strongly dominant perspective on social meanings, especially those involving moral considerations, still appears to be that of absolutism.

Presumably because they were deeply grounded in common sense, early sociologists took this absolutist perspective on social meanings in general and on social problems in particular. This led to the implicit assumptions about social problems made by sociologists for the first hundred years of their work: (1) there is no problem in defining the problems either in general or in particular; (2) everyone either agrees about what social problems are or, when they seem to disagree, their disagreements are only apparent; (3) there can be no real or sincere disagreements about the nature of social problems because the very nature of society (or God) makes it certain that some things are problems for men and some are not; and (4) social problems should be eliminated. Only very slowly did sociologists come to see the falsity of these assumptions and to see instead that social problems are actually highly problematic for the members of society and should be considered even more so by the sociologist.

The Theory of Social Pathology

Early students of social problems were so certain of their understanding of what those problems were that they took the same view of them that doctors take of illness or disease. Many of them called themselves *social hygienists* and proposed to clean up the problems of society in the same way a medical hygienist would go about cleaning up diseasecausing filth. For example, Parent-Duchatelet, one of the best known of the hygienists, did a massive study of prostitution in Paris to determine where this problem was most concentrated, where it came from, why it persisted, why girls got involved and in general, everything that would be needed to eliminate the problem of prostitution. As medicine developed and became more concerned with pathology, these sociologists came to call themselves *social pathologists,* a name that remained common until the 1950s.

Social pathologists believed that certain things were necessarily bad or harmful for society in the same way that certain things are necessarily bad or harmful for the human body. Just as no one except a madman or a would-be suicide would consider cancer cells to be good for his body, so would no one consider social problems to be good for society. Emile Durkheim was probably the best known proponent of the social pathology theory. As we can see in his treatment of suicide as a form of pathology, he believed it was easy for the sociologist to *objectively* determine what is socially healthy and what is socially unhealthy or pathological. Implicit in his argument about the pathology of suicide was his belief that what is statistically normal is generally identical with the socially healthy and that what is socially healthy is identical with what is useful or functional for society. Since he believed this to be the case, he believed that the sociologist need only look for the normal in any society to determine what is healthy for that society and what, therefore, the sociologist should direct his efforts at supporting. For example, suicide, crime, and similar "immoral actions" are abnormal in society, so the sociologist should direct his studies toward eliminating them or controlling them. Social problems are pathological for society; the pathological is abnormal; the sociologist, like any reasonable man, should strive for what is healthy, so the sociologist should strive for what is normal.

There were two unsolvable objections to this classic formulation of the theory of social problems as social pathology. First, there are clearly instances of abnormal social phenomena which most people, including Durkheim, would see as being healthy for society, as helping society to preserve itself. Second, any such absolutist theory of social problems mistakenly assumes that all members of society agree on what is good, or healthy for society.

Durkheim's recognition of the social usefulness, or functional value, of some abnormal phenomena is best known through his famous argument that crime, which is clearly not the normal state of society, performs some important functions, especially that of allowing the members of society to show everyone in that society what the rules are through the punishment of the offenders. Crime, with its consequent punishment, thereby helps to define and reinforce the rules of society: the abnormal and immoral can thus be useful to society, making it healthier for the great majority of citizens. But Durkheim also recognized another kind of situation in which the abnormal can be of great use to society. In any period of transition or social change we find that it is precisely that which has been abnormal under old conditions that now makes a society better able to survive the new conditions, hence healthier, just as a new, abnormal kind of organism is the one best able to adapt to a new environmental situation. Yet Durkheim himself recognized that Western societies have long been in a state of rapid transition, so how can we avoid the conclusion that in our time the abnormal in society is truly the more adaptive, the more healthy for society? As Roger Lacombe showed long ago in his brilliant analysis of Durkheim's application of sociology to the practical solution of social problems, Durkheim was forced by this argument to go back to recognizing that social "usefulness" or "health" was really dependent on the values or goals of a particular social analyst:

> Durkheim himself felt that the pursuit of the normal, as he defined it, could not always be our good. He recognized that

in "periods of transition, when the entire species is in process of evolution, without having yet become stabilized in its new form . . . the only normal type that is valid under such circumstances is the type from the previous condition, and yet it no longer corresponds to the new conditions of existence. A normal type can thus persist throughout the entire range of a species although no longer adapted to the requirements of the situation. It is then normal only in appearance. Its universality is now an illusion, since its persistence, due only to the blind force of habit, can no longer be accepted as an index of a close connection with the general conditions of its collective existence." In cases of this type, when we want to know if the fact is truly normal, it is necessary, according to Durkheim, for us to consider if it is useful to society as implied in its nature. It is necessary to connect it "up with the conditions of existence of the species under consideration, either as a mechanically necessary effect of these conditions or as a means permitting the organisms to adapt themselves." When, therefore, sociology finds itself with a universal phenomena but in an epoch of transition "he will go back to the conditions which determined this generality in the past and will then investigate whether these conditions are still given in the present or if, on the contrary, they have changed. In the first case, he may properly designate the phenomena as normal, and, in the second, refuse it this designation." Now, it seems to us that an important modification in the practice of sociology is introduced here: it is, in fact, "in the epochs of transition" and it will be best to proceed as we have said, but it seems clear that the most advanced societies are always "in a state of transition" because they constantly evolve. In any event, it is hardly to be doubted—and Durkheim would be the first to say so—that we are now in an epoch of this kind. Thus, the procedure which Durkheim would seem to consider exceptional enough would much rather seem to necessarily be the essential procedure of sociology, at least today. Now, it seems impossible to us to introduce it without abandoning the definition of the normal given by Durkheim. If in certain cases, perhaps the most frequent, the normal is different from the universal, then this universality cannot define (the normal). Consequently, Durkheim is obliged to distinguish a "normalcy in fact" which is characterized by universality and "normalcy by right" which is characterized by usefulness or, by default, necessity. But, since, according to Durkheim, when the two do not coincide it is necessary to realize the normalcy by right, which is the essential one? Thus, after having discarded it, Durkheim is obliged to implicitly return to the definition in terms of usefulness. Universality only constitutes an easier and grosser criterion that one can substitute for the real criterion; but it will not be thus in all cases, nor even likely in most of the important cases, as we have seen.[4]

In the end, it is clear that Durkheim's absolutist view of social problems, his view that social problems are obvious and that everyone in society can obviously be assumed to want to solve those obvious problems, is unjustified. He was implicitly making basic assumptions about society and was assuming that everyone would accept his value assumptions, which is unjustified:

> . . . it seems to us finally that the conception of a sociological art is not acceptable in the form given it by Durkheim. Sociology cannot give us orders, impose a given goal on our activity. It cannot show us the ends we should aim at. It is true that there is a goal on which there is the most frequent, almost unanimous agreement: we want society to live. Sociology can take this into consideration and build a system of rules which will permit us to achieve it. No doubt, as we have seen, this task will be difficult and, perhaps, will lead only to very relative certainties. But, still, this work is possible. The future will show if it can produce results. Only, sociology cannot pretend to imprison our activity in a

[4] Roger Lacombe, *La Methode Sociologique de Durkheim: Étude Critique* (Paris: Felix Alcan, 1926). (The translation is my own.)

system of rules. The preservation of social life is not necessarily the only goal we can pursue: one conceives of others which have a high value for us and which we seek to achieve by modifying certain institutions, even by trying to transform the structure of our society. One does not see by what right sociology could forbid us such activity and it is not right for us to attach less importance to obtaining these goals than to the preservation of social life. Sociology, therefore, leaves room for a search for ends: however these may be conceived, as speculation or as established fact, it is beyond the field of social science and social science can only intervene afterwards to furnish us with the means of achieving them.[5]

It was the independent recognition of these implicit value assumptions in the analyses of social problems by the social pathologists that led C. Wright Mills to the same conclusion several decades later in his famous paper on the social ideologies of social pathologists. As he argued, the social pathologists generally came from similar backgrounds and as professionals lived in similar social situations, so they tended to have similar value assumptions in their work:

If the members of an academic profession are recruited from similar social contexts and if their background and careers are relatively similar, there is a tendency for them to be uniformly set for some common perspective. The common conditions of their profession often seem more important in this connection than similarity of extraction. Within such a generally homogeneous group there tend to be fewer divergent points of view which would clash over the meaning of facts and thus give rise to interpretations on a more theoretical level.[6]

[5] *Ibid.*
[6] C. Wright Mills, "The Professional Ideology of Social Pathologists," *American Journal of Sociology,* 49 (Sept., 1943).

Because they made similar value assumptions in their work, because the value assumptions were those of the middle-class social groups in which they lived and from which their students came, and because these assumptions were those upheld by the officials (especially the police) with whom the social pathologists worked and from whom they took much of their data for analyzing social problems, they rarely encountered any critical analysis of their assumption that social problems can be treated as absolute, unproblematic phenomena—as sickness. The rapid changes in the social composition of sociology that began in the 1930s and has continued since then changed this view, but not before sociologists tried to modify their absolutist theories without giving them up.

Structural-Functional Theories

The structural-functional theories have always necessarily taken an absolutist approach to social problems because structural-functional theory in general is absolutist. Social problems, seen as totally unproblematic in the classical manner of the social pathologists, were seen as caused by the structure of society, especially by disjunctions between the values of society and the social patterns of life. This view is best represented by the classical theory of deviance, especially juvenile deviance proposed in "Anomie and Social Structure" by Robert K. Merton to explain deviance, especially juvenile delinquency.[7] Merton argued that the structural values of success were universally shared, while the chances for legitimate success were stratified, so that the anomic strains that produced the problems of deviance were inevitably created in society. Since the structural-

[7] Robert K. Merton, "Anomie and Social Structure," *op. cit.*

functionalists believed that social structures have functions in society and that anything created by society and the social structures must in some way serve the function of maintaining the social structure itself, they also argued that the social problems thus created by the social structure must serve at the same time to solve or prevent social problems. Consequently, we find a large number of works by the structural-functionalists trying to show that any social problem is also a solution to other social problems. Durkheim had already argued that crime serves the function of reinforcing the values of society and thereby prevents more crime, and Merton argued in another famous essay that the corruption of big-city political machines in America helped solve the problems of poverty for the immigrants in these cities by giving them access to funds and jobs that they would not otherwise have.[8]

This work by Merton will serve as a good example of the kind of absolutist thought involved in these many "yes-but" works by the structural-functionalists. Merton was basically arguing that, because we can assume the general principles of structural-functional theory to be correct about society as a whole, we can expect that there will always be some positive functions served by what members of society see as social problems. If we consider what all the members of America's cities had to say about social problems, we can see that Merton was at least right from the standpoint of one group of people, those immigrants and nonimmigrants who profited from corruption. But we would also find many other groups, probably constituting a majority, who would insist that corruption is a terrible social problem because it gives an unjust advantage to some people, makes police and most other officials the captives of the criminal minority through the pay-off system, and produces tremendous problems of inefficiency by making adminis-

[8] See Robert K. Merton, "Manifest and Latent Functions," in *Social Theory and Social Structure* (New York: The Free Press, 1957).

trative advance depend more on corruptability than on efficiency.

The important point here is that the plausibility of Merton's analysis really depended on the existence of conflicts over the social definition of what is a problem and what is not, yet this was precisely the fact that his whole structural theory denied. Merton and the other structural-functionalists were making use of the pluralistic nature of our society and the problematic nature of social problems to gain acceptance of their theory, while at the same time they were assuming the problems to be absolutely defined. Again, their theories assumed the problems to be absolute and clear to anyone, yet they were invoking *sociological omniscience* to argue that the great majority of Americans were wrong in not seeing the ways in which social problems are also solutions of other social problems. The structural-functional theory of social problems, then, contained an internal contradiction.

The more recent works by the structural theorists have proposed a modified structural theory which we might call the *structural-preconditions theory.* Merton himself later tried to analyze the social meanings of social problems. That is, he tried to determine the necessary and sufficient dimensions of meaning involved in the idea of social problems.[9] But this does not mean that he or the other structuralists have given up the assumption of absolutism. What they generally try to do is show that there are certain *structural preconditions* that produce the situations that lead members to define them as social problems. The rest of these analyses give almost no consideration to the great conflicts over social problems in our society and take us back to the same list of social problems dealt with by the social pathologists.

Probably the most developed work on the structural-preconditions theory of social problems has been done by Jerry Stockdale, who sees the basic problem as, "What structural pre-

---

[9] Robert K. Merton and Robert Nisbet, eds., *Contemporary Social Problems* (New York: Harcourt, Brace, 1961 and 1966).

conditions increase the likelihood of collective action in social systems?"[10] He agrees with Herbert Blumer and others (see below) that social problems must be seen as socially meaningful phenomena, but he regards the nature of these final definitions and the process by which they are arrived at as being unproblematic and focuses almost entirely on the question of what produces the collective action that results in the social definition of a social problem. He argues that five structural variables serve as necessary preconditions for the rise of such collective action: discontent, structural blockage of efforts to reduce the discontent, contact with others who suffer from discontent and might thereby be available for collective action, the probable efficacy of any such collective action, and an ideology supportive of such collective action. While there is every reason to continue looking for the social conditions that are associated with the development of social definitions of social problems, this structural-preconditions theory suffers from many of the problems of the structural theories of social problems and from the problems of the stage theories we shall discuss next. In addition, this kind of theory suffers from begging certain key questions. Discontent is presented as an explanation of the rise of a socially defined social problem, yet discontent apparently implies a sense of problem felt by the individual about his social situation. The crucial problem here is how the sense of problem, or discontent, comes about in the first place. This is compounded by treating the structural variables as nonproblematic and by failing to consider how they are to be derived from a social structure that is supposedly common to everyone. We must certainly seek the social situations or conditions that are important in the development of social definitions of social problems, but we cannot do this by trying to build a theory of such problematic definitions

[10] Jerry Stockdale, "Structural Preconditions of Social Problems," (Paper presented at the American Sociological Association, Washington, D.C., August, 1970).

upon a foundation of structural theory that denies all such problems of social meanings.

Although the social pathology theory and the structural-functional theories saw no difficulty in maintaining the absolutist perspective on social problems, other early sociological theories, while maintaining this absolutist perspective, did see a problem that was also encountered by the man of common sense. Since the sociological analysts used commonsense devices to solve this problem, we must first consider the way it was handled by men of common sense.

The Commonsense Explanations of Conflicts over Social Problems

While the commonsense actor assumes that the real social problems are quite obvious to any man of good sense, he certainly knows that there are others who disagree with his own definitions of what the problems are and, even more, with what should be done about them. These conflicts over social problems and their solutions are a sad fact of life with which he must successfully contend if he is to convince others that he is right about what the problems are and what should be done about them. In fact, it is precisely because he assumes that the real social problems are so absolute, and thus necessarily apparent to the other members of society, that he finds it so difficult and so maddening to explain that there are other seemingly sensible men who do not share his own conceptions of the social problems and social solutions: the seeming paradox demands explanation and the explanation is important in determining how to end the conflict, how to make the others see the truth. In addition, the assumption of absolutism is a fundamental one lying behind the kinds of explanations he does make for these conflicts.

While there are many subtle variations, there are only two generally used explanations of conflicts over social problems and solutions that seem important here: (1) the *misunderstanding theory,* and (2) the *conflicting interests theory.* Each is found in almost any explanation of conflicting ideas in commonsense discourse, since the same problem of explaining conflicts over the truths that are supposed to be absolute and therefore obvious is common to all such discourse. But there are certain aspects of these theories that have special importance in the study of social problems.

When someone is found to disagree with one's own ideas about social problems or solutions, perhaps the most common explanation used is that "he doesn't understand what you intended to communicate," or "he doesn't know the real facts about the situation," or "he doesn't really understand the importance of those facts." While the commonsense actor usually assumes that anyone else will see things as having the same meanings as they do for him, he also assumes that the other person may have to be shown just what he really meant or just what the situation is and just how it must be looked at in order to see the truth. Consequently, when someone disagrees with him, one of his first thoughts may be to try to show the other person what he really means, or what the facts of the situation are, or how to evaluate those facts.

An example of this kind of explanation is found in one of Stokely Carmichael's and Charles Hamilton's justifications for the use of agitation by blacks: if blacks continue to smile and act nice in the face of their problems, the whites, not sharing their situation, will not understand what the problem really is, so the black must react to his situation with truthful anger and demand changes:

> Anything less than clarity, honesty and forcefulness perpet-
> uates the centuries of sliding over, dressing up, and soothing
> down the true feelings, hopes and demands of an oppressed

black people. Mild demands and hypocritical smiles mislead white America into thinking that all is fine and peaceful. They mislead white America into thinking that the path and pace chosen to deal with racial problems are acceptable to masses of black Americans. It is far better to speak forcefully and truthfully. Only when one's true self—white or black—is exposed, can this society proceed to deal with the problems from a position of clarity and not from one of misunderstanding.[11]

The explanation of these conflicts in terms of misunderstanding seems to hold only under certain important conditions. First, the other person must be seen as a man of good sense, a man of normal mental and intellectual capacities. Second, he must be seen as serious, not joking about the differences in ideas. And third, and by far the most important condition for our purposes, he must be *trusted,* that is, he must be a man who can be assumed to be trying to find out the truth, not a man who hides from the truth or a man who lies. If any of these conditions does not hold, then the misunderstanding theory is not applicable. In case the first two fail, he is seen as too abnormal to see the truth, or else just joking. If he is not trusted for any reason, then his differences in ideas about the problems and solutions will be seen as lies. In conflicts over social problems and solutions we find that those with conflicting views are generally distrusted for one basic reason—conflicting material interests.

The man of commonsense complements his assumption of absolutism with his assumptions about the practical man. The practical man lives in the same world of absolute meanings, but he may have a different set of *situational contingencies* from those of another individual, and he above all accepts those situational contingencies as *realistic constraints* upon his life. It is assumed, then, that he will act within the limits of such

[11] Stokely Carmichael and Charles Hamilton, *Black Power* (New York: Vintage, 1967), pp. ix-x.

practical constraints like a practical man rather than like some wild-eyed idealist or hair-brained radical who is concerned primarily with going beyond the immediate, concrete situation of action and who, thereby, denies the overriding importance of the situational contingencies. As Egon Bittner has argued in his analysis of commonsense thought:

> One of the most widely accepted ideas about culture and normatively governed conduct in complex social setups concerns the existence of a heterogeneity of enforceable cognitive and evaluative standards. The objects and events that an ordinary person encounters, recognizes, judges and acts upon in the course of his everyday life do not have unequivocally stable meanings. This is not to say that recognition, judgment and action are not normatively governed, but that the ordinarily competent person *is required* to use practical wisdom to interpret the relevance of a rule to a particular instance of the typified situation to which the rule presumably pertains. To use a trivial example, when inside a church one normally uncovers his head, but it would be distinctly foolish to attempt to remove one's cast if one's skull were recently fractured. To fail to exercise a tolerable minimum of practical wisdom is colloquially known as naivete.
>
> Under ordinary circumstances a person moves from situation to situation informed by a stock of knowledge that is adequate to the solution of his practical problems and for the protection of his interests as he sees them, and by and large he succeeds often enough to retain his faith in his practical judgment as an instrument of intuition and as a standard to recognize the meaning and judge the conduct of others around him. He is typically devoid of the scholar's urge to investigate discrepancies and clarify ambiguities, although he is by no means unaware of them. He takes for granted that his conduct has consequences that are in accord with the intended meaning of his action; and he finds this supposition generally confirmed by his experience. Of course,

confirmation can only be guaranteed as long as the ordinarily competent person is willing to acknowledge in practice that his own actions and the actions of others do not have simply stable meanings. For example, he must know that what under some circumstances could be a lie, may in the next context be a required expression of tact; and he must be able to live with such ambiguities in relative comfort.[12]

This assumption of the overriding importance of the situational contingencies in determining what the practical actor will do leads us to distrust the definitions of situations provided by one whose situational contingencies are different from our own. In American society, and possibly all societies, material interests, which include all factors directly relevant to our economic and social influence or power, are commonly seen as the most important situational contingencies. Consequently, the most common form of this kind of explanation of conflicts over social problems and solutions is the *material interests theory*. The conflicting statements by individuals with different material interests are distrusted because these material interests are believed to be a determinant of their beliefs.

Material interests are believed to determine other people's ideas about problems and solutions (though almost never one's own) in two ways. In the first case, which generally seems to be one in which the other individual is seen as potentially trustworthy and well intentioned, the material interests are seen as merely causing *self-deception*: he could see the truth were it not for the conflicting material interests which lead him to hide from the truth. (This self-deception or hiding from the truth has been best described by Sartre in his descriptions of the insincere life.) In the second case, which seems to be the one in which the other individual can never admit the truth, his conflicting material interests are seen as the reason for his lying about the problems

<hr/>

[12] Egon Bittner, "Radicalism and Radical Movement," *American Sociological Review,* 28 (December, 1963), pp. 928-940.

and trying to deceive others about the existence of those problems. Both this self-deception theory and the lie theory can be seen repeatedly in the attempts by the black militants to explain why the whites do not share their conceptions of the horrible problems faced by the blacks. They insist that they alone are telling it like it is, while the others are all deceived or lying. Again, Carmichael and Hamilton present us with an excellent example of this, once again throwing in the misunderstanding theory to allow for those who are trusted but do not agree with their conceptions of the problems of the blacks:

> . . . there are statements in this book which most whites and some black people would prefer not to hear. The whole question of race is one that America would much rather not face honestly and squarely. To some, it is embarrassing; to others, it is inconvenient; to still others, it is confusing. But for Black Americans, to know it and tell it like it is and then to act on that knowledge should be neither embarrassing nor inconvenient nor confusing. Those responses are luxuries for people with time to spare, who feel no particular sense of urgency about the need to solve certain serious social problems. Black people in America have no time to play nice, polite parlor games—especially when the lives of *their* children are at stake. Some white Americans can afford to speak softly, tread lightly, employ the soft-sell and put off (or is it put-down?). They own the society.[13]

Both the misunderstanding theory and the material interests theory of conflicts over social problems and solutions are important commonsense devices by which the belief in the absolutism of one's own ideas about problems and solutions are retained and those of others are rejected. They are important, then, in serving to justify, maintain, and augment the conflicts over social problems. This is especially true of the material

[13] Stokely Carmichael and Charles Hamilton, *Black Power, op. cit.,* p. ix.

interests theory. An individual who is believed to be deceived or to be hiding from the truth is one whose ideas would be rejected with contempt; an individual who is lying about what the problems and their solutions are to protect his own material interests in conflict with one's own is an enemy guilty, not only of conflicting interests and a failure to agree, but of the absolutely immoral act of lying as well. His ideas are not only to be rejected, but to be attacked and subverted by any means available, frequently including counterlies as part of one's political strategy. Even if the sequence did not start with lying, the presumption of lying because of different material interests almost guarantees that it will end up that way and that the "truth" of who started it all will be lost in the confusing charges and countercharges. The conflicts will grow.

Early Social Science Theories of the Conflicts

Since the social sciences have been so highly grounded in commonsense experience and thought, it is once again not surprising to find the early social science theories beginning with and building on these commonsense theories. The misunderstanding theory is not often found these days, but it has had its day. A good example of this is found in Gunnar Myrdal's argument that preconceived general theories of functional and structural properties of social problems are the reason for the social scientists's failure to see American race relations as requiring basic social changes in order for the problems to be solved:

> The presence of this same static and fatalistic valuation in the hidden *ethos* of contemporary social science is suggested by some of the terminology found throughout the writings of many sociologists, such as "balance," "harmony,"

"equilibrium," "adjustment," "maladjustment," "organization," "disorganization," "accommodation," "function,"
"social process" and "cultural lag." While they all . . . have
been used advantageously to *describe* empirically observable
situations, they carry within them the tendency to give a do-
nothing (laissez-faire) valuation of those situations. How the
slip occurs is easily understandable: When we speak of a
social situation being in harmony, or having equilibrium, or
its forces organised, accommodated, or adjusted to each
other, there is the almost inevitable implication that some
sort of ideal has been attained, whether in terms of
"individual happiness" or the "common welfare." Such a
situation is, therefore, evaluated as "good" and a movement
in the direction is "desirable." The negative terms—dis-
harmony, disequilibrium, disorganization—correspondingly
describe an undesirable situation, as indicated by the
etymological connection of their prefixes to the word
"bad".[14]

This view of the other social scientists as suffering from
misunderstanding of the nature of social problems and social
solutions retains the assumption that the problems and their
solutions are in some way absolute: other scientists were wrong
simply because of the way they regarded the problems. This
theory has given way almost entirely to some variant of the
material-interests theory among those who retain the absolutist
theory of social problems. Among the structural sociologists, C.
Wright Mills, in his famous early work on the ideology of social
pathologists, forms a bridge between the misunderstanding and
conflict theories. In that work Mills argued indirectly that the
other sociologists defined social pathologies in terms of their
middle-class ideas. Though he did not make the direct inference,
this analysis seems to imply that they were wrong, not because

[14] Quoted by Howard Becker in "Introduction" to *Social Problems*
(New York: John Wiley, 1963).

they did not understand how others might see the problems, but because their middle-class material social positions determined their thinking about social problems. In his later works, Mills made this point more explicitly as he moved further in the direction of Marxist thought.

Marxism forms the basis for almost all of the sociological theories of conflicts over problems and solutions that assume the absolutist perspective. The Marxist theory is based almost entirely on the commonsense material-interests theory. We can see this theory in its simplest, most moderate, and most commonsense form in Norman Birnbaum's recent analysis of the supposed determination of American policies by material (economic and power) interests:

> That there is a long-term consonance of state and property interests in the conduct of foreign policy seems clear. What is less clear is the extent to which certain features of America's internal politics can be attributed to this consonance. Here, an enumeration may be helpful. Manpower is planned (through mechanisms like government educational policies and the workings of Selective Service) with a view towards strengthening the nation in international competition; economic policies and social investment generally are adjusted to "defense" spending (consider the enormous stupidity of the moon race, with its distorting effect on the entire nation's technological resources); above all, the limits of national consensus have been set at those compatible with a rapid psychological mobilization of the population in the defense of a schematic notion of the national interest . . .
>
> It is true that considerable economic benefits accrued to a good proportion of the entire population as a result of American foreign relations. In this connection, it is suggestive that the rhetoric of the two Kennedy brothers, their insistence that only a more equitably organized American

society can effectively prosecute a global mission, represents an enlightened version of American imperialism . . .[15]

Rather than emphasizing the lying aspect of this material-interests theory, the Marxists have focused on the self-deception aspect and from this have developed the *false-consciousness theory*. The Marxists see material interests as the basic determinants of ideas. However the proletariat, whose material interests conflict with those of the bourgeoisie, commonly agree with their bourgeois masters about social problems and the social action needed to solve those problems. If material interests are the cause of ideas, how can this happen? How can it happen that the proletariat do not see capitalism as their mortal enemy? How can it happen that they support and even die for "bourgeois democracy" in its struggles with "communist democracy"? This bitter paradox is resolved by the theory that it is all due to false consciousness.

We see the most extreme form of the Marxist false-consciousness theory in Herbert Marcuse's argument that the masses cannot even truthfully define their own needs in society today, whereas he and other Marxists can do so with perfect historical objectivity:

> We may distinguish both true and false needs. "False" are those which we superimposed upon the individual by particular social interests in his repression: the needs which perpetuate toil, aggressiveness, misery, and injustice. Their satisfaction might be most gratifying to the individual, but this happiness is not a condition which has to be maintained and protected if it serves to arrest the development of the ability (his own and others) to recognize the disease of the whole and grasp the chances of curing the disease. The result then is euphorian unhappiness. Most of the prevailing needs

[15] Norman Birnbaum, *The Crisis of Industrial Society* (New York: Oxford University Press, 1970), pp. 84-85.

to relax, to have fun, to behave and consume in accordance with the advertisements, to love and hate what others love and hate, belong to this category of false needs.

Such needs have a societal content and function which are determined by external powers over which the individual has no control; the development and satisfaction of these needs is heteronorous. No matter how much such needs may have become the individual's own, reproduced and fortified by the conditions of his existence; no matter how much he identifies himself with them and finds himself in their satisfaction, they continue to be what they were from the beginning—products of a society whose dominant interest demands repression.

The prevalence of repressive needs is an accomplished fact, accepted in ignorance and defeat, but a fact that must be undone in the interest of the happy individual as well as all those whose misery is the price of his satisfaction. The only needs that have an unqualified claim for satisfaction are the vital ones—nourishment, clothing, lodging at the attainable level of culture. The satisfaction of these needs is the prerequisite for the realization of *all* needs, of the unsublimated as well as the sublimated ones.

For any consciousness and conscience, for any experience which does not accept the prevailing societal interest as the supreme law of thought and behavior, the established universe of needs and satisfactions is a fact to be questioned—questioned in terms of truth and falsehood. These terms are historical throughout, and their objectivity is historical.[16]

Marcuse's false-consciousness theory of social problems emphasizes the *structural determination* of "false definitions of social problems," that is, the ways in which the overall modes of technological thought and production supposedly prevent most individuals from really seeing the problems. But the false-

[16] Herbert Marcuse, *One-Dimensional Man* (Boston: Beacon Press, 1964).

consciousness theory has also commonly produced the *conspiracy theory* of social problems, which is a special variant of the material-interests theory. Almost inevitably, the Marxist finds a bourgeois power elite somewhere that is manipulating the thinking of the masses through the mass media, religion, and so on. For example, while C. Wright Mills's later views of social problems are highly structural and are given credit by Marcuse for greatly affecting his own thinking, Mills, too, inevitably found a power elite, though his sociological knowledge of American society led him to see this power elite as a highly complicated "near group."

The general Marxist theory of social problems is inadequate because it assumes the social meanings to be absolute, and it thus cannot make any theoretical sense out of the facts about the conflicts over social problems in our society. It is unacceptable as well because either it is fundamentally dishonest or else it destroys all possibility of objective social thought. If it is true that ideas are determined by one's material social position, then the Marxist must in all honesty be just as subject to this determinism as anyone else. If others' ideas are subject to false consciousness, then the Marxist ideas must also be. To insist that only the Marxist can stand outside of this iron law of social determinism is an act of intellectual dishonesty. But if the Marxist honestly recognizes and accepts his own subjugation to the iron law, then he accepts solipsism, that is, he then agrees that all ideas about our problems are equally necessary and therefore equally true, so the definition of the situations is entirely up to each individual and there is no way out of this. Having accepted solipsism, he would then have to recognize that the truth goes to the victor, so he would have no justification for sounding so moralistic about the bourgeois propaganda or false consciousness. Though there have been many different attempts to salvage Marxist though from these traps, any Marxist theory, however revisionist, will rest on foundations that lead inevitably to such traps. The Marxist theories of social problems are better viewed as political proclamations intended to stimulate political action against the bourgeoisie than an attempt at serious sociological thought. At best, they are inspired more by sympathy for the poor than by passion for scientific truth.

Interactionist Theories

True to their basic principle of the symbolic nature of human action, the symbolic interactionists have long argued that social problems must be considered primarily from the standpoint of their social meanings for the members of society. True to their other basic principle, that meanings are not given to human beings, but must be *constructed* by human beings out of their interactions with their fellow human beings, the interactionists were the first theorists to begin the investigation of the social processes by which social phenomena are defined as problematic.

The first interactionist approach to social problems was the natural-history or, more specifically, the *natural-stages theory* proposed by Richard Fuller and Richard Myers. First, because they took seriously the interactionist injunction to study the definitions of things used by the members of society, Fuller and Myers recognized the need to consider the conflicts over social definitions of problems. Yet they were still unwilling to give up the certainties of sociological analysis provided by the absolutist assumption. This led them to a dualistic theory that distinguished between the *social meanings of social problems,* which they saw as the subjective element, and the *objective social conditions* of the problems, which they believed the sociologist was able to uncover:

> A social problem is a condition which is defined by a considerable number of persons as a deviation from some social norm which they cherish. Every social problem thus consists

of an objective condition and a subjective definition. The objective condition is a verifiable situation which can be checked as to existence and magnitude (proportions) by impartial and trained observers, e.g., the state of our national defense, trends in the birth rate, unemployment, etc. The subjective is the awareness of certain individuals that the condition is a threat to certain cherished values.

The objective condition is necessary but not in itself sufficient to constitute a social problem. Although the objective condition may be the same in two different localities, it may be a social problem in only one of these areas, e.g., discrimination against Negroes in the south as contrasted with discrimination in the north; divorce in Reno as contrasted with divorce in a Catholic community. *Social problems are what people think they are* and if conditions are not defined as social problems by the people involved in them, they are not problems to those people, although they may be problems to outsiders or to scientists, e.g., the condition of poor southern sharecroppers is a social problem to the braintrusters of the New Deal but not to many southern landowners.[17]

While they thus introduced serious consideration of the social meanings of problems, Fuller and Myers, like Robert K. Merton and Robert Nisbet after them (see below), tended to assume that any community would tend to be homogeneous, so there would be general agreement within the community about what is and is not a social problem. It was this assumption of homogeneity that the later interactionists rejected. Howard Becker, Herbert Blumer, and others agreed that social problems are what people think they are but insisted that there are many different groups in our society with conflicting views of what constitute social problems. According to Howard Becker,

The difficulty with the Fuller-Myers approach to the sub-

[17] Richard C. Fuller and Richard R. Myers, "The Natural History of a Social Problem," *American Sociological Review,* 6 (June, 1941). pp. 320-329.

jective aspect of social problems is that it does not specify who the "people" are in the formula "social problems are what people think they are." They seem to suggest that a community will reach a consensus about what does or does not constitute a social problem, and they fail to consider the possibility of different definitions of the same problem by people differently placed in the society.

A problem is not the same to all interested parties; indeed, there will be as many definitions of the problem as there are interested parties. When we speak of adolescence or race relations, the terms do not define a problem. They only point to phenomena someone defines as a problem; the definitions will not all be alike.

Consider race relations. Although clearly an area of major social concern, it is not clear what the "problem" is. For the Negro and for many white citizens as well, the problem is how to achieve as rapidly as possible the full participation of the Negro in American society. For other whites the problem is different: the possible loss of social advantages they have long enjoyed at the expense of Negroes. For many politicians and for some social scientists the problem is the tension and violence of a situation in which Negroes demand rights that whites are unwilling to grant. For professionals—social workers and educators, among others—the problem is to undo the harm done by generations of segregation and discrimination so that the Negro will be equipped to take advantage of his rights. This does not exhaust the list: parents worry about preserving the neighbourhood school, realtors worry about the effect of open housing laws on their business, and diplomats worry about the effect of our racial crises on the leaders of the new African and Asian nations.[18]

Failure to recognize how problematic the social meanings of social problems are led Fuller and Myers to argue that all

---

[18] Howard Becker, "Introduction," *Social Problems, op. cit.*

social problems develop through a sequence of invariant *natural stages*. They argued that a society will come to define a social condition as a social problem only if; (1) there arises a shared (public) awareness that the objective condition is a problem; (2) this is followed by official policy determinations of what to do about the problem; and (3) this leads to social reform aimed at ending the social problem. They also argued that the crucial awareness stage is characterized by the gradual involvement of more and more people in the discussions of the problem, the spreading of the message through the mass media, and the formation of informal and formal groups to deal with the problem by spreading the word and affecting the official policy stage in the process. They argued that at the next stage policy formation took place on three levels that were closely inter-dependent: (1) informal discussion among the people experiencing the problem; (2) more organized discussions by the pressure groups formed to deal with this specific problem; and (3) discussions among experts and officials. The discussions in the first two levels were supposed to be concerned with the goals of the people involved, such as the definition of the problem and getting something done about it, while in the final stages the discussions were supposed to be focused on the means to be used to produce the needed reforms. In the third stage of reform, Fuller and Myers argued that the efforts of the groups, experts, and officials would result in a reconciliation of the conflicting values and interests that had originally given rise to the sense of problem that became the basis for the whole process: the problem is solved by the experts and officials for the people.

This natural history picture of the process of defining and solving social problems involved assumptions about the grass-roots nature of democratic political action in our society and about the responsiveness of the experts and officials to the will of the people. Perhaps because of this, and because this view also presented the whole process as only minimally problematic with an absolute set of stages and happy outcomes it had for years a great influence on much sociological work, in spite of the fact that the Fuller and Myers work was based on little more than an illustrative study of the social problem of trailer camps in the Detroit area.

In 1951 Edwin Lemert published the results of a long over-due test of this stage theory of social problems. Though he studied the same supposed social problem of trailer camps, the only difference being that his study was done throughout the state of California, he found that the natural history picture presented by Fuller and Myers did not hold at all. While the development of trailer camps and the personal sense of problem was similar in California and Detroit, Lemert and his coworkers "were promptly struck by the relative absence in newspapers of controversial reporting and editorial discussion of such establishments. In none of the cities, as far as we were able to determine, did anything like a public interest and concern with trailer camps come to a critical focus in the newspapers. Certainly in contrast with the stormy controversies perennially aired in Los Angeles newspapers over vivisection, traffic difficulties, communism, and smog, trailers and trailer camps received only the most cursory and limited coverage."

What Lemert found most striking was that the whole nature of the definition of trailer camps as a problem, the degree to which the camps were seen as a problem, and the degree to which these definitions of the camps as problems became shared varied greatly. Far from being an invariant process it was quite varied because of the problematic nature of the symbolic representation of the camps and their effects on people:

> Is all of this to say that there was no awareness of trailer camps as problems in our five California communities? By no means can this be said to be the case, as the most casual kind of inquiry of public health officials and zoning administrators revealed. Trailer camps at different times

and at different places have been and continue today to be sources of annoyance and irritation to individuals and to groups both public and private. Importantly, however, the specific irritations have varied greatly with respect to their substance and with respect to the context of symbols in which they were publicized. In one community the trailer camps were seen primarily as a health problem, in another as a sanitation and housing problem, in another as a fire hazard, and in still others as a police problem.

Neighbourhood awareness of trailer camps as problems manifested itself only in sporadic and attenuated forms. . . .[19]

Very importantly, Lemert found that there continued to be great differences and conflicts among groups over whether, or to what degree, the trailer camps were problems:

At this point we may summarize by saying without reservation that in none of the communities we studied did an awareness of trailer camp problems become the generalized, multi-group, multi-sided phenomenon that was claimed for it in Detroit. Instead, awareness of the problem took the shape of segmental reactions of individuals or of one or two groups with special interests at stake, or else it was the harried awareness of a small number of administrative officials in whose jurisdiction the trailer camps happened to fall. In several instances the awareness of the problem gave indications of having been organized and solicited by an individual or a single group.[20]

In addition, Lemert found great variation in the way in which policy was created to deal with any such problem. For the most part, rather than responding to grass-roots pressures, the officials evolved policies for dealing with trailer camps over long periods of time with relative lack of concern for the grass-roots opinion:

[19] Edwin Lemert, "Is There a Natural History of Social Problems?" *American Sociological Review,* 16 (1951), pp. 217-223.
[20] *Ibid.*

Policies have been formed with but a minimum of spontaneously generating public opinion as an antecedent. An arresting demonstration of this comes from the survey of trailer camps previously alluded to, in which it came out that 23 communities in the state had trailer camp ordinances without, however, any trailer camps to regulate. In other words here we find the policy formed but no problem and no history of the problem in most of the cases. Why and how does policy get formulated under conditions in which the objective situation toward which it is directed is absent? Clearly the answer has to be sought in the anticipatory, positive conception of much governmental administrative action, and in the special nature of urban civic participation which abets it. . . .[21]

Equally importantly, Lemert found no clear direction in efforts at reform or in the consequences of such efforts, and he concluded that a basic reason why reform efforts were so uneven was that the legal meanings of trailer were fundamentally problematic for the members of society: "In searching for evidence of such a stage of reform in our investigation of trailer camps in California cities we were everywhere impressed by the limited and uneven success of efforts at reform and by the continued frustration of administrative regulation. The absence of any real reform in these communities was clearly a function of the failure of policy-forming groups to reach a decision on the basic question of *whether trailers are vehicles or whether they are dwellings.*"[22] In general, although the natural-stages theory of social problems recognized at least partially the problematic nature of the social definition of social problems, it did not see how fundamental these problems were, and it greatly underestimated the complexity, variability, and uncertainty of the process by which problems and their solutions are defined in our society. The theory failed to see how complex the processes are

[21] *Ibid.*
[22] *Ibid.*

in good part because it was based on too little research into the natural histories of our many social problems. Lemert's work, as he well recognized, was also too narrow, but it clearly showed the right directions to be taken, showing how problematic the definitional processes are even for one very limited kind of social problem. While little has been done thus far to correct this lack of research, we now have a much clearer idea of how fundamentally problematic the processes are and thus know that we will find no simple set of stages through which social problems are defined and solved.

The *collective behavior theory of social problems* proposed by Herbert Blumer is the most thoroughly interactionist theory and builds on certain ideas of the natural-stages theory while modifying them to avoid the earlier errors. Blumer is aware of the fundamentally problematic nature of the social definitions of social problems and of the resulting complexities and uncertainties involved in the actual processes by which problems are defined. It is this that lies behind his argument that social problems are defined through complex collective behavior processes:

> . . . social problems lie in and are products of collective definition. The process of collective definition is responsible for the emergence of social problems, for the way in which they are seen, for the way in which they are approached and considered, for the kind of official remedial plan that is laid out, and for the transformation of the remedial plan in its application. In short, the process of collective definition determines the career and fate of social problems, from the initial point of their appearance to whatever may be the terminal point in their course. They have their being in this process of collective definition and not in some alleged objective area of social malignancy.[23]

[23] Herbert Blumer, "Social Problems as Collective Behavior," unpublished paper presented at the Convention of the American Sociological Association. Washington, D.C., August, 1970.

Recognizing their complexity and uncertainty. Blumer does not believe that the definition processes involve any specific set of stages of natural events. He does argue that our studies of social problems should be guided by five analytical stages, but these are seen as complexly interdependent.

First, there is *the emergence of the social problem,* which is seen as highly problematic: The most casual observation and reflection shows clearly that the recognition by a society of its social problems is a highly selective process, with many social conditions and arrangements not even making a bid for attention and with others falling by the wayside in what is frequently a fierce competitive struggle. Many push for societal recognition but only a few come out at the end of the funnel.[24] Second, there is the *legitimation of social problems,* which is necessary if a social problem is to proceed to the next stage of mobilizing action: . . . after gaining initial recognition a social problem must acquire social endorsement if it is to be taken seriously and move forward in its career. It must acquire a necessary degree of respectability which entitles it to consideration in the recognized arenas of public discussion. . . . If the social problem fails to get legitimacy it flounders and languishes outside of the arena of public action.[25] Third, if the problem gains legitimacy, it now enters the arenas in which social action is mobilized. This is a very complex set of arenas in which the specific processes of mobilization are important in determining the directions that action will take:

> If a social problem manages to pass through the stages of societal recognition and of social legitimation it enters a new stage in its career. The problem now becomes the object of discussion, of controversy, of differing depictions and of diverse claims. Those who seek changes in the area of the problem clash with those who endeavour to protect vested

[24] *Ibid.*
[25] *Ibid.*

interests in the area. Exaggerated claims and distorted depictions, subserving vested interests, become commonplace. Outsiders, less involved, bring their sentiments and images to bear on their framing of the problem. Discussion, advocacy, evaluation, falsification, diversionary tactics, and advancing of proposals take place in the media of communication, in casual meetings, organized meetings, legislative chambers, and committee hearings. All of this constitutes a mobilization of the society for action on the social problem. It seems scarcely necessary to point out that the facts of the social problem depends greatly on what happened in this process of mobilization.[26]

Fourth, if social action is sufficiently mobilized and effective, an *official plan of action* will now be formulated which will in part redefine the problem for official action: This stage in the career of social problems represents the decision of a society as to how it will act with regard to the given problems. It consists of the hammering together of an official plan of action . . . (which) is almost always a product of bargaining in which diverse views and interests are accommodated. . . . It represents how the society through its official apparatus perceives the problem and intends to act toward the problem.[27] Fifth, if such a plan is formulated, then it generally will lead to some attempts at implementation, but the *implementation of the official plan* is also problematic and may well be very different from what the officials originally expected, especially because implementation ushers in new conflicts over the problem and its solutions:

Invariably to some degree, frequently to a large degree, the plan as put into practice is modified, twisted and reshaped, and takes on unforeseen accretions. . . . The implementation of the plan ushers in a new process of collective definition. It sets the stage for the formation of new lines of action

---

[26] *Ibid.*
[27] *Ibid.*

on the part of those involved in the social problem and those touched by the plan.[28]

The interactionist theory of social problems, especially as developed by Blumer, constitutes the most important development thus far in the theory of social problems but has barely outlined the nature of the theory we must develop and does involve some important weaknesses. While it treats social problems as being fundamentally problematic, it does not offer any explanation of this. It therefore does not show us any way in which the sociologist can contribute to the members' understandings of these problems and thereby help them to find at least partial resolutions to their conflicts. Although the collective behavior theory sees the definition of problems as necessarily the outcome of political action, it sheds little light on this political activity. Moreover, while this theory does at times treat public, official and expert actions as being partially independent determinants of the social meanings of problems, the theory as actually developed reintroduces some of the problems of the earlier natural-stages theory, especially that part which sees official action as following and being precipitated by grassroots, public pressures. What is called for is a more general theory of social problems that is built on the analysis of the reasons for the fundamentally problematic nature of social problems and social solutions, that develops the implications of this analysis for our understanding of social problems, that deals with the highly complex processes by which social problems and solutions are defined, and that draws the implications of all this for sociological involvement in the study and solutions of social problems.

[28] *Ibid.*

SUGGESTED READINGS

Emile Durkheim never wrote extensively on the specific subject of social problems, but his major works reveal clearly what his thought was on those problems. *Suicide* (translated by John A. Spaulding and George Simpson, New York: Free Press, 1951) is not only his most famous, but also his most important, work in the area of deviance and social problems. We see in this work that he believed sociological knowledge would make it possible to displace old values with scientifically determined values. He tries to show that suicide is a form of social pathology, at least in all of the Western societies. Sociologists should study suicide, and by implication, all forms of social problems, in the way a doctor studies illness. This work eventually became one of the cornerstones of the whole field of social pathology, which dominated the approach of American sociology to social problems in the 1930s and 1940s.

An interesting sequel to Durkheim's *Suicide* would be *The Social Meanings of Suicide* by Jack D. Douglas (Princeton, N.J.: Princeton University Press, 1967). The first half of the book is a historical and critical analysis of Durkheim's book and all the major succeeding sociological works on suicide. The final half analyzes the the absolutist conceptions that underlie all of those works and tries to show that actions such as suicide must be studied from the standpoint of the actors. Rather than imposing their own ideas on such actions, sociologists must be fundamentally concerned with determining what the actions meant to the actors.

C. Wright Mills's essay "The Professional Ideology of Social Pathologists" (*American Journal of Sociology,* Vol. 49, Sept., 1943) is the earliest and most famous attempt by sociologists to analyze the assumptions that underlie the theories of social pathology and, more generally, the absolutist approach to social problems. Mills was especially concerned with showing that the middle-class positions of sociologists determined their views of social problems. Unfortunately, in his later works he never considered how his own social situation might affect his equally absolutist conceptions of social problems. Mills never saw the need to study social problems from the standpoint of the members of society.

In his early work, "Anomie and Deviance," Robert K. Merton took an uncompromisingly absolutist view of social problems. The work is about deviance in general, but it focuses on delinquency statistics. Merton saw delinquency as an important social problem with specific properties that justified its being categorically distinguished from other kinds of crimes. In his book *The Creators of Delinquency* (Chicago: University of Chicago Press, 1969), Anthony Platt shows that delinquency is really a twentieth-century conception created by reformers and officials who had their own goals in mind in creating the category. Rather than being an absolute form of a problem, delinquency is clearly a very relativistic one.

Deviance and Respectability: The Social Construction of Moral Meanings (New York: Basic Books, 1970) is a collection of original essays edited by Jack D. Douglas which discusses the problems of deviance and crime and is concerned with the ways in which the members of society interpret and use social rules, including criminal laws, to achieve their own purposes in given situations. It shows that even crimes, which sociologists used to see as absolutist social problems, are relative to specific societies, specific individuals, and specific situations. Many of the essays are concerned in one way or another with the importance of politics in defining what will be a crime and what will not.

Labeling Theory by Edwin Schur (New York: Harper, 1971), is a fine presentation, analysis, and critique of the symbolic interactionist labeling theory of Herbert Blumer, Howard Becker, and many other contemporary sociologists of deviance and other social problems. Labeling theory is defined too broadly, so that it becomes almost indistinguishable from other theories (especially the phenomenological theories considered in the next two chapters), but the broad scope is also one of the values of the book.

The final chapter, on labeling theory and social policy, is most relevant to a critical assessment of the strengths and weaknesses of labeling theories for the study of social problems. The author concludes the book with a call for more consideration of the relevance of the micro-sociological studies to big social problems.

chapter 4

The Problematic Definitions of Social Problems

The interactionist theory of social problems was the first to systematically reject the traditional absolutist theory of social problems that sociologists had relied on since the work of the nineteenth-century public hygienists. Because of its rejection of an absolutist view of social problems, the interactionist theory is the first example of what we can call a *phenomenological theory of social problems.*[1] All phenomenological theories share four basic ideas about social problems: (1) *the sociologist must first study social problems and their solutions from the standpoints of the members of society*; (2) when the sociologist does study social problems in this way he finds that *the meanings of social problems to the members of our society are highly problematic*; (3) the problematic nature of social problems means

---

[1] For a full discussion of phenomenological sociology see *Understanding Everyday Life, op. cit.* My own work on the problematic meanings of social problems was greatly stimulated by a paper by John Lofland on "Disputes About Social Problems," delivered at the Convention of the American Sociological Association, Washington, D.C., August, 1970.

that *there will be basic conflicts among the members of our society in defining social problems*; and (4) these conflicts mean that *the sociologist who is committed to providing objective and practically useful information and explanations of those social problems must analyze the ways in which conflicting groups construct the meanings of social problems and solutions to those problems.*

Social Problems from the Actors' Standpoints

As we have seen, the absolutist sociologist assumed he knew what social problems are. All he had to do was introspectively analyze his own thoughts about social problems, give a formal definition of social problems, study those problems empirically, develop a theory, and tell the members of the society what to do to solve the problems. The members would surely agree with those definitions and would see the proposed solutions as the best solutions. If they didn't, then they needed to be better educated or simply ignored. The absolutists had great contempt for the "vulgar" ideas of common sense: common sense was to be discarded, not studied. The elitist and tyrannical aspect of this approach did not seem to bother even the American sociologists.

The phenomenological sociologist does not think up what social problems are; he does not provide *ad hoc definitions of social problems.* Instead, he begins by empirically determining what social problems are by analyzing what the social actors say these are, and are not, in their everyday, practical communications. Unfortunately, this procedure is not nearly as simple as it may sound.

As in most of their communications, the members of our society do not use one term to communicate ideas about social problems. Instead of simply using the one term "social problem" to communicate their ideas about such problems, they use many different terms: "social failings," "social sufferings," "social tensions," "social weaknesses," and so on. Moreover, people commonly use abbreviated terms to mean the same things: "our problems," "our failings," etc. Worst of all, the members of society commonly take it for granted that whoever is listening to their communications will know all of what they mean even when they use only indirect or very partial references to that meaning. These references are called *communicative glosses* and consist simply of a kind of mental shorthand we use to avoid going to all the trouble of spelling out everything we want to say.

A fine example of the complex use of various terms to communicate about social problems is found in the following statement by Stewart Alsop in his essay "The Mysterious American Disease":

> The United States is rather like a man whose annual physical checkup shows that he is in dandy shape, and who feels perfectly horrible all the time. Moreover, the doctors really have no idea what ails the poor fellow. Recently the head doctor came close to admitting as much. . . .
>
> All the signs suggest that the long economic boom which gave Mr. Average his 34 per cent growth in real income is coming to an end. If there is a recession—is there any if?—the racial tensions and economic frustrations which have led to "the greatest unrest in America in a hundred years" are sure to increase.
>
> Then there will be a great national temptation to resort to authoritarian measures to deal with those problems which seem otherwise so insoluble. In fact, much as it goes against the American grain to admit it, there are some problems which are inherently insoluble, just as there are some diseases which are inherently incurable. At least the mysterious American disease does not appear to be lethal, and it

is worth bearing in mind that an authoritatian cure can be much worse than a democratic disease.[2]

The term "disease" is used by Alsop here in roughly the same way he is using the term "problems." At least, he seems to use the two interchangeably, using the term "disease" to show the reader what he means by "problems," presumably because the reader can be expected to have a more direct understanding of "disease" than of "problems."

In general, members of our society, precisely because they assume that they know what these social problems are and that others will see them in the same way, commonly refer to social problems without using the term and frequently without using a related term. This means that in order to get at the meanings of "social problems," we have to rely on systematic comparisons of their statements, including statements in which they do not use the term social problem, but in which our previous experience with their uses of that term indicates they probably mean the same thing as when they use the term. Such an analysis of the social meanings of social problems quickly reveals their problematic nature.

The Problematic Meanings of Social Problems

Sociologists have come increasingly to recognize that *the definition of social problems is highly problematic in our complex society.* Whether something is considered a social problem or not is dependent on the values and ideas of those looking at it. Since there are many conflicts over beliefs and values in our pluralistic society, there is a great deal of conflict over the definition of what is and what is not a social problem. This has become

---

[2] Stewart Alsop, "The Mysterious American Disease, *Newsweek* (February 9, 1971), p. 98.

especially clear in recent years, as various large interest groups have struggled to get the federal government to see their situations as social problems. Consider, for example, the great social debate over poverty: is poverty a social problem? Millions of people in our society, especially those who see themselves as liberals, argue vehemently that poverty is a social problem, a problem caused by the nature of society, and that society should therefore do something to end poverty. Millions of others, especially those who see themselves as conservatives, argue just as vehemently that poverty is an individual problem, not a social problem, and that therefore the individuals, rather than society, should do something to end their own poverty. There are even more extreme conflicts over the definition of social problems today, as we can see in the case of those who argue that the police are the social problem, not the criminals, which would have been an unthinkable idea to the social pathologists.

The social meanings of any communication are said to be problematic when they are uncertain to the members of society and when the members disagree about them among themselves. The social category of social problem and related categories are highly problematic for the members of our society for *two reasons.*

First, the category is problematic because even in the abstract it has at least three distinct meanings. These meanings overlap, so they are said to have what Wittgenstein called *family relationship meanings,* but they are also partially independent. This can be seen by considering a typical kind of statement about social problems: "Use of marihuana has become a 'frightening social problem,' Attorney General Thomas C. Lynch told California lawyers and judges. . . ." [3] This statement can mean, first, that smoking marihuana is a social problem because it is something done by many people and is "bad" or "wrong." This is the *moral meaning* of social problem that used to be so common.

[3] Reported in the *Los Angeles Times* (Sept. 11, 1969), Part I, p. 3.

This same statement could mean that marihuana smoking is a problem in that it produces a problem, such as suffering, anxiety, tension, etc., for a large number of people in society. In this sense, a social problem is *any problem shared by a significantly large number of people in society; it is social only in the sense of being shared.* (What constitutes a significantly large number is itself problematic for the members of society, and they sometimes argue over whether the number involved is large enough to matter.) Someone who believes poverty is widespread may believe it is a social problem in this sense even if he believes it is something caused by individual laziness. This second meaning is what we call *the weak meaning of social problem.* Both of these two meanings of social problem, however, have apparently been gradually going out of use and are being replaced with a *strong* (the third) *meaning of social problem,* that is, *any problem that is both socially shared and socially caused.* In fact, when we look at the context of the use of the term in the statement by Attorney General Lynch, we can see that he was using the term in this sense, since he went on to argue that the youthful offenders are largely the result of a failure by members of the legal profession to act effectively: "What youth does with its years ahead is pretty well their problem, their decision," he said. "But, at least society should provide them with a solid and sound foundation from which they can make their future decisions."

Lynch said, "the willful lack of knowledge of law" can be attributed largely to the legal profession, which should have been the first to awaken youth to the fact that legal machinery is a social instrument for their use and protection.[4] Because this meaning of social problems—that of a problem that is shared and caused by society—is the most common meaning, we shall always use the term "social problem" in this sense unless otherwise stated.

---

[4] *Ibid.*

This kind of analysis of meaning is the foundation of the famous definition of social problems given by Merton and Nisbet,[5] but they add a fourth dimension of meaning—the belief that something can be done to solve the problem. The trouble with adding this fourth dimension is that members of our society commonly believe that we have social problems about which it is not practical to do anything. Death is not a social problem, not because we cannot do anything about it, but because it is not normally socially caused. Diseases, such as cancer, are often considered social problems even when we can't do anything about them. Smog was always considered a great social problem in cities such as Los Angeles even when it was believed nothing could be done about it, even before it was discovered that smog was caused by the presence of too many cars. It is true that people are not apt to talk about such *hopeless* social problems, but this is because they see nothing that can be done about them. The belief that there is a realistic solution to a social problem is very important in leading to more communication and action about the problem, but it is not part of the meaning of social problem.

The second and most problematic aspect of the social meanings of social problems consists of the disagreements over the shared nature of problems and over their causes, that is, over what is and is not a social problem, rather than disagreements over the abstract meanings of the term "social problems." While we shall be analyzing a number of instances of this in the next chapter, it is useful to look at one example which starkly contrasts the definitions of problems and nonproblems. In this example Richard Barnet and Marcus Raskin argue that "pacified Americans" see some things as nonproblems even though many experts and all "depacified Americans" see these things as problems, and they argue that "pacified Americans" must come to

[5] See Robert K. Merton and Robert Nisbet, eds., *Contemporary Social Problems, op. cit.,* pp. 775-823.

see these things as the real problems facing us before it is too late to save ourselves:

> When future historians and archaeologists sift the wreckage of our civilization, they will be impressed by the well-documented warnings we treat as ritual. No society ever faced disaster with more facts. Every catastrophic step in the nuclear arms race has been predicted and publicized. Every impending crisis has its own team of Cassandras. We have experts who tell us that the automobile will make the city uninhabitable and will eventually kill the urban population. We have other experts who tell us that we cannot poison the rivers and oceans indefinitely without risking the oxygen supply needed to support life. . . .
>
> Pacified Americans believe that they will have peace by pursuing war, but they are uniting the world against them.
>
> Pacified Americans believe that they can hold onto their riches only if they intimidate the rest of mankind, but they will exhaust themselves in the process.
>
> Pacified Americans believe that they can exploit the material resources of the earth to satisfy their every whim, but their children will pay for the destruction of the earth. . . .[6]

There are two general reasons why such disagreements over which concrete situational phenomena constitute social problems and which do not are necessary, or inevitable, in our society: (1) the pluralistic structure of our society means that different groups will inevitably differ in their experiences and in the meanings they give to those experiences; and (2) even within any particular group for which there is shared experience, or a common life situation, there will inevitably be conflicts over the concrete meanings given to experience, especially when it comes to explaining the causes (social vs. individual) of that experience.

---

[6] Richard J. Barnet and Marcus G. Raskin, *An American Manifesto* (New York: New American Library, 1971).

Though there are still arguments among sociologists over whether American society is becoming more pluralistic or more homogeneous, the evidence seems pretty clear that it is still quite pluralistic.[7] There are certain commonly shared patterns of life and social meanings, such as our common language, a common commitment to our democratic form of government, a common conception of ourselves as Americans, and so on. But while these are important in determining certain things about our society, especially the nature of social order, we must not be misled by them into believing that American society is homogeneous *in general*. As I have previously argued in *American Social Order,* these common meanings and ways of life are especially apt to mislead in this way and to obscure the vast diversity of our society, precisely because they are the public elements of our society. There is considerable homogeneity in the public realm of life, which we might call, with some exaggeration, the *Howard-Johnson's front of American society.* But lying behind this public facade, which is itself continually broken by great conflicts, is the private reality of America's vast differences: the continuing strength of ethnic and racial identities, the ancient regional differences, the chasm between the giant cities and the lonely farms, the lengthy social ladder that divides the poor from the rich, the generation gap that divides the young from the old, the differences in world view of the many professions and occupations, the cleavage between white collar and blue collar workers, the growing differences between the educated and the uneducated, and many more.

These many differences, however complexly overlapping and crosscutting they are, make up many different life-situations, and these produce or reinforce many basic differences in shared meanings. Part of these consist of the differences in definitions of social problems. Some life situations lead people to see some

[7] For a full description of the issues over pluralism see *American Social Order, op. cit.*

phenomena as "social problems," while other situations lead people to see other phenomena as problems. Moreover, even when there is agreement on what the problems are, the differences in life situations may lead people to see these problems from very different perspectives with very different priorities. As many people have pointed out, the man who lives in the slum may see rats as a great social problem and not see inflation as a problem at all, while the man who only sees the slum from the windows of the New Haven railroad on the way to his Manhattan office may see inflation as a great social problem and rats as no social problem.

We see then that the differences in shared perceptions and shared meanings produce differences in the conceptions of problems held by different groups at a given time. Because these are differences in the same time period, we can call them *synchronic problems* in the definition of social problems. Although these are generally the difficulties in defining social problems that concern us most, they are not the only ones.

Because each group in our society is normally changing quite rapidly, both in its actual life situation and, even more, in its social definitions of that life situation, we also find that the social meanings of problems are problematic over a period of time for these groups. These *diachronic problems* in the definition of social problems pose an especially difficult task for social policy makers because they make it pretty certain that any one social arrangement that satisfies people today can come to be seen by the same people tomorrow as a terrible social problem simply because of changes in their subjective definitions of things, even if the external events remain the same. (The problems of social policy makers are actually worse than this because the external arrangements are changing as well, which means that they are caught in many crosscurrents of relativistic changes that defy any totally rational analysis). An excellent example of this diachronic problem involved in defining social problems, which we shall see more of in our analysis of the second progressive era in Chapter 6, is given by Milton Friedman in the following argument that the very "successes" as he defines them of American society give rise to a growing sense of social problems:

> If Apollo was a victory for U. S. engineering genius, it could not disguise American failures at home . . . If we can put men on the moon, why can't we build adequate housing? Or feed all citizens adequately? Or end social and economic injustice?" This particular quotation comes from *Time* magazine, but it might have been lifted from any of dozens of comments on the spectacular moon landing.
>
> The widespread acceptance and repetition of this cliche is a depressing testimonial to the superficiality and lack of historical perspective in so much that passes for informed commentary on current affairs . . .
>
> The cliche about Apollo is itself ironic testimony to our success at home. That success has raised our aspirations to levels never before dreamed of. In other times and places, the goal of "adequate" housing and food for all and the *end* of social and economic injustice seemed as fantastic as a voyage to the moon. The example of U. S. success has made both goals seem equally attainable.
>
> Yet they are not. We may, and we all hope shall, continue to attain higher incomes, have more and more adequate housing, and reduce social and economic injustices. We must face and meet today's problems and not rest on past glories. But no matter how well we succeed, our aspirations will continue to rise, and will continue to exceed our attainments. "Ah, but a man's reach should exceed his grasp, or what's a heaven for?"[8]

Perhaps the most important kind of diachronic problem in the definition of social problems is that produced by changes in

---

[8] Milton Friedman, "On Lunacy," *Newsweek* (Sept. 29, 1969), p. 94.

the *feeling of general social satisfaction and dissatisfaction.* While there do not seem to be any clear and distinct criteria by which people judge how satisfying or dissatisfying their social lives are, they clearly do have some vague sense of what they expect to get out of life, against which they can judge how well things are going. It is this that lies behind the so-called revolution in rising expectations that seems to have led so many people around the world to feel more dissatisfied with their present social conditions, even though these conditions are clearly better in any objective terms. As we shall see later, there is reason to believe that such rising expectations lie behind much of the discontent over poverty and many other problems in American society in recent years.

Even a seemingly physicalistic social problem such as air pollution can be greatly affected by changes in the implicit criteria we use to judge our air. As Matthew Crenson has argued very persuasively, the actual amounts of sulphur dioxide and dirt particles in the air of American cities is probably much less today than it was thirty to fifty years ago, yet we are vastly more convinced that we face a grave social problem of air pollution today because our criteria have changed:

> . . . there is reason to hope that the dangers have been subsiding. Shortly before World War II, the U.S. Bureau of Mines published a compilation of sulphur dioxide measurements that had been made in a number of American cities between 1914 and 1939. When these figures are matched up with comparable data for the 1960s it becomes apparent that there has been a general decline in sulphur dioxide pollution during the past thirty or forty years. In some cities, the sulphur dioxide content of the air today is only one-third or one-fourth what it was before World War II. A similar observation can be made concerning the air-borne dirt particles that enhance the lethal potential of sulphur dioxide. Since 1957, the U.S. Public Health Service has been measuring suspended particulates in a large sample

of American cities. By 1966 (the last year for which published data are available), the average amount of floating dirt in city air was lower than it had been in 1957.

The government data on suspended particulates show a substantial decline in the average from 1957 to 1961, followed by an increase from 1961 to 1966—although only a slight increase.

In some ways, at least, city air is probably cleaner today than it was thirty or forty or fifty years ago. The city of tenements, with its coal-burning factories, furnaces, and locomotives, was probably a good bit dirtier than today's city. But today cities are clogged with automobiles, and they present a new order of air pollution problems. The most notorious form of automotive pollution is photochemical smog, a brownish haze which has annoyed the residents of Los Angeles and other cities for more than twenty years.

Among the constituents of smog, there are potentially lethal gases and cancer-producing substances. In spite of all this, smog investigations have not revealed any relationship between variations in mortality. Photochemical smog cannot be given credit for any pollution disasters like the New York incident . . .

It is curious, therefore, that public alarm about the pollution problem has clearly been growing. If we are not moving toward a pollution crisis, then why has the outcry become so enormous? The likely answer is that the rising chorus of complaint about dirty air comes less from any sharp change in the quality of the air than from changes in the human beings who breathe it. Today people are probably more fastidious about the air that they breathe than they were a generation ago. Some evidence to support this notion comes from an opinion survey conducted in the St. Louis metropolitan area about seven years ago. Although medical evidence suggests that older people have more to fear from air pollution than do younger people, the St. Louis survey evidence showed that people under forty were much more likely to complain about air pollution than were people over forty who lived in similarly polluted neighborhoods. One likely implication of the survey results is that there has been an increase, from one generation to the next, in people's intolerance of dirty air. Pollution levels that were acceptable in the past are no longer tolerable to many younger urbanites.[9]

We can also see the basic aspect of such diachronic problems by considering the specific argument over crime in the streets. The social category of crime in the streets has been used generally to refer to those kinds of crime that involve actual violence or potential violence against strangers, such as murder, assault, rape, and armed robbery. Such criminal acts as these have probably been seen as a social problem by a large percentage of the American public at any time, but although the evidence on earlier periods is not very good, there seems to have been a steady increase in the concern and anger over this social problem in the last few decades. No one has voiced this concern and anger more strongly than J. Edgar Hoover: "These statistics [on violent crimes] represent an epidemic of crime and violence, which has affected virtually every segment of American society. The mugger, the rapist, the hoodlum stalk our streets in frightening numbers. Fear of venturing outside the home at night has become a fact of urban life."[10] People in urban areas seem to be increasingly convinced that the problem is getting worse all the time, meaning specifically that there is more and more of it; and this growing concern and anger over the rising tide of crime in the streets has produced increasingly harsh federal and local legislation to deal with it, including laws that many legislators have attacked as violations of civil rights.

There is no reason to believe that this increased fear is the

[9] Matthew A. Crenson, "Is Air Pollution Really a Threat?" *The Johns Hopkins Magazine,* XXI (December, 1970), pp. 23-26.
[10] J. Edgar Hoover, *Vital Speeches of the Day,* XXXV (November 1, 1968), p. 42.

result of any actual increase in the experience of such violent crimes on the part of urban Americans. Rather, we find it is due partly to a simple ignorance of the facts, which allows the actors to read their own feelings into the situation, and partly to basic changes that have taken place in the actors' interpretations of the world, independently of the external changes.

The ignorance of facts in the area of crime is very common, if for no other reason than the relative lack of direct experience of most members of society with the things they are trying to analyze. The extent of such ignorance is illustrated by the report of a United Press International reporter on a police blotter from New York City in 1906:

> Most, if not all, of the people mentioned in the dust covered blotters of the 64th Precinct stationhouse now are dead.
>
> But, the so-called "blotter"—or official journal of the day-to-day activities of the stationhouse—presents a vivid picture of life when time moved a lot slower, life was much simpler and, although there indeed was crime, it was on a much lower plane than now—or so it would seem.
>
> Thumbing through the pages of the blotter of the then two-year-old, three-story building, one cannot even find a mention of narcotics, one of the most common crimes listed today.
>
> High on the list of arrests or crimes committed involving investigations and arrests now involve either narcotics directly—or burglaries to get the money to pay to supply a "habit."[11]

The reporter was quite right in noting the total lack of any arrests for narcotics violations in 1906 and the high frequency of narcotics-related arrests in 1970. But he obviously did not realize that the only reason there were no arrests for narcotics in 1906 was that there were no laws against the use of narcotics

---

[11] Edward V. McCarthy, "Turn of Century Crime Mostly Minor Offenses," *Los Angeles Times* (Dec. 11, 1970), Part I-A, p. 6.

in 1906. This ignorance of basic facts allows him to conclude that in 1906 crime "was on a much lower plane than now," thereby supporting the popular myth of a great crime wave sweeping the nation, especially the myth of the rising menace of heroin addiction. The available facts indicate that the rate of opiate use and addiction was probably as great in 1906 as in 1970, especially because it was so widely used in Laudanum to calm down crying babies and soothe the nerves of old ladies, and that while other nonaddictive drug use has soared in recent years, opiate addiction has probably not expanded. A knowledge of such facts would quickly lead one to see that what has changed is the social concept of narcotics and of the whole crime problem.

When we look at the other facts on violent crimes we find the same thing. If we take the Uniform Crime Reports (U.C.R.) of the F.B.I. as valid information of these crimes, we find, as Leroy Gould has shown, that the picture is a very mixed one:

> Since 1933, the rate of homicide has declined and the rates of forcible rape and aggravated assault have increased. Robbery, prevalent in 1933, declined in frequency until about 1945; it has been increasing irregularly since then, although the 1933 high has not been reached again. Overall, the U.C.R. index of crimes against the person shows a general decline in these four types of crimes from 1933 through 1943 and a general increase since 1944.
>
> Even if these figures are accepted as accurate, however, problems of interpretation still exist because the four crimes do not demonstrate the same trends. Noting, for example, that most of the recent increases in crimes against the person are due to increases in assaults, and that the number of homicides has actually decreased, it is hard to say whether the incidence of serious crimes against the person have been rising or falling. To answer this question, one must be willing to equate assaults with homicides or at least, in terms of seriousness, be willing to say that a certain number of assaults are as serious as one homicide. Few people would

be willing to make such a comparison; certainly, the crime commission was unwilling.[12]

But there is in fact no valid reason to accept these official statistics as good indications of what has been going on in American society. Sociologists have shown conclusively that the official statistics on crime are highly biased. They are probably more dependent on the desire of police and other officials to publicize a slightly increasing rate of crime to justify increased budgets and power for themselves than on what is happening in the rest of society. Consequently, we have more reason to believe that the actual experience of crime by urban Americans is quite independent of this growing fear of crime in the streets. We have, then, a situation of great national importance that may affect the civil rights of us all, one in which the social definitions of the problem of violent crime have changed greatly over the last few decades; yet there is no good reason to believe that the actual experience of such crimes has changed at all. If anything, we have better reason to believe that the extremely violent crimes are decreasing.

Conflicts over the Definitions of Social Problems

Given the necessarily problematic nature of the social definition of social problems, conflicts over the definition of social problems in our society are inevitable. Since an understanding of these conflicts is crucial for any sociological analysis of the problems and for any realistic policy proposals for dealing with such problems, we must analyze several of the most important kinds of conflicts.

[12] Leroy C. Gould, "Crime and Its Impact in an Affluent Society," in *Crime and Justice in American Society,* op. cit., p. 85.

While all social meanings of social problems are subject to some disagreements in our society, there is great variation in the degree of disagreement. There are some phenomena which are almost universally seen as social problems, at least in the weak sense of a shared problem, if not in the strong sense of a problem that is both socially shared and socially caused. Murder, starvation, hunger, and similar phenomena are such nearly universally agreed upon (weak) social problems in our society. Environmental pollution, or at least smog, is probably the most recent example of such a *consensus* social problem. When we analyze the different social problems on which there exists such a consensus we find that they are almost always directly related to the common human physical and physiological needs. Because our body and its needs in relation to the physical universe are shared by us all, there are certain things and certain feelings that can be counted on with a high degree of reliability to be seen by human beings as necessary or inevitable. Almost all human beings expect starvation, hunger, and death to hurt or frighten, and thus they represent problems that anyone would like to solve. These consensus social problems, then, can be called naturalistic or *physicalistic social problems.*

When we look at American discussions of starvation, hunger, murder, smog, etc., we do in fact find that almost everyone considers them to be (weak) social problems. Hunger is an excellent example of this. There are almost no Americans who argue that hunger is not a social problem or who argue that hunger is good for you and we should have more of it. In a nation with millions of mystics, astrologists, know-nothings, and organized extremists on every side, there is not yet a National Committee to Support Hunger. There has, apparently, been a Murder Incorporated, though it received very little popular support. The difference between this and hunger would seem to be that no one directly benefits from others' hunger, even if they indirectly benefit from the conditions that produce that hunger; thus no one goes against the consensus view of hunger as a great social problem.

There have been great national conflicts over the question of the actual extent of hunger; those who believe it is very restricted would argue that it is not an actual social problem. But they agree that it would be one if it were extensive. Here we simply have a disagreement over facts. We have also had great arguments over the concrete meanings of hunger, as we do over all of the other psychological aspects of social problems. Many social critics have argued that we must define hunger in terms of the medical definitions of adequate nutrition or in terms of standard nutrition. However, as soon as they move away from the almost universally shared physiological experience of hunger, which everyone finds to be a form of suffering (except the minimal degree that tantalizes), and thus a problem, they immediately enter the realm of more problematic meanings and, consequently, the conflicts over the definition of hunger as a social problem grow.

We can see the same factors at work in the definition of environmental pollution as a social problem. The more directly something can be linked to a universal physiological experience, the more likely it is that there will be agreement as to its being a (weak) social problem. Smog is probably the one form of pollution that has a universal and immediate effect on the human body. While sensitivity to it differs greatly, no one is immune to the stinging eyes and the aching chest that come from a strong dose of smog, so everyone sees it as a (weak) social problem. When we move to other forms of pollution that are less immediate and universal in their physiological effects on human beings, such as thermal pollution, we find the definition more problematic; consequently, we find more conflicts over the definition of such pollution as a social problem.

In addition to these physicalistic social problems, we find a second type of problem that is partially derived from them:

least-common-denominator social problems. These are problems such as economic depression, high mortality rates, high disease rates, and war. They themselves are not physiologically experienced, but they are seen by almost everyone as related to physiologically defined problems: economic depression is seen as causing hunger, mortality rates as indicating death, war as producing death and maiming, etc. It is because they are cast in global terms that apply to the whole society (everyone is potentially affected by depression, high mortality rates, war) that they are a form of *least-common-denominator social problems,* about which there is at least a medium-to-high range of consensus as social problems. Partly because of this, policies aimed at solving them have become least-common-denominator goals for our pluralistic nation. Politicians of all parties use depression, threat of war, and so on, as rallying cries to create consensus for their policies. Since agreement about them is even more widespread, we can expect to see the same use of smog and pollution in the future.

The importance of the least-common-denominator social problems in producing a consensus about both the nature of social problems and the social policies for dealing with them is made especially clear by a consideration of the problematic meanings and resulting conflicts over "poverty," which, as the term has been used in recent years, provides us with an excellent example of our third type of social problem, *the relativistic social problem.* One might expect that poverty, which presumably involves much direct suffering on the part of individuals, would be more generally defined as a social problem. To the degree that poverty is interpreted to mean starvation, hunger, or disease, we find this to be so. But these aspects of poverty are not what poverty most commonly refers to in our society today, perhaps because they have become so relatively rare that they are no longer of concern to many people.

The fact is that poverty is one of the most problematic

social categories found in the realm of social problems today; as we would expect from this, we find great conflicts over the use of the term and over its definition as a social problem. When we look at the actual uses of the category of poverty today we find a vast number of different meanings, even among the experts on the issue. At one extreme we find John Kenneth Galbraith asserting in *The Affluent Society* that poverty has been virtually eliminated in American society—and that was in 1958 before the War on Poverty and the decade of prosperity in the 1960s. At the other extreme we find Michael Harrington insisting in 1962 in *The Other America* that there are at least fifty million poor people in America. The difference between virtually zero and fifty million indicates considerable disagreement over the meanings of the term, made all the more striking by the fact that the two estimates were made by men who share a reasonably common "liberal" view of American society. An analysis of the many other formal definitions of poverty shows the same disagreement—even confusion—over the meanings of the term.

The analysis of the term poverty, like the category of "social problem," reveals family relations of meanings. That is, the term is found to communicate a number of different dimensions of meaning that overlap at various points, but that are also partially independent of each other. Because of this, it is quite possible for different people to use a category like poverty and seem to mean the same thing while actually meaning quite independent things.

In the nineteenth century and the earlier part of this century, the term "poverty" was used to refer primarily to the kind of grinding poverty to be found in the London slums studied by Charles Booth or in the "Hell's Kitchens" of American slums. Because of this, we sometimes still find the term used this way today, in which case it refers primarily to the first dimension of meaning of the term: *lacking in material goods to the point of physical suffering from hunger, weather or disease.* It was probably this sense of the term that Galbraith had in mind when he estimated that poverty had virtually disappeared from America. (Even in that sense he was probably being too optimistic, as revealed by congressional studies of the rural south in the 1960s.)

In this earlier sense of the term we find an emphasis on *absolute or objective criteria such as hunger.* Most uses of the category still rely heavily on this idea of an *absolute amount of material goods relative to absolute needs of human beings,* but, as starvation and the related sufferings of grinding poverty disappeared or were relegated to unseen pockets of society, the absolute criteria changed and in fact became *social criteria* rather than physicalistic or physiological criteria; this meant that they actually became less absolute and thus less agreed upon. In this second sense poverty came to mean *lacking the material goods necessary to meet (absolutely agreed upon) human needs of health.* Rather than actual suffering being the criterion, the criterion was now any diet which could be shown medically to produce less than adequate physical development. The factor of housing adequate to maintain physical health was also included, but the concentration was on nutrition. This is sometimes called the "nutrition adequacy definition." It was this dimension of meaning of poverty that led Rose Friedman to write that in 1965 Americans with an income of less than $2,195 for an average family of four (but ranging from $1,295 for two to $3,155 for seven) could be considered poor.[13] This led her to conclude that only 4.8 million families were poor.

Using the same kind of standard, but with different weightings or parameters, the U.S. Chamber of Commerce *concluded* that poverty is not massive and that it is not a serious issue, which might mean that it is not even a (weak) social problem.

---

[13] Rose D. Friedman, *Poverty* (Washington, D.C.: U.S. Government Printing Office, 1965).

We see, then, that any definition of the category of poverty in terms of human needs that does not rely on universal physiological experience such as hunger, cold, or disease, immediately introduces problematic meanings. This adequate nutrition criteria introduces the least amount of problematic meanings, since it is tied to standards set by medicine, but even doctors disagree greatly over such things. Should one concentrate on "minimum daily adult requirements" or on optimal requirements?" But what is an optimal requirement? Presumably, it is one defined in terms of health and is a diet that produces the best health. But there is no absolute standard for health, no standard based on physiological experiences universal to human beings; health is culturally relative and means very different things to the cross-country runner, the weight lifter, the office worker, and the slender suburban matron. In terms of "standard caloric requirements," some wealthy American women are terribly impoverished. What is presented as an absolute, physiological definition turns out to be very unphysiological and very problematic for the members of our society. Such an "absolute definition" may be more useful as political rhetoric than as a resolution of the problem of defining poverty.

The third dimension of meaning given to poverty extends the idea of basic human needs into the realm of supposedly shared social ideas as to what constitutes a decent standard of living: *poverty is defined as lacking the material goods necessary to enjoy a decent standard of living.* This is the idea behind the famous official definition of poverty proposed by the Social Security Administration and used as the basis of the legislation for the Office of Economic Opportunity. As Ben Seligman has summarized this official estimate:

> . . . the SSA Poverty Index specified the minimum money income required to support an average family of given size at the lowest level consistent with a decent standard of living. In essence, it specified an acceptable level of con-

sumption, thereby providing broad limits to the relative incidence of poverty. A new poverty line was drawn separately for 124 different types of families. These were classified by sex of the head of family, number of other adults, farm versus urban, and number of children under the age of eighteen. Then the amount of income was determined that would buy an adequate diet based on Department of Agriculture criteria, and excess income over this amount was used to set the various poverty lines. While in the main the food bill was estimated at a third of total income requirements, different ratios were used for different sizes of families. The total sum necessary to meet the needs of a family headed by a man, based on the "economy" diet, was $3,220 a year; for a family headed by a woman, $2,960. The actual income medians were found to be $1,760 and $1,300 respectively. Again, the estimate of the number of poor persons came to 35 million for 1963.[14]

Other analysts have argued that these figures around the average of $3,220 are grossly inadequate. They have added to the problematic meanings of the category by adding additional factors such as "standard education costs." Some of these estimates of the average "poverty line" run as high as $10,000 or more for an average family in New York City, where living costs are very high, and some estimates place America's poor at one third or even one half of the total population. All of these indexes, however, still attempt to tie the meanings of poverty to some idea of either a physiological absolute standard or a supposedly social absolute standard.

This is not true of the completely relativistic meaning of poverty. A growing number of the analysts of poverty have explicitly given up any idea of tying the meanings of poverty to such absolutes. They have noted that continuing prosperity,

---

[14] Ben B. Seligman, *Permanent Poverty* (Chicago: Quadrangle, 1968), pp. 29-30.

with average increases in personal income equal to those of the 1960s, has led to a steady decrease in poverty and would lead to an elimination of poverty by about 1990, if poverty is defined in terms of the average (real) income level of $3,220 per year for an average family. But they insist that any such decrease in poverty or elimination of poverty would not be truly meaningful to the poor because, they insist, the poor themselves think of their social situation in terms of their general socioeconomic status relative to that of everyone else in the society. In this way they conclude that *poverty is any condition that falls at the lower end of the socioeconomic scale.* In terms of this completely relativistic meaning of poverty, they then try to show that poverty has not decreased at all in the United States over the last several decades and may have actually increased. They argue that when we look at the income distribution in the United States we find, as Seligman has estimated, that:

> While there has been some improvement as contrasted to pre-World War II periods, the fact remains that income distribution patterns are substantially unchanged since the mid-1940s. The lowest fifth of consumer units in 1965 had an average personal income of less than $2,900 and received only 4.6 per cent of total family personal income. In the main, reductions in income inequality have occurred only in the top half of the distribution scale; there are very few changes for families located in the lower half. At the same time, the share of net worth that goes to the top 2 per cent of families increased (from 58 to 61 per cent between 1953 and 1962), while that going to the lowest fifth of income receivers fell from 11 to 7 per cent.[15]

Regardless of whether or not it is true that the members of our society now commonly define poverty in such completely relativistic terms—an important point to which we shall return—

[15] *Ibid.*, p. 35.

it seems clear that such a relativistic definition produces the maximum of social conflict over the definition of social problems. The reason for this is very simple: once we make no attempt to show that the meaning of the social problem is a necessary one, independent of the wills and intentions of the different members of society, we make the selection of any particular group's social definition of poverty entirely arbitrary. What is there to constrain us or anyone else in society to accept the meanings of poverty shared by those who regard themselves as being poor? Why not accept the Chamber of Commerce's definition? If a millionaire insists that he feels poor, should we thereby include him in the category of the poor? Again, should we take the findings by Cantrel that almost no one in America considers himself a member of the lower class to be an indication that, in fact, there are no lower-class people?

The argument over the nature of the social problems of poverty shows us this extreme example of some actors' purposefully choosing to make their categories completely relativistic and, thereby, producing great conflicts over the meanings of the problem and its solutions. But as we shall soon see, most of the problems over meaning and most of the conflicts over social problems are not purposeful. Rather, they come about as a result of factors not available to the actors for analysis and, consequently, produce conflicts that cannot be solved by the actors by common-sense rational analysis. Some of the arguments over poverty show this shortcoming, but it is even clearer in the great arguments over whether the order of American society is a social problem, which are generally cast in terms of healthy society versus sick society.

SUGGESTED READINGS

As Stanford Lyman and Marvin Scott explain in beautifully clear detail in *A Sociology of the Absurd* (New York: Appleton-Century-Crofts, 1970), the sociology of the absurd is founded on the premise that the world is absurd, by which they mean inherently meaningless. Man is born into a meaningless world, yet he must have meanings that order his world for himself and his fellows if he is to live at all. He must, then, construct a world of shareable meanings. This book is a fine introduction to the fundamental ideas of the many different kinds of phenomeno-logical sociology, though it tends to be focused on the analysis of how the members of society give "accounts" (explanations, justifications) of their activities in daily life, which aligns the work predominantly with the school of Alfred Schutz.

The Social Construction of Reality (Garden City, N.Y.: Anchor Books, 1967) by Peter Berger and Thomas Luckmann is the classic introduction to Schutz's phenomenological sociology and is especially valuable for those who do not wish to get involved with all the issues dealt with in Schutz's classic work *The Phenomenology of the Social World* (Evanston, Illinois: Northwestern University Press, 1967). It deals with many of the basic problems involved in the construction of social meanings and social order. While it is in basic agreement with the perspective of the present book, it differs by placing far greater emphasis on the fact that social meanings are shared social meanings and less on the pluralism (or multiple realities) of American society.

Understanding Everyday Life, edited by Jack D. Douglas (Chicago: Aldine, 1970), covers a broader scope of the phenomenological sociologies than the two just reviewed and is more empirical and more oriented toward so-called ethnome-thodology and social linguistics. It is more difficult in its later chapters, but it begins with the simpler aspects of phenomeno-logical sociology and builds on these. The first chapter,

"Understanding Everyday Life," compares phenomenological sociologies with absolutist sociologies and analyzes the relations among the many different types of phenomenological sociologies. In one way or another, all of the essays are concerned with how the members of society go about constructing social meanings to deal with the problematic aspects of their everyday lives.

The classic study of the changing social definitions of the problem of opiate addiction and of how individuals come to define themselves as addicts is Alfred R. Lindesmith's *Opiate Addiction* (Bloomington, Ind.: Principia Press, 1947). Lindesmith shows that in the nineteenth century opiate addiction was thought of as an individual problem—and often was not seen as a problem at all. It was only in the early years of this century that the federal government defined it as a social problem. Since the passage of the Harrison Stamp Act after World War I, opiate addiction has progressively been looked on as a social problem.

An important work patterned on Lindesmith's book is Howard Becker's *Outsiders* (New York: Free Press, 1963). It applies the same ideas to marihuana use, going on to develop a very important, general theory of deviance—labeling theory. Becker not only shows how relativistic and changing the social meanings of the problem of marihuana use have been, but also how the legal definition was constructed by Congress, especially the important part played in this by the Federal Bureau of Narcotics. Becker argues that all social rules and their concrete uses must be seen as at least partially problematic.

The Social Organization of Juvenile Justice by Aaron Cicourel (New York: Wiley, 1967) is based on extensive field research comparing the juvenile police divisions of two different cities. Cicourel shows how the definitions of the social problems of delinquency by individual policemen vary and change and how these definitions affect their methods of dealing with delinquency. Since the definitions of the problem affect what is done about delinquency, including how much effort is put into "discovering" it and reporting it to the community through the mass media, these individual definitions have a great effect on the more general social definitions of the social problems of delinquency.

Most people would probably assert that, even if most social problems are problematic and must be defined for concrete situations, at least a physical problem like blindness must be certain, so there would be no problematic constructions of the meaning of this problem. *The Making of Blind Men* by Robert Scott (New York: Russell Sage, 1969), a highly readable study of the social definitions of blindness in our society, shows this is not true. Scott shows how highly problematic the social definition of blindness is and what practical considerations, such as desire of government agencies for funds, have gone into defining the problem. The formal definition is so different from the common-sense definition that Scott actually argues that experts must teach people to be "blind," especially when they can read newspapers by sight.

chapter 5

Conflicts over the Definitions of Social Problems

We have seen that the problematic meanings of social problems are a basic cause of conflicts in our society. But they are not the only causes of such conflicts. The highly problematic nature of the basic commonsense ideas about individual persons and societies also causes such problems. In fact, some of these problematic meanings of persons and society, especially those concerning the causality of events and the responsibility for such events, are so basic that they probably produce conflicts that cannot be resolved by any commonsense rational, or scientific analysis that does not tyrannically impose its solutions on the members of society. These basic problems of meaning are most apparent in the conflicts over law and order or over the healthy society versus the sick society.

Since human beings, singly and collectively, are so necessary for the survival and happiness of the individual, it is little wonder that much of our thinking in every realm of life is concerned with understanding people. And, since the necessary freedom of human beings and the complexity of their relations with their world make it inevitable that human beings will be highly problematic for each other, it is little wonder that much of their thinking and communication is concerned with each other, especially with the problems they encounter in living with each other.

It is this which has led men to be so aware of the *problems of social order*. Not only has the problem of social order been the basic one of intellectual social thought and of the social sciences, but it has also been cardinal to much of *commonsense social theory*—or those sets of ideas that the members of society use to understand, explain, and affect their social lives. Just as Plato, Augustine, Hobbes, and Durkheim saw the problem of social order and disorder as fundamental to any social thought or social science, so have most men of common sense seen this problem as basic to their social lives. While it would be easy to give thousands of examples from the many sources of commonsense ideas, one recent example will suffice to show the general nature of these ideas. Robert E. Fitch, a theologian, was asked in an interview what he thought of recent acts of violence in the United States. Referring to acts of youthful vandalism and what he thought was a failure of parents to deal with these acts, he argued: "Certainly such incidents, on a broad scale, are the road to anarchy—to the complete ruin of everything human society seeks for itself in the way of justice and order. We simply cannot live as human beings in a society that is helpless to deal with disorders of this kind."[1] We see here the overriding fear of anarchy, or general social disorder, and many specific ideas about the relationship of various actions to the production of such disorder.

Anarchy, or the lack of social order, is probably the most feared and most commonly agreed upon problem of social order, but there are others. Any condition that is seen as a problem

---

[1] "Is America Really 'Sick'?—Interview with a Noted Theologian," *U.S. News and World Report* (June 10, 1968), pp. 44-49.

that emanates from the very nature of the society or that affects the whole social system is such a problem. Probably the problem of social order that is the second most generally agreed upon today is the "healthy" versus the "sick" society—the *problem of social pathology*. There is a great conflict today within the United States over whether the whole American society (or social system) is healthy or sick, that is, whether the basic nature or structure of American society is such that it produces primarily good things or primarily bad things. (It should be clear that the ideas about the problem of social pathology have a direct bearing on the ideas about the problem of general social disorder. It seems to be commonly believed that failure to solve the problem of social pathology produces the problem of general social disorder: a sick society causes anarchy.)

This great conflict over whether America suffers from a problem of social pathology ranges from the systematic, balanced appraisal of Arthur Schlesinger, Jr. in *The Crisis of Confidence* to the shrill denunciations of the underground newspapers and the bland counterassertions of the chambers of commerce and the Optimists. The clearest contrast is, of course, found between the positions of those at opposite extremes, those who see everything about America as sick and those who see nothing but healthy signs. These extremes, however, only show the pluralistic nature of American values, beliefs, and feelings. It is those who share general views about what our current social problems are, but who disagree completely about the general meanings of these problems for our society as a whole (that is, whether ours is a sick or healthy society), who show most clearly the basic reasons for the conflicts over these problems of social disorder. Typical of the statements that American society is a healthy society, though one with roughly the kinds of social problems enumerated in the many views of American society as sick, is the statement by Robert Fitch in his article, "Is America Really 'Sick'?":

When people no longer live in the past or in the future, but only for the moment, civilization is at the point where disintegration sets in. Yet I think we have the basic health and resources to overcome this danger, which arises mostly from the doings of a small minority in this country. . . . I think the large majority of Americans are basically sound. Yet it will take time to outlive the consequences of many years when affluent, permissive and egalitarian homes were breeding a generation of pampered brats.[2]

Another example typical of this view is found in an article, "The Good Things about the U.S. Today," in which the views of American Society as sick and healthy are contrasted:

At home and abroad, America now is being pictured as an ailing giant.

Racial strife, student anarchy, a rising wave of crime, dissent over the war in Vietnam—these and other troubles are leading many in the world to conclude that the United States is on the road to decline and downfall.

Yet a close look at the facts of life in the America of today turns up quite different conclusions. The nation's strengths are found to be great and varied. . . .

Far from being a "sick" society, Americans in the majority are showing themselves to be strong and morally responsible.[3]

Given this general agreement about what our problems of social order are, what is it that produces such great conflict over the evaluation of their significance for social order in American society. From an absolutionist, commonsense standpoint there should be no such conflict at all; for surely people who agree on the existence of our obvious social problems, on how numerous they are, and on how deep they run today should be able to see

---

[2] *Ibid.*
[3] "The Good Things about the U.S. Today," *U.S. News and World Report* (Sept. 2, 1968), p. 50.

that there is necessarily something basically wrong with our society, that it is somehow sick and needs to be made well by means of some basic changes. This is, in fact, the view taken by most current analysts of our social problems. Consider, for example, the conclusion drawn by Arthur Schlesinger, Jr. from an enumeration of our current problems:

> At home we see our cities in travail and revolt; rising mistrust and bitterness on the part of minorities; unraveling ties of social civility; a contagion of violence; a multiplication of fanaticisms on both far right and far left; a spreading impulse, especially among the intellectuals, the young and the blacks, to secede from the established order; and three terrible murders in five years of men who, through their ability to mobilize American idealism, might have held the country together. Abroad we see our nation increasingly disbelieved and disliked, our motives misunderstood and traduced, our labors unavailing. The failure of half a million American soldiers with nearly a million allies, employing the might of modern military technology, to defeat a few thousand guerrillas in black pyjamas has shaken our faith in our power, as the destruction we have wrought in the pursuit of what we conceived as noble ends has shaken our faith in our virtue.[4]

This absolutist standpoint leads to the view that those who don't see something sick about a society with so many problems are simply wrong. Yet the fact is that neither side can show the other side why they are wrong, at least not in such a way as to induce the other side to admit its error and change its position. At this point the absolutist view often gives way to the conspiracy theory, in which the opposing side is seen as lying about the obvious truths for some reasons of personal gain. This theory may lead to an attempt to force the conspirators to accept the

---

[4] Arthur M. Schlesinger, Jr., *The Crisis of Confidence* (New York: Bantam Books, 1969), p. x.

truth. But we have seen plenty of reason already to believe that such differences are usually sincere and important. How, then, can we account for them? Probably the most obvious reason for these conflicts is the complexity of our views of the world and our accepted methods of managing this complexity. There are a great number of different aspects of the world that we consider to be important in judging the fundamental nature of our social order; the methods of thought we use to do this judging are highly complex; and *there is no set of determinate rules of rationality that allow us to manage this complexity in such a way as to arrive at determinate judgments.* There are at least two general factors involved that seem crucial in producing such conflicts over the problems of social order.

Conflicts Resulting from the Problematic Nature of Factual Arguments

The complexity of man's view of the world and the difficulty that arises in dealing with it is first apparent in the *factual arguments* over the nature of specific social problems. When the practical man realizes that there is some conflict over the general condition of our society, he turns first to those aspects of the argument on which he expects the most certain agreement—the facts. As one journalist stated, "A close look at the facts of life in the America of today turns up quite different conclusions"; he had concluded that the facts have resolved the conflict in favor of the view that American society is healthy.

But the other side doesn't see it that way. First there are disagreements over the nature of the facts themselves, specifically, over what methods of observation produce "real" facts (as opposed to what merely *appear* to be facts). At its most basic level this conflict is derived from disagreements over the meanings of the categories in terms of which the observations are made, such as the disagreements over the meanings of poverty, which we have already analyzed. But the conflict is also based on disagreements over the *criteria of factuality*. For example, some people believe that only quantitative data, or statistics, can be taken as facts, while others believe you can prove anything you want with statistics. Some believe that government information can be trusted, while others believe you can't trust anything you don't see with your own eyes (or "seeing is believing".) Some take accounts in the newspaper or other media to be facts, while many insist that you can't believe anything the columnists say.

Secondly, disagreements over the facts about problems of social order are common even when individuals accept the same methods of observation and use the same sources of factual evidence. This is especially illuminating when we consider the alternate plausible presentations of the facts by one individual. An excellent example of this is found in the following speech by William Lindholm, President of the Chesapeake and Potomac Telephone Co., delivered in Elkins, West Virginia:

> Almost every day we have been reminded of our woes as magazines, newspapers, and the airwaves have chanted the catechism of failure. According to these reports we are a nation in which millions wallow in poverty and millions are functional illiterates. According to them there has been little or no racial progress. We are a nation of haters. Unemployment is rampant and getting worse. We are choking on polluted air and gagging on polluted water in our decaying cities. We ignore hunger in the midst of plenty. We have student anarchy, a rising wave of crime, dissent over Vietnam while at the same time we are charged with suppressing dissent. Of Americans themselves, we hear that we don't care for one another, that it's every man for himself, that we are miserable, tense and worried, and sit shamefacedly in collective guilt.

Before I go any further, let me say clearly that I cannot refute some of these charges. I cannot say they are false because regrettably many have some basis in fact. Neither do I agree with some who say that the news media have been malicious and conspiratorial in their reporting of our problems. It's the job of the news media to report the news as they find it, and I think for the most part they have done that. I do think that more weight has been given to editorial comment than is justified. And I think that more attention, too repetitive attention, has been given to the dark side of the news than is perhaps necessary.[5]

Having generally accepted the forms of evidence used by those who paint the gloomy factual picture, and having generally agreed on the nature of the factual information used, Mr. Lindholm goes on to present other facts which he believes show conclusively that the first presentation of the facts is insufficient and hence presents a distorted picture, and that, instead of being sick, America is very healthy and strong:

And what have our strengths and abilities led us to do? To create the healthiest, wealthiest, most generous nation in the history of the world.

A few statistics will give you some idea of just how successful we are. These figures were reported by *U.S. News & World Report* and they're a real eye-opener.

Just listen to this:

With 7 per cent of the world's land area and 6 per cent of the world's population, we account for one-third of the world's production of goods and services.

Our farmlands produce 13 per cent of the world's wheat, 46 per cent of its corn and 21 per cent of its meat— enough to feed 200 million Americans and much of the world besides.

Our factories produce a flow of goods almost equal in

[5] *Vital Speeches of the Day,* XXXVI (Nov. 1, 1969), pp. 56-59.

size to the combined output of the Soviet Union and Western Europe.

Fifty-three per cent of all the cars in use throughout the world are found on American streets and highways.

Per capita disposable income in America (1967 figures) comes to more than $2,700—45 per cent more than in Canada and the United Kingdom and 70 per cent more than in France.

No other country can even come close to matching a record like that. We're immensely successful and there's no reason to be ashamed of it.

That's the record of the free enterprize system. . . .

We are the strongest nation the world has ever seen, and we have shared our wealth as no nation has ever done.

Since the end of World War II, we have supported the hopes, the welfare, and, by and large, the unity of the whole non-communist world.

Contrary to what some of our critics say, we are not imperialists. We are not sick. We are not on the downhill. The problems we face are problems of success, and of all the ills we could suffer, success is by far the best.

Now let's look specifically at some of the problems we face. First, the problems of poverty, unemployment and lack of racial progress. We must admit that those do exist in America today. But we do not have to accept the reports that imply that little or nothing is being done about them. The fact is that we have made enormous progress in these areas.[6]

The reason for these disagreements about the facts, even when there is agreement on the types of observations and facts to be used, is that the people involved in the arguments implicitly agree on the need to *aggregate the facts,* so they are really using *aggregate facts that can be put together in different ways.* It is agreed that there will be many facts about any one social

[6] *Ibid.*

problem, especially a problem concerning the whole society, and that these must somehow be related to each other; but it is almost never recognized that the need to aggregate the facts introduces non-factual elements into the factual argument, elements which are very much affected by subjective factors.

The first element of disagreement comes from the necessity of *selecting* the facts. There is a potentially infinite number of factual observations that can be made about any problem, so selectivity is necessary; yet many people commonly do not note this necessity. Instead of discussing how to select the facts and possibly reaching an agreement about that, they make their own selections on the basis of their own implicit criteria. These vague criteria are the determinants of what the people see as important or relevant facts, so they implicity determine that some kinds of facts will be sought and used to evaluate the problem while others will not. But what are the criteria that determine this relevance? Presumably, there are many of them, including vague feelings, hunches, and individual inclinations derived from many different sources. But some of these criteria are especially significant for the problem of understanding the argument about social problems: these are the criteria of *optimism versus pessimism,* which are not merely general attitudes of the individual, but are also directly tied up with what the individual intends to do with his analysis of the social problem, especially whether he intends to use the analysis to praise, damn, destroy, or reform. If an individual is concerned with the problem for the purpose of doing something positive to solve it, then he puts an optimistic frame around it and looks for those facts that can lead to such positive action. If he is concerned with the problem as a means of damning the society, he chooses a pessimistic framework to select his facts, often using the facts to show that nothing can be done to solve the problem within the present social order. In fact, sometimes we even find individuals explicitly arguing that we must make a choice between such an optimistic or pessimistic framework for our considerations of the facts and our evaluations of their significance for understanding our problems. For example, in the speech we have been considering, William Lindholm argues that we must purposefully look for the facts indicating our strengths and the possibilities of solving the problems.

Our incessant attention to our problems and weaknesses has had the demoralizing, debilitating effect upon us of the first kind of psycological tool. We have had all too little of the kind that unites us, encourages us and gives us hope that we can ever overcome our difficulties.

And the effects upon us are as devastating as a broadside from a cannon. We are a people with faith in one another, and when we lose that faith, we become weak, however heavily we may be armed.

The dangers of always hearing how bad we are, are first that we might believe it; that we might become what our critics say we are. And second, that we might dissipate our energy in frenzied activity trying to answer all the alarms at once without doing anything really productive.

The point I'm making is that when we've got so "psyched-up" about our problems, we can waste a lot of energy just worrying about them or running around in circles, without ever really accomplishing anything productive.

I think it's a mistake to allow ourselves to become so preoccupied with our problems and failures that we forget our strengths and successes.

As the German poet Goethe noted, "If one treats a person as if he were what he ought to be and could be, he will become what he ought to be and could be."

I believe that. And I believe it applies to nations as well as individuals. So now in the remaining minutes I would like to speak of our strengths as individuals and as a nation, as a way of reminding ourselves of what we are and what we can become.[7]

In this example the conclusion of the argument, i.e., whether the society is sick or healthy, is predetermined by the selection of the facts from which the conclusion is to be drawn. In this way the facts selected and the conclusions drawn about social problems become *reflexive;* that is, each becomes a determinant of the other. The necessity of selecting and evaluating the facts, then, means that the facts alone can never resolve the arguments over what our social problems are. Rather, they commonly provide a reinforcement of the argument, especially when the individuals look at the facts as being absolute, since they sometimes then feel that their conclusions about social problems are irrefutable and that the other side must be lying. It is significant to note that in the speech being considered, even though there is an explicit recognition of the necessity of making a problematic selection of the facts, there is no conclusion that this would make the alternate argument, the one in the pessimistic framework, just as plausible. Rather, the optimistic criterion used in selecting the facts is not regarded as in any way undermining the absoluteness of those facts. In this particular case, however, the author does conclude that those on his side and those on the other "should not bicker and harangue or curse one another as we decide how best to heal our wounds and cure our ills. We can love this country without hating others. And we can continue the debate on how we can become what we've yet to be." Even the assumptions of absoluteness are problematic in their applications to concrete problems.

The arguments also continue because any aggregation of facts necessitates some way of comparing or *balancing* the facts, which necessitates weighing *or evaluating* the facts. Each fact of "health" could be compared with each fact of "sickness" and a

---

[7] *Ibid.*

simple measure be taken, but most members of society agree that some forms of each kind of fact are more important than others, so they must be weighted. This, for example, was argued by Donald S. Macleod:

> I would like to talk about the one thing that is occupying so much of our attention today—the state of the nation . . .
>
> In the United States in the year 1968:
>
> 96,459,483 men did *not* commit a criminal offense.
>
> 4,896,720 college students did *not* participate in a campus demonstration.
>
> 201,489,710 citizens did *not* use illegal drugs.
>
> 17,613 baby doctors did *not* publicly condemn the draft law and protest the war in Vietnam.
>
> Those are majority groups. Those are some of the people who have been almost forgotten and are now being ignored. Why? Because their minority counterparts—those who *did* commit a crime, participate in a campus demonstration, use illegal drugs, and publicly protest the draft law —got all the attention.
>
> The majority is made up of more than numbers. These are living, breathing people with opinions, responsibilities, and rights. In them is found the moral and philosophical fiber of which the nation was built. If they have a fault, it's that their influence is not as great as their numbers—that their voice is not as loud as their convictions are strong.
>
> They are the silent majority. The social commentators, editorial writers, playwrights, novelists, essayists, television news media and angry young men ignore them. They conduct an audit of our society that is lop-sided and wrong. They give inordinate weight to the numerically small minority. They concentrate almost exclusively on our national liabilities. This, to me, is an unacceptable audit.
>
> The headlines bombard us daily with stories of violence, corruption and outrage. We hear that the very foundations of American society are crumbling. Responsible Americans have told us that if we don't solve our problems without

undue delay, we face the prospect of our cities disintegrating into political, economic and social chaos. Some citizens have questioned whether this nation will survive as a free republic to celebrate its two-hundredth anniversary seven years from now.

We have problems in this country, and I'll not minimize their seriousness. And certainly these statements have in them an element of truth—truth, that is, for some members of our society. The question is: For how many people in our society are they true? Are they true for all our people? For most of them? For many? For a majority? Or are they true only for a small minority?

This, I feel, is a crucial question of our times . . .

We've got to apply tough accounting principles to any social balance sheet we try to draw up today. We can't use numbers which are weighted against the real facts of a working democracy. We can't use numbers just to kid ourselves.[8]

Weighing and evaluting are problematic for social actors and produce conflicts among them for the same reason the selection of facts does. In this speech we find the same statement of the need to choose between an optimistic and a pessimistic framework and the same reflexive relation between the conclusions and the facts that we found in our last example. In this case, however, we also find a strong contention that the proper balancing of facts will produce an absolute answer; this is the optimistic answer the author has insisted earlier we must adopt in order to see the right weighting of facts: "We've got to start with a balance sheet that is so accurate as to be unchallengeable. Only from this base can we guide ourselves to a secure, free future for ourselves and our children." The balancing of the facts, which were chosen in the light of the optimistic conclusion, is to assure us of the attainment of that optimistic outcome.

[8] *Vital Speeches of the Day,* XXXVI (Oct. 15, 1969), pp. 17-21.

Conflicts Resulting from the Problematic Nature of Commonsense Theories of Persons and Societies

Though in many cases they are not explicitly referred to, there are many commonsense theories of persons and society lying behind most arguments about the facts of social problems. Understanding what these theories are and that they are the context in which the factual arguments are being made is often crucial for understanding the factual arguments themselves, just as an understanding of the nature of the factual arguments is often crucial for understanding the theories of persons and society. Much of the difficulty for the sociologist trying to understand the meanings of the commonsense arguments over social problems comes from the fact that these commonsense theories are not only taken for granted by the members of society using them, but are also commonly *deep meanings of any communication;* that is, they are so taken for granted by the members of society that they are not generally recognized by them to be part of their own thinking about the problems, until a sociologist systematically demonstrates that they are there.

Certainly one of the most basic of all commonsense ideas about persons and society, and probably the most important one in understanding the conflicts over social problems, is that of *causal interdependency.* There are three aspects of causal interdependency in commonsense thought that greatly affect the arguments about social problems: (1) causal interdependency between the individual and his social situation, (2) causal interdependency between individuals (which can be looked at as a special case of the interdependency between the individual and his social situation, but which necessitates special consideration), and (3) the complex causal interdependency between the many different segments of society.

Conflicts arising from interdependency between individuals and their social situations. When the members of our society ask themselves how or why something has come about in society, such as a problem that is shared by many individuals, they can plausibly see the problem as the result of something they themselves chose to do, something that happened to them, something that came from outside of them, or, rarely, something from inside their own bodies that is not subject to their volition. That is, they can see any events involving human beings either as caused by human beings, as accidents not caused by human beings, or as some combination of the two. If they see the events as caused by human action, they can see these actions as the result either of something that is part of the actors (something internal to the actors) or of something external that has caused them to perform those actions, or as some combination of these. If he intended to perform certain actions that brought about the problem, any human actor seen as the original cause in any sequence of actions is regarded as *responsible* for the actions and, thus, for the consequences of those actions.[9]

Our shared commonsense understandings of our social world provide us with a vast number of ideas that we use in trying to decide who is responsible for any social action or event. For example, we can see these ideas being used in any of the vast number of decisions concerning such things as who is responsible for a murder, who is responsible for a divorce, who is responsible for a child's delinquency, and so on. We are all familiar with such ideas as the following: Any parent who neglects her child is responsible for the child's going wrong and any man who treats his wife cruelly is responsible for her leaving. Different groups and different individuals have varying ideas of this sort, but regardless of the groups or individuals involved, we find that

---

[9] For an analysis of the social meanings of responsibility see my essay in *Deviance and Respectability: The Social Construction of Moral Meanings* (New York: Basic Books, 1970).

there is almost inevitably disagreement among them concerning the allocation of responsibility for any action or event. *In some way, the meanings of social causality and, thence, of social responsibility are problematic for the members of our society; these problematic meanings produce conflicts over the decisions about who is responsible.*

The primary reason for this problematic meaning of social causality is the essentially problematic nature of intention, which is generally seen as necessary in considerations of responsibility for any action. But the problem also seems to be the result of the assumption that *man is so fundamentally social that anything he does is by necessity partly determined by his relations with other individuals.* Whatever the basic reason, we find that individuals considering the question of responsibility for any act or event can almost always construct plausible arguments to impute causality both to the individual who did it and to the other individuals involved in the situation in which the action or event took place.[10] Moreover, this tendency to consider the individual's social situation responsible for his action seems to have greatly increased over the last century, as the belief in individualism and free will has waned and the belief in social determinism has increased. The belief in two theories would seem to be about equal today, so we may be experiencing the greatest amount of problems in allocating responsibility. It these trends continue, we will eventually find few problems in allocating responsibility, since most people will use the argument of social determinism; but there are some important indications that countertrends are increasing, especially from existentialism, so beliefs in individual responsibilities may continue.

Excellent examples of the conflicts that arise from the equally plausible nature of these two theories of social causality

---

[10] See my discussion of the social meanings of causality in *The Social Meanings of Suicide, op. cit.*

and responsibility can be seen in communications such as those following the assassinations of John F. Kennedy, Martin Luther King Jr. and Robert F. Kennedy. Consider, for example, the following article, written after the death of Robert F. Kennedy. First the authors present the rationale of those who viewed the assassinations as caused by something in American society, something about Americans in general:

> Once again, 200 million Americans are being asked to stand trial for the assassination of a noted leader.
>
> In 1963 the murder of President John F. Kennedy in Dallas by Lee Harvey Oswald first produced the idea that all Americans share "guilt" for such a crime.
>
> The same theory was heard again in April of this year with the murder in Memphis of the Rev. Dr. Martin Luther King, Jr., Negro Minister and civil-rights leader. Accused of the slaying is James Earl Ray.
>
> This time it is the assassination of Senator Robert F. Kennedy in Los Angeles—by Jordanian immigrant Sirhan Sirhan, says an indictment—that is raising the cry of collective "guilt".
>
> Back of this view is a widely publicized contention that nearly all Americans in recent years have been condoning political extremism. The effect, it is said, is a "climate of hatred."
>
> Psychiatrists, sociologists and other authorities on human behavior find much to concern them in America. Preponderantly, however, they appear to feel that increasing violence probably would result more directly from specific factors—spreading urbanization, rapid communications and other causes—than from political hatreds among Americans.[11]

As these authors view the situation, the people who believed the murders were caused by the society (and therefore the

---

[11] *U.S. News and World Report* (June 24, 1968), p. 37.

responsibility of us all, rather than simply the responsibility of those who committed the acts) argued that there were various social situations which had arisen, presumably as a result of the intentional actions of most Americans, which led to an increased tendency for a few people to commit such acts of violence. The authors of this article completely disagree with this theoretical analysis of those people and argue that, on the contrary, the only real causes and the only people really responsible were those who committed the acts:

> The three men accused of these assassinations bear little resemblance to most other Americans.
>
> One was a convict, another had been classified as in need of psychiatric treatment, and the third was inflamed by nationalism. None could get along with other people, or hold steady jobs.
>
> Such persons, it is pointed out, have existed since the beginning of recorded history. But today, opportunities to commit murder multiply with the growth of technology and population.
>
> Eric Hoffer, San Francisco's long-shoreman–philosopher, said of Robert Kennedy's assassination:
>
> "To accuse America because an Arab committed this crime is the most slanderous thing in the world."
>
> Similarly, President Johnson warned against concluding that America "has lost its sense of direction, even its common decency." He added:
>
> "Two hundred million Americans did not strike down Robert Kennedy."[12]

The authors argue that only the individuals are responsible because of at least three factors: (1) these men are not like most Americans, (2) each one has something peculiar about him which led him to commit such acts independently of other Americans, and (3) such murderous acts have occurred in all societies and

---

[12] *Ibid.*

are happening in our own society with seemingly greater
frequency because of greater opportunities, not because they are
actions increasing numbers of Americans have chosen. But it
would be easy for any member of our society to see the kinds of
equally plausible counterarguments that could be offered to these
counterarguments also based on what is commonly held to be
the factual evidence in these three cases. He could argue that
the men who committed these assassinations are just like millions
of other Americans who have been classified as requiring
psychiatric treatment (after all, one team of psychiatrists studying
Manhattan found that almost 50 per cent of its residents needed
such help), who have been inflamed by nationalism, and who
have been convicts. He could also then argue, exactly as others
have done, that all of the "peculiar" things about these men
were actually caused by certain aspects of American society.
These are aspects that show it is a sick society that causes just
such murders: the terrible urbanization, the lack of adequate
medical care for the mentally disturbed, the teaching and
encouragement of the kind of nationalism that involves killing
others for the sake of national policy, the emphasis on violence
in the mass media, etc. He could argue that the existence of such
murders in other nations begs the question and also that to argue
that the growth of technology and population in our society
causes more opportunity for such acts is an admission that it is
something about the society itself, something for which we are
all responsible, that indirectly causes such things. Therefore the
acts are in fact socially caused. I leave it to any competent
member of our society to provide the plausible countercounter
arguments to these. Any such member should now be able to see
that it is possible to go on endlessly spinning out plausible arguments and that the discussion can only be stopped by insisting,
on the basis of evidence and theoretical beliefs that are entirely
independent of the present situation, that some theories of society
and individual action are true and others are false. For example,

an insistence that individuals are free to choose such actions, regardless of their social histories and immediate situations, resolves the argument very nicely in favor of those who see these acts as individually caused, whereas an insistence on social determinism resolves it the other way. But the insistence on either theory of causality is justified only on the basis of some preconceived theory of man and society, one which no one could rationally prove with the limited evidence available in these cases.

Conflicts arising from interdependencies between individuals. In addition to the conflicts over social problems that arise from the problematic relationships between the individual and society that we find in the commonsense theories of man and society, we find conflicts arising as well from the problematic relationships believed to exist between individuals. Most importantly, because individuals are believed to be so greatly affected by other individuals and because their actions are seen as greatly affected by the concrete interactions between the individuals in any situation, we find the causal explanations of concrete actions and events and, thus, the concrete imputations of responsibility for those actions and events to be highly problematic for the members of our society. Consequently, we find a great number of conflicts revolving around the issue of *who caused whom to do what* in any concrete situation.

While the increased belief in social determinism has produced more conflicts over social causality and responsibility, there have always been such arguments in Western societies. One of the oldest forms of the argument is a result of the ancient *temptation theory of evil action.* This theory is still used extensively in allocating responsibility for such social problems as crime and unmarried teenage pregnancy. While many people argue that it is the boy's fault if an unwed, teenage girl gets pregnant, there are many others who will argue that it is the girl's fault because the boy could not have impregnated the girl had she not provided him with the temptation. This same kind of argument is seen very nicely in a mother's statement about her son's car theft in a letter to Ann Landers:

> Dear Ann Landers: Our 16-year-old son and his friend are in serious trouble because some stupid person put temptation in front of him. Being human, they couldn't resist it.
>
> Juddy and a 15-year-old pal were walking along the street last evening and they saw a 1970 Chevrolet with the key in the ignition. On a moment's impulse they decided to go for a little ride. These boys didn't mean to steal the car—they just wanted to have some fun . . .
>
> Please say something about irresponsible adults who tempt kids and expect them to be superhuman.
>
> —Proud of Our Boy.[13]

The conflicting point of view about such actions is that regardless of the existence of temptations, any individual is responsible for choosing to do certain things, including giving in to temptation. As Ann Landers replied in this case:

> Dear Parents: Granted, ignition keys should *never* be left in cars. But your letter is a beautiful example of what is wrong with many of today's youth. Parents like you have been making excuses for your children for so long it is pitiful. Surely you are aware that life is filled with temptations. Kids who have not been brought up to resist temptation are destined to be in trouble forever . . .[14]

Conflicts over social causality that are based on such ancient beliefs as those involved in the temptation theory may be due largely to the pluralistic differences in our society, and theories such as this may be largely restricted to the millions of people who form the fundamentalist Bible Belt of America. Many people may reject such arguments as being simply the result of faith or

---

[13] *The Indianapolis Star* (Dec. 7, 1970), p. 16.
[14] *Ibid.*

of an inability to look at situations rationally because of a lack of education. But there are plenty of examples of analogous arguments about social causality and responsibility among the most educated and "modern" members of our society, showing that the arguments are the result not only of pluralistic differences in beliefs, but also of the very nature of commonsense, rational discourse.

Consider, for example, the conflicts in the late 1960s over who was responsible for the steady escalation in campus protests and violence, which came to be seen as one of our most pressing social problems.[15] After the shooting of students at Kent State in 1970, the conflict tended to center on the issue of who was responsible for the protest movement, the violence, and the killings at Kent State. There were, of course, the conflicts over the causal relationships within the general social situation, the actions of the president over Cambodia, the relationship between the actions (or nonactions) of the administrators and those of the students, the relationship of all of these to the development of the student protests, and the relationship between the protest movement and violence; We shall discuss these kinds of conflicts below in our considerations of those conflicts arising from the problematic relationships among the segments of society. All of these conflicts formed the background for the central question in the foreground of public attention: given the confrontation of students and National Guard units at Kent State on the fateful day, were the students or the National Guard responsible for the shootings that took place? For the most part, the students and administrators insisted that the Guard was responsible, while the Guard and the Ohio courts insisted that the students were directly responsible (and the administrators indirectly responsible because of the *background causal relationships* considered below).

---

[15] I have previously discussed many of these arguments in *Youth in Turmoil* (Washington, D.C.: U.S. Government Printing Office, 1971).

In such arguments over social causality and responsibility, we find a clear recognition of the interdependent nature of human actions in any concrete situation: *actions are seen to be the result of other actions, to be determined by sequences of actions and reactions.* The conflict seems to be mainly over the issue of who was the actor and who the reactor. Because of the common-sense view of causality, which necessarily involves a temporal sequence with the cause coming before the effect, it becomes crucial to determine who acted first, who started the sequence of actions and reactions. To someone not involved in this whole conflict, the argument may seem easily resolved: the students had to have started it or there wouldn't have been any National Guard there. But this resolution was not acceptable to the participants because any such commonsense theoretical explanation of interdependent actions breaks the actions and reactions up into a number of interdependent sequences of actions and reactions. It is not simply a question of who did the very first thing, but of who did the first thing that produced the general sequence of actions and reactions that in turn led to the first action within the specific sequence of actions and reactions that produced the deaths of the students. In the case of Kent State, for example, does one see "*the* beginning," the first demonstration, or the administration's call for help, or the Guard's decision to use live ammunition? And how is each related causally to all the others? In any argument of this sort there may be many such *embeddings of sequences of actions and reactions.* Since there will be arguments over just what the relationship is between the situation and the actions, there will be disagreements in the first place over how to break up the sequences of actions and reactions. But added to this conflict will be those growing out of the necessarily problematic nature of considerations of the complex interdependencies among the sequences of actions and reactions: *when we have interdependencies among interdependencies, the total outcome of the arguments considering what is cause and what is effect, what is action and what is reaction, cannot be completely resolved by the use of commonsense criteria of rationality.* In fact, the argument becomes so problematic that even the actor who wishes to be most sincerely rational is forced to rely upon his judgments of actors and actions, rather than upon his specific considerations of these concrete events, to decide what is the most likely relationship of causes and effects and thus who is most likely to be responsible. But this means that even the most rational commonsense actor will have to rely in part upon preconceived judgments about who is most likely to be responsible for such actions, so that the imputations of responsibility will necessarily be in part reflexively related to the kinds of actors and the kinds of actions one already believes are involved; that is, *responsibility will be allocated according to what one thinks of the people and the actions involved in part independently of the situation one is judging.* This is why we find such a strong tendency in those who trust the students and who believe they are idealists committed to doing good things to help society to see the students as innocent and the Guard as responsible for the murders, while those who trust the Guard and see them as protectors of law and order tend to see the students as guilty and as getting what they deserved.

This kind of conflict over who is responsible for a problem is by no means isolated. Even when we restrict our attention to the social problem of campus disturbances and student violence, we find this conflict in most of the arguments between the supporters and attackers of the students. We find it in the arguments over the violence in Chicago in 1968 between the police and students. While most Americans seem to have concluded that the students were clearly responsible for the riots that occurred in Chicago, and that the police were the victims, the millions who supported the students argued that it was clearly the actions of the police that had caused the riots: the police were the responsible actors, while the students were merely the reacting victims of police brutality. Henry Resnik has summarized this view very well in arguing that the "Chicago Seven," charged by the government with conspiring to produce the violence, were not really responsible for the violence:

> Consider the attitude of the Chicago authorities, especially Presiding Judge Julius Hoffman, from the first Yippie requests for park permits to the handing down of the contempt sentences. Whatever one thinks of the defendants' undeniable crudeness and deliberate disruptiveness, most of the real violence emanated from an overreaction to the protesters's rhetoric, and a vigorous condemnation of the youth movement long before it came to Chicago.[16]

Here Resnik argues that, while it may be true that the students started the action and might thus seem responsible for the whole thing, it is still true that their subsequent violent attacks on the police and upon property were caused by the *over*reactions of the police to the initial rhetoric of the demonstrators. Even when there is agreement on the facts of what happened and on the overall nature of the sequence of action and reaction, there is complete disagreement over who is responsible for the specific actions which everyone agreed were violent. This same position was taken by the so-called riot commission and completely rejected by the police and other authorities.

This same theory of action, overreaction and reaction was extended by many to the explanation of the whole social problem of student violence. While most people probably took it for granted that those committing the violence were responsible, thereby agreeing with people, such as Nixon, Agnew, and Reagan who denounced the violent students as the responsible agents, millions of other people turned the whole argument around and denounced the denouncers as the real cause of most of the violence. They argued that the political rhetoric in reaction to

---

[16] *Saturday Review* (Dec. 12, 1970), p. 28.

the student rhetoric and action constituted an overreaction that was the subsequent cause of student violence. The embedded aspect of the sequences of interdependent action and reaction is most obvious in the argument of those who attack violence as being the cause of subsequent violence. This same kind of argument has been applied to other social problems. For example though it has not received the widespread publicity, it has been argued that the Northern attacks on Southern racism are a real cause of the worst aspects of Southern racism because they inflame the Southerners against the Negroes.

We see, then, that the complex, embedded interdependencies of the commonsense theories of personal causality and responsibility produce an inevitable problem, or a rationally irresolvable indeterminacy, in these considerations of social problems. This same kind of problem is found in all of the other commonsense theoretical ideas about social problems and their solutions. That is, *in each theoretical explanation of an action or event it is always possible to introduce a second plausible theoretical explanation that conflicts with the first one, because the commonsense theories used to explain the action or event involve complexly interdependent factors whose various effects cannot rationally be separated by analysis.* The result, once again, is that conflicts in the explanation of actions and events are inevitable.

Conflicts arising from interdependencies among the segments of society. The complex interdependencies existing among the many parts or segments of society produce necessary problems and conflicts as well. Consider, for example, the eternal argument over the relationship between art and society. This argument has complex bearings on all kinds of issues of social policy, especially in a day in which a large percentage of the population has come to expect the government to do something about everything. Once people become concerned with the health or sickness of a society, they often look to the wellsprings of creativity for an indication of how healthy or sick the society is. Many people argue that, since all segments of society are *equally interdependent,* we can tell directly from an analysis of art just what the condition of society is. For example, many people taking this view argue that modern man is anarchic because modern art is anarchic. The additional argument over the actual state of modern art merely compounds the problems. But there are others who reject this whole argument of equal interdependency and argue instead that the relationship between art and society is complex or even completely indeterminate. Consider, for example, the following argument by Robert Evett, which he made in the context of his considerations of the best social policy to adopt toward art education and governmental support of art:

> First, there is a very real question of how much of the substance of a civilization is reflected in its arts. Do the moral and ethical principles of a legal system show up in sculpture and architecture? Is there a linking together of situations and events that produces a sort of cultural mass guilt? Can a civilization that produced a Mozart be all bad? Well, why not? The eighteenth-century civilization that produced Mozart was bad in so many ways that it would be hard to find anything good to say about it except that it produced a great deal of great art and some good science and philosophy; and that in these fields the pressure of the civilization was felt—for instance, in the arts, where style and content conformed to the social contract between the patron and the artist; which proves nothing at all except that art and life are not the same and never have been.[17]

This problem is compounded for Mr. Evett by the partially indeterminate relations between creativity (or even the nature of creativity) and artistic work:

> As for the divine spark of creativity, perhaps it does exist

[17] *Atlantic Monthly* (Jan. 1971), pp. 77-78.

in everybody. Certain creative acts—making pottery or jewelry, or cooking delicious food—can give pleasure not only to the creator but to other people as well, and these modest arts are within the grasp of almost anybody. Is the creativity that goes into making a soufflé the same as what goes into a piano concerto? It would be hard to answer this question with any finality, because it takes not only a different kind of technique but a lot more of it to write a piece of music than it does to cook a dish. But in cookery, you can do it well by doing it right; the composer has to have not only enough technique to execute a work but enough imagination to conceive it, and there is no indication whatever that these two indispensable elements are normally found together. Unless they are found together, there is no reason to assume that someone has a vocation to or a talent for musical composition.[18]

Mr. Evett then concludes from his argument that all kinds of mistakes in social policies regarding art education have been made because of a failure to see these indeterminate relations.

Two other examples of such interdependent causal arguments will illustrate further the nature of the problems created by the commonsense theories of social problems. First, the argument over pornography and its effects on society illustrates the way in which the assumed interrelations among the parts of society can be used to arrive at completely contrary conclusions as to whether something constitutes a social problem and as to what the social policy should be toward it. One example of this is found in the argument between President Nixon and those who wrote the report issued by the National Commission on Obscenity and Pornography in 1970. The Commission argued that there was no evidence that pornography, which itself is subject to very different social definitions, causes deeds that would be seen as criminal or immoral, such as rape and child

[18] *Ibid.*

molestation. Those who share this point of view commonly argue as well that, if anything, eliminating the legal controls over pornography accomplishes two things: it leads quickly to a falling off of public interest in such things because the public becomes jaded and it clears up many problems of police corruption and inadequate manpower by eliminating the need for police work in this area. But those who might accept this evidence, and even those who might agree with these particular conclusions about the relationship between pornography and society, may still argue, as did three dissenting commissioners on this national commission, that "pornography has an eroding effect on society, on public morality, on respect for human worth, on attitudes toward family love, on culture." As President Nixon said in rejecting the report's conclusions, "The warped and brutal portrayal of sex in books, plays, magazines, and movies, if not halted and reversed, could poison the wellsprings of American and Western culture and civilization." As a judge in a small Iowa city was reported to have said of the citizens' negative reaction to his decision that a pornographic movie was legal: "Part of this, I suppose, is that people feel threatened by the severe breakdown in religion . . . And some people lump the whole thing into a Communist conspiracy . . ."[19]

The typical structure of this argument is now apparent: even if you are right in arguing that factor x (pornography) does not cause factor y (sex crimes), it is still true that, because of the complex interdependency of all factors in society with the underlying structure (wellsprings) of society, factor x will cause direct problems at the underlying, structural level, which will eventually cause problems in all other segments of society, probably including factor y. Lying behind all concrete events and actions, then, is a fundamental structure of interdependent relations: there is a social system that causes concrete social

---

[19] All of these quotes are from *Newsweek* (Dec. 21, 1970), pp. 28-29.

events. Because this social system theory in one form or another is so basic to commonsense theories of social action and events, it is always plausible for an individual to argue that changes in one realm will produce changes in another realm and that what might appear to be an isolated event is found upon investigation to be the result of complex causal relations with the underlying structure or system of society. This in itself is sufficient to make any argument potentially indeterminate and problematic, but the indeterminacy and problems are further increased by the fact that the members see different elements as comprising *the* underlying structure or system of the society.

For example, for millions of Americans today the relations between man and God, as represented by religious practices, are still the one overall determinant of everything else in society; they try to explain any social problem, such as crime, in terms of man's relation to God. This ancient theory, which was the basis of a large proportion of all sociological research and theory in the nineteenth century, is illustrated by a contemporary explanation of crime, and evil in general, by Billy Graham, one of America's most famous and respected men (In this particular statement we also find an explicit acceptance of multicausal theories, which, as we have already seen, adds to the problematic nature of the argument. It might also be noted that this argument led Mr. Graham to conclude that the clergy is to blame for much of today's crime because its members are the ones who are most responsible for determining the relations between men and God.)

> When belief in God goes out, doubt and cynicism rush in. This is usually followed by tyranny and repression. A terrifying intellectual, spiritual and moral tide of evil has already loosed us from our spiritual mooring . . .
>
> Some of the great principles that guided our country in the past are fading from the scene. I am convinced that only a great national religious revival in America can restore them . . .

> One of the reasons for crime, perversion and the evils of the modern man is that he has lost his belief in the certainty of the judgment of God.
>
> Most of our pulpits are silent on the subject, and this accounts in great measures for the noise and clamor of rebellion and crime in the streets.[20]

But it is entirely plausible for someone who agrees entirely with the analysis of our age as an age of evil and crime to argue that the breakdown in the relations between man and God are not the causes of this evil. Rather, one who believes that the underlying system or structure of American society is its secularism, its commitment to material interests, and its ambitiousness can argue that crime and evil are caused by the nature of that ambition and secularism, as we find in the following analysis of certain actions by Supreme Court Justice Fortas:

> Justice Fortas had to resign, because he had been guilty of an impropriety which made his continued presence on the Supreme Court embarrassing to him, to his fellow Justices and to the country. But his withdrawal will not cure, will not even alleviate, what has become a national failure of social conscience. The Fortas case is only one of a succession of scandals and when Fortas returns to his law practice that succession will continue, because the causes will remain deep in the American ethos.
>
> Why did Mr. Fortas take $15,000 for three lectures, a legal but indiscreet action for one in his position? Why did he accept $20,000 from the Wolfson Foundation and not return it until it was, in a sense, hot money? Was it because of irrational greed stemming from early poverty? Certainly nothing in his present circumstances could explain his behavior. But if one goes beyond his present income, past income, his wife's income, etc., some light is thrown on plausible causes of his behavior. For most of his life Mr.

[20] Reported in the *Los Angeles Times* (Dec. 21, 1970).

Fortas has been part of a vast maze of relationships in which some decent things are done (the Fortas law firm defended Owen Lattimore without fee), but in which powerful individuals take advantage of the main chance, right up to the edge of ethical impropriety . . . Justice Fortas became an important man, a confidant of Presidents, and finally almost Chief Justice of the United States, by manipulations and circumventions much like those for which he is now castigated. He lived in an atmosphere of such stratagems; for many years, we may assume, he had little or no contact with people other than those who pursued similar aims, by similar means. There was no pressing reason for him to change, so he did not change . . . This will ruin a mass; it can destroy a nation.[21]

When the belief in the systematic causal interdependency of the parts is carried to the extreme, we find that commonsense theories once again become totally reflexive and thereby produce irresolvable conflicts. Consider, for example, this argument about the relationship between financial success and crime. It is first argued that the commitment to financial success is a basic, structural, systematic aspect of all American society. (In line with this it is commonly argued that being poor, not having achieved this success, is a basic cause of crime, and this is used to explain the high official crime rates of the poor. We see this aspect of the commonsense theory in the famous sociological theory of deviance proposed by Robert K. Merton.) To be financially successful, then, is a good thing to be sought by all, and the achievement of financial success is supposed to produce satisfaction and certainly not crime. But it is found that even the very rich commit crimes, and financial crimes at that. Does this invalidate the commonsense theory about the American social system. Not at all; it simply shows the need to properly interpret the theory in the light of the newly considered facts.

[21] Editors, *The Nation* (May 26, 1969).

It now becomes apparent that the very success that was a good to be sought by all produces crimes that are against the basic rules of the social system and that may, indeed, ruin the whole social system that has produced it. Rather than being rejected, the theory is now seen to rationally produce the very opposite conclusions from those it first appeared to produce: the "facts" and the "theory" are adjusted in such a manner that they support each other and are seen to have always done so. We simply didn't see the "right interpretation" until we discovered the new "facts."

Conflicts over Social Responsibility and Solutions to Social Problems

The members of our society are concerned not only with the causality of social problems, but with responsibility as well. Responsibility includes all the ideas of causality, for those individuals or groups are generally believed to be responsible for a social problem only if they are believed first to have caused the problem. But responsibility involves more than personal and social causality. It also involves the idea of *moral choice, of intentionally choosing to do what one knows will have the consequences that constitute the social problem even though one is theoretically free not to choose that path of action.* Both intention and freedom of choice are generally necessary elements of any action for which an individual is considered morally responsible.

Because responsibility presupposes causality, the imputations of moral responsibility for a social problem are subject to all of the problems and conflicts resulting from the problems and conflicts involved in imputing responsibility for a social problem. But, because responsibility involves the additional element of morality, the imputation of responsibility is subject to the problems and conflicts involved in imputing moral meanings in our society. There are three kinds of problematic meanings that are especially important in producing these conflicts over moral responsibility. First, the imputation of intention to anyone is necessarily problematic because it is an entirely internal phenomenon not subject to direct observation and can, conse- qently, always be plausibly denied to some degree by arguing that there was an alternative intention or motive involved. Second, it is generally possible to argue plausibly that, even if a given person intended to commit the actions involved, he did not intend to produce the consequences that constitute the problem. Third, one can also argue that, even if he did intend the actions and did know their consequences, he still did not have any free choice in the matter, so he cannot be considered morally responsible.

Automobile accidents and pollution both provide us with excellent examples of the kinds of conflicts that arise from these problematic meanings of moral responsibility for social problems. The deaths, injuries, and financial costs resulting from auto accidents were not commonly considered to be (strong) social problems until Ralph Nader [22] and others publicized the ways in which the construction of automobiles, the structure of roads, and so on, were clearly known to be determinants of the rates of accidents and, especially, of their consequences. Once this view was accepted, events that had previously been seen as "accidents" beyond the control of men were now seen as at least partially subject to the decisions of men and, therefore, as socially caused events. Since they were seen as socially caused events, they were also seen as events for which some individuals presumably bore responsibility. While there now seems much less conflict over the question of whether they are socially caused events, there is still

[22] Ralph Nader, *Unsafe at Any Speed* (New York: Grossman, 1965).

great conflict over the question of who is responsible for these events.

Those who take the position of Ralph Nader argue that the manufacturers of American automobiles, especially the heads of the giant corporations that determine policies in the manufacture of automobiles know about the relationship between the construction of automobiles and accidents, intentionally decide to pursue construction policies they know will produce larger rates of accidents resulting in deaths, injuries, and financial costs for repairs, and are in fact free to change these policies whenever they decide to do so. The heads of the corporations thus charged and their supporters contend, on the other hand, that they are not in any way responsible for accidents and their consequences. They so contend largely on the grounds that, while they do recognise the relationship between construction and the consequences of accidents, they are not free to build cars differently. They deny they have this freedom on two grounds: (1) in some cases they do not have the technical knowledge to change construction; and, more commonly, (2) when they do have the required knowledge they are not free to produce cars in accord with that knowledge because customers will not buy such cars; this, therefore, will not lead to safer cars, but rather to financial disaster for their companies, which would be considered a failure on their part to live up to their clear moral responsibility to make money legally for their shareholders.

The argument about pollution, especially smog, follows a similar path, with many of the same arguers taking part, the accusing side trying to show that the corporate side freely and intentionally chooses a path of action producing pollution, knowing full well the consequences of such actions, while the corporatic side concentrates on denying the freedom to do anything about it. In the case of pollution, especially smog, the denial of freedom is made far more on the grounds of lack of technical knowledge needed to do anything about it. The accusing side then reasserts the corporate side's responsibility for it all by insisting that they purposefully chose not to invest in the kinds of research that long ago would have made that knowledge available for use today. The corporate heads then generally deny that they ever intentionally made such a decision. Much of the ensuing argument is centered on trying to establish intention not to invest in research that could reasonably be expected to produce such knowledge.

These arguments over responsibility for causing social problems are sometimes pursued for their own sake, simply to bring about moral condemnation of someone believed to be committing evil deeds. But the greatest importance of such arguments, and no doubt the major reason most people make them, is their implications for the preferred or appropriate solutions to the social problems involved. The implication is simple: he who is shown to be guilty of an immoral deed has an obligation to stop it and, less clearly, to make amends for past immoral deeds. The argument over moral responsibility for social problems, then, is often an argument directed at solving the problem by showing *who* should stop doing *what* is believed to be causing the problem. In many cases, however, the problems today are seen as complexly interwoven with other activities which few people would like to see stopped, so the implications for solutions are more problematic and, therefore, more subject to conflict. For example, while few people want to see auto accidents or pollution continued, few people want to see an end to automobile production or to the industrial activity producing the pollution either. For those who take this more complex, gradualist approach to solving social problems, the preferred solution generally lies in the direction of investing money to prevent the problem in the first place, normally through technological developments, and to control or clean up the problem after the fact. The argument over responsibility is then concerned with who is to be responsible for investing that money, with the bill going in most cases to the one believed responsible. Since the costs involved could be enormous, the problematic aspects of the ideas of moral responsibility for social problems are used to the utmost by all sides involved to support their own constructions of moral responsibility.

Conflicts over Weak Problems, Strong Problems, and Solutions

We saw in the first part of this chapter that there are a number of basic reasons why even the facts about social problems are necessarily problematic for the members of our society. But it should also be apparent that they are less problematic and, therefore, less subject to conflicts than any statements concerning the causes of social problems. Statements about the causes of problems are subject both to conflicts over the facts and to conflicts arising specifically from the nature of the commonsense theories of causality and responsibility. The problematic meanings of statements about the causes of social problems, then, are compounded.

The first immediate implication of this is that statements about weak social problems will be less subject to conflicts than will statements about strong social problems. Since statements about weak social problems are concerned only with the nature of the problem and the facts about its sharedness in society, they are subject only to the problems involved in defining that nature and those facts. Statements about strong social problems, on the other hand, are subject both to all of these problems and to the problematic meanings of the commonsense theories of social causality, so the chances for plausible conflicts are inevitably greater. In turn, one implication of this is that we can expect conflicts over socially defined social problems to increase in the future simply because the term "social problem" has come increasingly to mean a problem not only widely shared in society, but also socially caused. As we have also seen, however, there are more important reasons why we can expect increasing conflicts over social problems.

Our argument also leads us to conclude that the conflicts over solutions to social problems will be the greatest of all. Ideas about social solutions include all the problematic meanings of the facts and social causality, since solutions can only be proposed for factually defined problems and since any solution depends in part on some understanding of the causes of the problem. For example, the idea of solving air pollution by eliminating automobile exhaust particles and gases of various kinds was only possible once it was discovered that these emissions are the most important cause of smog in most parts of the country. But the ideas about solutions also involve all the problems associated with imputations of moral responsibility and all those involved in choosing the *"best practical alternatives"* proposed for solving a social problem. Choosing the best practical alternative not only involves additional problems derived from the problematic theories of persons and society but also introduces all of the elements of private interest into the arguments, thus making the argument very important for many powerful groups in our society.

As we argued at the end of the last chapter, conflicts over solutions tend to be maintained and reach a maximum when the criteria used to evaluate whether a problem has been solved or still exists are completely relativistic criteria, that is, when the solutions are defined as some stable proportion or percentage relative to the whole. For example, when we argue that the social problem of poverty is represented by the lower two fifths (or any other arbitrary percentage) of the income distribution regardless of absolute values, and then argue that no solution is possible until that two fifths at the lower end does not exist, we maximize conflict over any attempts to "solve the problem" in that way. Edward Banfield and others have argued that this kind of relativistic criteria of solution is increasingly being applied to urban problems and problems of poverty and that, aside from causing conflicts over the problems and solutions, this may produce some very harmful results:

> To a large extent . . . our urban problems are like the mechanical rabbit at the racetrack, which is set to keep just ahead of the dogs no matter how fast they may run. Our performance is better and better, but because we set our standards and expectations to keep ahead of performance, the problems are never any nearer to solution. Indeed, if standards and expectations rise *faster* than performance, the problems may get (relatively) worse as they get (absolutely) better . . . there is danger that we may mistake failure to progress as fast as we would like for failure to progress at all and, in panic, rush into ill-considered measures that will only make matters worse . . .
>
> This danger is greatest in matters where our standards are unreasonably high. The effect of too high standards cannot be to spur us on to reach the prescribed level of performance sooner than we otherwise would, for that level is by definition impossible of attainment. At the same time, these standards may cause us to adopt measures that are wasteful and injurious and, in the long run, to conclude from the inevitable failure of these measures that there is something fundamentally wrong with our society. Consider the school dropout problem, for example. The dropout rate can never be cut to zero: there will always be some boys and girls who simply do not have whatever it takes to finish high school. If we continue to make a great hue and cry about the dropout problem after we have reached the point where all those who can reasonably be expected to finish high school are doing so, we shall accomplish nothing constructive. Instead, we shall, at considerable cost to ourselves, injure

the boys and girls who cannot finish (the propaganda against being a dropout both hurts the morale of such a youngster and reduces his or her job opportunities) while creating in ourselves and in others the impression that our society is morally or otherwise incapable of meeting its obligations.[23]

The only solution that is possible when one is using a relativistic criteria in this way is complete equality or homogeneity. For, as long as there is any distribution, there will be a lower two fifths to be impoverished. Since attempts to produce complete equality will produce maximum conflicts with all the other three fifths of the population, we can see that such solutions produce maximum conflict.

Conflicts and Agreements

In the last two chapters we have emphasized the problematic meanings of social problems and the conflicts over definitions that grow out of such problematic meanings. This, however, must not be interpreted to mean that everything is problematic or that there are no agreements. On the contrary, we have even argued that there are certain kinds of social problems, especially the physicalistic ones that easily become consensus problems. Moreover, the whole idea that there are conflicts among major groups in a pluralistic society over the meanings of problems is based on the implicit assumption that there are some agreements *within* the conflicting groups over how to define problems and solutions. Of course, there may also be problematic meanings and conflicts over definitions *within* groups as well as between them.) We have emphasized both the conflicts and the problematic nature of the meanings because the fundamental importance of

[23] Edward Banfield, *The Unheavenly City,* op. cit., pp. 21–22.

these has so commonly been overlooked by earlier analysts and because the partially problematic nature of the meanings involved becomes the basis for seeing that *our whole theoretical approach must be oriented toward explaining how the members of our society go about constructing agreements and disagreements about social problems.* How do the members of our society make use of the shared meanings and the nonshared meanings to try to convince each other that something is a problem or not a problem, a solution or not a solution? It is this that must concern us most of all in developing our sociological theory of social problems.

SUGGESTED READINGS

American Social Order (New York: Free Press, 1971) by Jack D. Douglas, is an attempt to describe and explain social order in American society from a phenomenological (existential) perspective. It is based in good part on the argument that American society is highly pluralistic—though there are many crosscurrents of both pluralism and homogenization going on today—and that this pluralism makes social meanings and social order highly problematic for us. Much of the work is concerned with showing how Americans construct social meanings and social order in this highly problematic situation. Some preliminary considerations are given to the problems involved in constructing the meanings of social problems and the effects of these constructions on social order.

Beyond the Melting Pot (Cambridge, Massachusetts: M.I.T. Press, 1964) is a highly readable description and analysis of the present pluralism of New York City. The authors, Nathan Glazer and Daniel Moynihan, show that all of the rhetoric about American society as a melting pot of ethnic identities has largely been just so much rhetoric. New York, like most other great American cities, remains a pluralistic world of ethnic identities, ethnic residence patterns, ethnic businesses, and so on. Moreover, as Milton Gordon has also concluded in a more general analysis of ethnicity today (*Assimilation In American Life,* New York: Oxford University Press, 1964), there are good reasons to believe this ethnic pluralism will continue into the forseeable future.

Henry Kariel's *The Decline of American Pluralism* (Stanford, California: Stanford University Press, 1967) is probably the best known and most scholarly work attempting to show that the ancient forms of pluralism in American society are rapidly declining. Actually, most of the evidence considered is concerned with the rapid contralization of American businesses. This trend, which has also been documented in a massive work by W. Lloyd Warner and his coworkers (*The Emergent American Society,*

New Haven, Conn.: Yale University Press, 1967, Vol. 1), is certainly an important one and must be weighed in any analysis of American pluralism. But this trend must also be weighed against other trends, some of them quite new.

Two works that form an excellent comparison and contrast in the definition of the social problems of urban poverty in American society today are Edward Banfield's *The Unheavenly City* (Boston: Little, Brown, 1970) and Kenneth Clark's *Dark Ghetto* (New York: Harper, 1965). Kenneth Clark's book has been one of the most important sources of the argument that the problems of the urban poor, at least of the blacks in urban ghettoes, are definitely great and growing and that something must be done about them immediately if the society is to avoid catastrophes. Edward Banfield is probably the best statement of the highly subjectivist view of urban problems of poverty as being "what you make them" or how you "see them." Both works suffer from failing to see that such problems are a combination of problematic and more certain meanings, but a reading of such contrasting points of view is very important in understanding the definitions of social problems in our society.

These three books form an interesting contrast in views of the social problems of the conflict of generations, which we have heard so much about in recent years. Louis Feuer's massive scholarly work, *The Conflict of Generations* (New York: Basic Books, 1969), is grounded in basic aspects of human personality, society, and history. The conflicts are cross cultural and largely beyond the influence of individual, meaningful interpretations because they are basic responses to unconscious forces. The problems are seen as being more within the individual. *The Greening of America,* Charles A. Reich's very popular argument about the recent revolutionary rise of "Consciousness III", takes an equally absolutist view of the definition of the problems but turns completely around and argues that the problem is not within the young rebels at all, but rather, entirely within the materialistic, inhuman society that oppresses them. The problem is just as absolutely certain but it is in the society, not in the rebelling individuals. *Youth in Turmoil* (Washington, D.C.: U.S.

Government Printing Office, 1970), by Jack D. Douglas, attempts to show how it is that the young and adult members of American society have come to see each other as social problems in recent generations. How do the various sides, including both the rebelling youth and the cooperating youth, both the angry adults and the sympathetic ones, define the problems and why?

chapter 6

Constructing the Meanings of Social Problems and Social Solutions

The phenomenological analyses of social action that have been carried out by sociologists in recent years have shown that all social meanings and, therefore, all social actions are problematic to some degree. They have also shown that the degrees of problems vary greatly: some meanings and actions are highly routinized and shared and, thus, vary little within a society from one situation to another and from one individual to another. In American society, for example, the procedural rules of democracy, such as the rule of the majority, are highly shared and not very problematic within the realm of electoral activities; again, the symbols of the flag and the star-spangled banner are highly shared and not very problematic in their applications throughout our society. There are even some activities, such as parent-child incest, whose meanings are relatively shared and unproblematic in their applications in all societies. Most meanings and activities are considerably more problematic than these for Americans. For example, even generally shared ideas such as "all men are created equal" or "equal justice before the law" are subject to great problems in their definitions for use in concrete situations and thus produce great conflicts over the concrete policies for education, employment, court proceedings, and many other realms of our everyday lives. As we have seen, the meanings of social problems run the gamut from relatively unproblematic, as in those directly tied to common physical experiences, to exceedingly problematic, as in the relativistically defined social solutions.

The phenomenological analyses of social meanings and actions in general have revealed that these problems of meaning make it necessary for the members of society to *construct specific, concrete meanings and paths of actions for each concrete situation they face in everyday life.* That is, the members must put together specific interpretations of their shared meanings (values, beliefs, ideas, feelings) that seem to them to be relevant and plausible for the situations at hand. Also, as one would expect, the more problematic the meanings applied to any concrete situation are, the more *constructive or interpretive work* the members must do to construct plausible, acceptable meanings to deal with that situation. Much of phenomenological sociology has been concerned with showing how they go about doing this, especially with showing what leads to one construction of meaning and action rather than to others.[1]

When applied to the analysis of social problems, this general analysis leads us to expect that the problematic meanings of social problems make it necessary for the members of society to construct concrete meanings of social problems, and *the more problematic the meanings of any social problem or social solution are, the more constructive work the members must put into defining it.* In addition to the fundamental work of investigating the specific problems members encounter in defining social

---

[1] See especially Chapter 6 of *American Social Order, op. cit.*

problems which we did in Chapters 4 and 5, the sociology of social problems is primarily concerned with working out the details of how this kind of constructive work is done and with its implications both for practical activities aimed at solving the defined problems and for the sociology of social problems.

The sociological theory of social problems, then, has come increasingly to be seen as the theory exploring and explaining: (1) the problematic nature of meanings and actions concerning social problems and solutions; (2) the ways in which the members go about constructing concrete meanings of problems and solutions; (3) the effects of these problems and this constructive work on attempts by the members of society to solve the problems they have defined; and (4) the implications of these problems, this constructive work, and their effects on society for the sociology of social problems. Since there are still important gaps in our factual knowledge about the processes by which social problems get defined, gaps which will remain until much more research on specific problems has been completed, much of this work necessarily remains exploratory, and it would be self-defeating to try to develop any highly formal set of explanatory principles. Nevertheless, we do know enough about the concrete processes of definitions to develop the fundamental ideas and principles that reveal the basic properties of social problems and solutions in our society and that will guide us to ever more fruitful empirical investigations.

Public Problems, Official Problems, Expert Problems, and Potential Problems

Almost all earlier sociological works that have seen the need for a theory of social problems, as opposed to having taken the absolutist stance of taking the nature of the problems for granted, have implicitly assumed that the problems of concern to sociologists will be defined as problems by the general public. This is true even of those interaction theorists who have accepted Lemert's findings and argument that there is no single path that can be followed in the definition of social problems. While they agree there are many paths followed, they still believe there is a single outcome; a social problem is implicitly defined by them as being widely shared by the public, though how widely is not discussed. Howard Becker, for example, has explicitly assumed this point of view:

> Little research has been done on the stages of development of social problems, so we cannot present a commonly accepted scheme of analysis. Instead, we can indicate the kinds of questions that might be raised in exploring the process in the case of a specific problem.
>
> The first step in the development of a social problem comes when some person or group sees a set of objective conditions as problematic, posing a danger or containing the seeds of future difficulties . . .
>
> After a problem has come to someone's attention, concern with it must become shared and widespread if it is to achieve the status of a social problem. The person who originally noticed it must point it out to others and convince them the situation is dangerous enough to require public action. We can raise the same kind of questions about the second step in the process as we did about the first. What kinds of people will the original definer of the problem be able to convince that his argument is sound? Who, on the contrary, will think his view foolish or mistaken? What tactics are most successful in winning support for the definition of a condition as a problem? What is the role of the mass media of communication—newspapers, magazines, radio, and television—in promoting widespread concern with a problem, and how does a person who wishes to define a new social problem get access to them?

> When widespread concern has been aroused, it must be embodied in an organisation or institution if the problem is to achieve lasting existence as a defined social problem.[2]

The interactionists have probably made this assumption as a result of an overconcentration on traditional social problems and problems about which a concensus develops. Problems such as crime, prostitution and corruption have always been with us, and what varies is normally the urgency with which the public feels something needs to be done. These problems are commonsense social problems, easily appreciated by anyone with good sense. They are commonly problems that wellup from the general public as a result of situational factors. When they do, the public demands action from the officials, the officials react, and the problem is temporarily "solved". This happens over and over again with such problems as crime, prostitution, and corruption. Commonly, the process begins with a little mass-media entrepreneurial activity: a reporter or editor begins a campaign against the "rising menace of prostitution on our streets." He demands immediate action by the laggard officials and police to stop the menace. Sometimes this activity leads to grass-roots decency movements; at other times it is the movements that produce the mass-media entrepreneurial reporting. Whichever way it goes, the officials and police almost always find it in their best interests first to deny the validity of the criticism and then to carry out their own campaign against prostitution by greatly increasing surveillance in the pestilential areas, questioning more people, running them off the streets, telling the known prostitutes they had better stop, pulling many in for questioning, booking many more than usual, pressing for prosecution and conviction, and sometimes calling for more stringent laws and sentences. The general result is that the prostitutes, criminals, and other "socially undesirable elements" move to nearby areas that have been

[2] Howard Becker, "Introduction," *Social Problems, op. cit.,* pp. 11–12.

denuded of patrols to saturate the criticized areas. The business goes on pretty much as usual, unless there is a general crackdown resulting from great pressures, but the social problem has been "solved" by disappearing, only to be rediscovered next year.

These traditional problems are similar to the problems of poverty and generational conflict, except that public concern over the latter comes and goes over much longer time periods. (Poverty and generational conflict were both major social problems in the 1920s and 1930s that were temporarily "solved" by disappearing from public attention during the 1940s and 1950s.) These traditional problems are ones with wide public definition and can best be called *public social problems* or *publicly defined social problems.* They do seem roughly to follow the general path of definition outlined by both Blumer and Becker: initial definition by isolated individuals, collective action consisting of informal talks and the spreading of more formal means of communicating the definition, legitimization of the definition of the problem by public and official acceptance, official response to the problem, research by experts, planning by officials, and execution, followed by solution as defined by the public so that the problem disappears. They probably follow this general, vague path because these officials act mainly as the result of pressures from the grass roots, rather than initiate actions themselves. Officials of this sort, especially at the local levels, traditionally follow a *foxhole strategy;* that is, they keep their heads down on most social problems, preferring to let sleeping dogs lie and agreeing with Calvin Coolidge that most social problems will disappear if you just wait long enough, but they come out fighting when the dogs begin to howl and the problems cannot be evaded.

These publicly defined social problems are still very important, especially in an era of progressivism in which large segments of the public have changed their criteria for defining social problems and are, thereby, easily mobilized for any constructive work aimed at defining a new social problem or generating action on old ones. But the publicly defined social problems have been progressively eclipsed in importance by those that are dependent for their definition on more specialized kinds of knowledge and which, therefore, are generally not initiated by men of common sense.

As knowledge and American society become more complex, the definitions of social problems, including those social problems that eventually receive wide public acceptance, are increasingly initiated and controlled at each stage by experts and officials. It is of value, then, to make a general distinction among those kinds of problems that are defined as problems by experts, those defined by officials, and those defined by the general public. We should distinguish among *public social problems, expert social problems,* and *official social problems.* In addition, as should be clear from the earlier discussions of the problematic nature of social problems, we must commonly consider which particular groups of experts, officials, and the public see something as a social problem, and we must also be concerned with how certain they are in their definitions.

Probably the most striking evidence of the importance of expert activity in defining social problems today comes from the area of pollution.[3] Only a few of the problems of pollution, especially air pollution in the form of smog, are immediately accessible to commonsense observation. Most forms of pollution are detectable only by analyses and measurements that can be performed only by experts, such as chemists, radiologists, and oceanographers. The experts, of course, are generally unsure about the effects of various pollutants on the human body, especially because the commonsense problems involved in specifying individual and social causality (see Chapter 5) are paralleled by the problems of specifying the effects of a specific

[3] See Carol A. B. Warren, "Pollution as a Social Problem" (Paper presented at the Convention of the *American Sociological Association,* Washington, D.C., August, 1970).

substance on a complex system, such as the human body, by the problems of specifying causal relations among parts of the body, and by the necessary problems in defining "safe levels," "acceptable levels," "harmful levels," "lethal levels," and so on. The result is that the experts themselves have great conflicts over whether there is a problem or, if they can agree on the problem's existence, over how serious it is and over what kind of action the seriousness calls for. All of these conflicts and problems are apparent in the arguments over such pollutants as mercury and radiation.

Mercury pollution is an excellent example of the importance of both experts and officials in defining social problems today. It has been known for a century or more that working with mercury in sufficient quantities for long enough periods of time will cause severe damage or death. For a number of years there have been some scientists who have argued that the continued disposal of mercury by means that lead to its increased concentration in the oceans was endangering fish and, thereby, the human beings who ate the fish. There were even some strong statements to this effect published in newspapers in the 1960s, but there was very little public attention and, while more and more experts were coming in greater numbers to define mercury pollution as a social problem, the general public certainly did not do so. In fact, the efforts of scientists to arouse public concern may have been counterproductive because those efforts probably looked to many people like the scare tactics of crackpots. In the early 1970s a chemist almost accidentally discovered that some frozen swordfish contained high concentrations of mercury. The report of this in the mass media and to the Food and Drug Administration led the FDA chemists to discover that there were also much higher concentrations of mercury in canned tuna than had been assumed. The public almost overnight come to see mercury pollution as a grave social problem. In many ways the public response was so great that it clearly had the overtones of the mass hysteria that has often been associated with social problems at the height of collective or public involvement in them.

The public definition of radiation and its side effects as pollution problems depends even more obviously upon the work and public statements of experts and officials. These problems are not detectable by commonsense means. Even the causes of the few deaths that have occurred from accidental overdoses could only be detected by the experts, since the physical symptoms normally do not show up until a few days after the accident.

Widespread public definitions of social problems as the primary means by which something gets done about problems are also being slowly eclipsed by the increasing power of government officials to initiate definitions of problems and resulting lines of action, rather than simply to respond to public demands. Big government is not simply a responder but an initiator as well. (As we saw in Chapter 3, Lemert found the same thing to be true even for local officials dealing with such obscure problems as trailer camps.) Increasingly, the government bureaucracies are responding directly to each other, rather than proposing something to the public and then waiting for the public to tell them that they should do something about it. As a result, we now have social problems defined and reacted to by government agencies with little participation by the public. An excellent example of this is the social problem of suicide, which was considered an important enough problem by officials of the National Institutes of Health to create a Center for Studies of Suicide Prevention but which has never been given much consideration by the general public, in spite of extensive efforts by the government officials to get people more concerned about it. While most people *might* agree, if asked by an official, that suicide is a social problem, very few of them treat it that way in their daily lives, and probably very few of them are aware that the officials have long been claiming that we must do more about it because it is the tenth-most-frequent cause of death.

In fact, while this process of official definition of social problems has become so much more visible in recent years because of the vast increase in such governmental initiatives and powers, there have long been quiet, even secret, efforts by government officials to define and deal with social problems in their own terms, regardless of the interests of the public in such work. For example, this is very clear in the area of water pollution. While there have probably always been some Americans who were concerned with the growing pollution of rivers and harbors, the general public has only recently become concerned with it. Various government officials, on the other hand, have defined it as an important social problem for approximately a century and have taken many steps to deal with the problem.[4] Public hygiene officials in the nineteenth century were the first to see the social problems of typhoid fever and other diseases associated with the general practice of dumping raw sewage into the rivers and lakes. They got laws passed to deal with this problem without great public involvement, and at least one such law against water pollution was used a hundred years later in an attempt to stop industrial pollution. Again, Donald Carmichael has shown that official and legal concern with water pollution has been strong in Wisconsin for a hundred years. This concern was far more related to the economic interests of small groups in the state than to any public outcry.

John Johnson's study of the changing parts played by the officials of the U.S. Children's Bureau in defining the social problems of children during this century shows the ways the officials tried to spread their definitions of the problems (especially by relating them to the big issues of the day that gripped the public) and the increasing cooperation between the

[4] *Ibid.*

officials and the experts in these attempts to construct the problems:

The first White House Conference on the Care of Dependent Children was called in 1909 for the specific purposes of focusing national attention on the social problems of children and to dramatize the need for a federal bureau to investigate and report on such matters. The subsequent establishment of the U.S. Children's Bureau three years later symbolized a political victory for the loose alliance of moral reform groups which had dedicated several decades of political struggles to the moral transformation of the lower classes into respectable middle-class citizens.

Following the establishment of the Children's Bureau, the White House Conferences have been used dicennially to promote the official conceptions of the social problems of children. While the abstract language of the Conferences tends to exploit the image of the symbolic salvation one allegedly attains by making a world which is better for one's children, and tends to politicize every conceivable moral concern of Mankind, the concrete policy recommendations were always grounded within the context of more immediate concerns. Thus, the 1919 White House Conference abstractly called for "the conservation of childhood," while its policy recommendations were more in keeping with the attempts of other officials to extricate the country from the immediate economic crises. It was much the same story for the 1930 White House Conference of Child Health and Protection. The 1940 White House Conference on Children in a Democracy was held in the context of an impending war, and proposed developing "a frame of reference for equipping American children for the successful practice of democracy." Following the war, the 1950 Midcentury Conference on Children and Youth evidenced a concern for "democracy's responsibility to produce socially-minded, cooperative people, without sacrificing individuality." By the time of the Midcentury Conference, the decades of Children's Bureau success in mobilizing the forces of officials against the lower classes and their children had been realized only at the cost of their own bureau autonomy and research hegemony in these matters. By the end of the war the White House Conferences became less and less of a front used by the officials to dramatize their conceptions of social problems and to promote their existing (or proposed) programs. By the 1950 Conference, "which followed a decade of profound discoveries in the field of dynamic psychology," increasing numbers of social scientists and others presenting social problems expertise rushed to such conferences to attempt the difficult tasks of translating the recent discoveries in the respective fields into official policy. Bureau officials became less involved in actual research and increasingly involved in the many tasks of co-ordinating numerous conferences, dispensing research funds to eager academicians, organizing various projects and demonstration grants, and co-ordinating the various "Citizen's Committees" which have been used since 1950 to take the messages of the White House Conferences back to the state legislatures for the purposes of updating the various laws and statutes in accord with the newly discovered or newly promoted conceptions of social problems.[5]

The argument that the social definitions of social problems are necessarily problematic and that part of this necessity arises from the pluralistic nature of our society leads us inevitably to expect and to study the conflicting definitions of social problems of different groups. We might, of course, simply argue that we should study all the different definitions of problems by all the different groups or individuals. In some cases, especially when we are interested in the developments of a social definition at a

[5] John M. Johnson, "Making Good Kids: The Role of the Children's Bureau in Defining and Creating Children's Social Problems" Paper presented at the Convention of the *American Sociological Association,* Washington, D.C., August, 1970.

very local level or on a very microscopic level, this is precisely what we should do. But for most purposes this becomes impossibly involved. Moreover, for most purposes it is not important to differentiate among all the different groups or individuals in the society, both because smaller groups tend to align themselves with larger *socially defined political social positions,* such as the "liberal position," the "conservative position," or the "black liberation movement," and because for most situations most groups and individuals are not nearly so important as the groups of the general public, the officials, and the experts. For most purposes these three natural types of group positions on social problems are so much more important as to justify a qualitative distinction from the other natural types of groups involved.

In addition to the three natural types of social problems, it is of increasing importance to distinguish an analytical or theoretical type of social problem, that of *potential social problems.* Just as it has become increasingly important to predict future social situations in general (see Chapter 1), so has it become increasingly important in particular to predict what specific social situations or conditions will be defined by what specific groups and members of society as social problems. These predictions about the future social meanings of problems are potential social problems. They are of the greatest importance in trying to do any social planning simply because the planner must know not only what people want now, but also what they will want in the future for which he is planning. Since we know for a fact that the definitions of what is a problem, including the very criteria used to define what is problematic, change greatly over time, bringing about diachronic changes in social problems, we can easily predict that social planning based on the simple assumption that people tomorrow will define problems and nonproblems the way they did yesterday will be wrong. Recognizing that problems are relative over time as well as among groups and individuals must make us even more pessimistic about ever actually producing a situation in which people feel there are fewer problems, that is, in which they would be happier with their society than they are now. Moreover, attempts to predict the future meanings of future external (objective) conditions become so tremendously problematic that we cannot expect to be very successful at them. Nevertheless, analyzing a few key potential social problems seems both possible and very important to anyone concerned with social planning to solve social problems.

Most social scientists who have been concerned with predicting future social problems have concentrated almost entirely on predicting the objective social conditions of these problems, simply because they have tended implicitly to make the absolutist assumptions about social problems. For example, in the best of these works, such as the attempt by Herman Kahn and Anthony Wiener to predict "Some Twenty-First Century Technological and Economic Issues," [6] we find detailed considerations of such problems as "computerized records," "excessively illusioned attitudes," and so on. Almost all of these are based on the value assumptions of Kahn and Wiener with no explicit discussion of them, yet they recognize in other parts of their paper that American society is pluralistic and changing and that part of this change consists in changes in the values and feelings of Americans, precisely the things that will determine whether they see such things as problems at all in the future.

At the present time it is undoubtedly utopian to try to predict the social meanings of social problems beyond the near future, especially since it is difficult enough to deal with the problems in the present. But it is possible and important for social scientists to deal with potential social problems in one way. In fact, it is necessary for us to try to do this if we are to

[6] Herman Kahn and Anthony J. Wiener, "Faustian Powers and Human Choices: Some Twenty-first Century Technological and Economic Issues" (New York: The Hudson Institute, 1968).

be anything more than mere cataloguers of what the public, the officials, and other experts have already come to define as social problems. What we can do, and what many of us already do, is try to show that, in terms of current trends in social meanings and in physical or social conditions, we can predict that, if nothing is done to change the situations, then Americans will come to experience certain conditions as social problems—possibly even as catastrophes. A recent example will help to make this whole process clear.

Regardless of the problems involved in specifying just what is meant by it, and the conflicts over its meanings in concrete situations, few people would doubt that most Americans are deeply committed to personal "freedom" and that they define any social condition that they believe decreases their freedom unnecessarily as a social problem. Moreover, while there would be more disagreement over the meaning of this freedom it seems reasonably clear that most Americans would agree that any trend that takes important decisions about their daily lives out of their hands, turning these decisions over to unseen bureaucratic officials and experts who cannot be controlled even indirectly through representative government, would be an important problem about which something should be done to reverse the trend. But, precisely because the officials and experts are so unobservable to most citizens and because the complex kinds of decisions involved and their complex and conflicting effects are very difficult to estimate even when one knows about them, the vast majority of citizens in our society do not have any clear idea about whether such trends exist. What they have is a sense of malaise, of something going wrong that makes them less free. It is the sense that somehow part of their everyday lives seems to trap them, as C. Wright Mills said:

"Nowadays men often feel that their private lives are a series of traps. They sense that within their everyday worlds, they cannot overcome their troubles, and in this feeling, they are often quite correct: What ordinary men are directly aware of and what they try to do are bounded by the private orbits in which they live; their visions and their powers are limited to the close-up scenes of job, family, neighbourhood; in other milieux, they move vicariously and remain spectators. And the more aware they become, however vaguely, of ambitions and of threats which transcend their immediate locales, the more trapped they seem to feel."[7]

Also as Mills argued, most men do not have the knowledge or the time to systematically trace out the relationship between their own immediate situations and those of other men in other places and, very importantly, other times. Seeing the so-called structural relationships between their situations and those of others today is difficult enough, but what is needed is more than this: what is needed is a systematic view of the directions or trends of things, for it is the trends above all which allow us to decide how general, how deep, how serious these developments are; this is fundamental to deciding whether we should simply ride it out, or muddle through, or shore up the foundations of our freedoms with minor changes in society, or make some more basic changes.

What is demanded, then, is a systematic consideration of potential social problems of freedom and tyranny.[8] A growing number of social scientists and social philosophers have in fact turned their attention to consideration of this vital potential problem. Rather than seeing the problem as simply one of big government or big business that takes the power of decision out of our hands, which is roughly the way men of common sense on both the right and the left see it today, these social analysts have generally concluded that the basic trends are being deter-

[7] C. Wright Mills, *The Sociological Imagination* (New York: Oxford University Press, 1959), p. 3.
[8] See *Freedom and Tyranny, op. cit.*

mined primarily by scientific and technological forms of thought and work. And they have concluded that, however mixed the trends may be, the general trend is toward less freedom for individuals in their everyday lives and toward more unrepresentative and secret (tyrannical) powers of officials and experts to make the decisions that determine the kind of situations the individual will face in his everyday life. More specifically, they have argued that:

> Our traditional personal freedoms, our civil rights were built largely on private ownership of the decentralized means of production, an educated citizenry capable of understanding complex problems of government decisions, and liberal forms of pluralism in government and private life which prevented the concentration of power in any one part of the society. The technological society thrives on centralization, massive size, and expert decision making—all of which have served to undermine the foundations of our traditional freedoms and their direct threats to these freedoms appear to be growing at an accelerating rate as technology itself grows at an accelerating rate.[9]

The general argument of these analysts, then, is that, given present and long-standing American values, ideas, and feelings about freedom and tyranny, which can be expected to continue for some time, and given our analysis of the basic social trends in America today, we can predict that Americans will come to see future situations as ones involving greater tyranny and, therefore, as constituting a great social problem—unless they do something to reverse these trends. The purpose of the scientific analysis is to anticipate the problems that would be experienced *if* they were to come about so that we can do something about the potential problem before it becomes an actual problem.

[9] *Ibid.*

Background Assumptions and Constructing Social Problems

Regardless of the kind of social problem or the social path followed in defining it, *all constructions of the meanings of social problems are dependent on the context of assumptions taken for granted by those doing the constructive work of defining the problem*. This unspoken context of assumptions constitutes the *background meanings* of the social problem: these are basic determinants of the meanings of the explicit communications about problems but are left in the background, unstated, and commonly unrealized even by the persons making the explicit statements.

Background assumptions are necessary in social communications partly for practical reasons: if people had to make explicit all the ideas involved in any communication, they might never get done. But this practicality is not something planned by human beings, or even understood by most. It is the way the human mind functions—the mind always constructs meanings for any concrete situation *in the context of* background, taken-for-granted meanings. While we can certainly stand back and theoretically consider the assumptions that underlie our concrete communications, we rarely do so when we are involved in everyday, practical communications, and then we generally make explicit only those assumptions that seem most immediately relevant to showing the rational structure of our argument to someone who has disagreed with or questioned our explicit communication.

Communications about (strong) social problems and solutions are also necessarily dependent on a context of background assumptions for the additional reason that the causal arguments and evaluations involved in constructing the meaning of any concrete problem are necessarily problematic, as we saw in Chapter 5. That is, there are inevitably rational gaps and indeterminacies, such as those resulting from the embeddedness of the ideas about social causality and responsibility, and these are bridged or made determinate by the members by being placed in a context of assumptions about society and persons *in general* (or typically). These general assumptions about society and persons do not have to be rationally demonstrated for the concrete situation the individuals are considering at a given time, so they provide a *presumptive rationality* to the specific communication about social problems. (Since any science of society necessarily remains partially grounded in common sense and thereby differs from common sense only in degree, it is obvious that our scientific ideas about society differ in this respect from commonsense ideas only by basing themselves on fewer and more explicit and precise assumptions.)

In commonsense communications about social problems the most important background assumptions made are those we can call the *metaphysics of man and society*.[10] These are the assumptions made about men and society without regard to the concrete persons and situations faced. The most important metaphysical ideas are those revolving around pessimism vs. optimism, trust vs. distrust, belief vs. disbelief, and so on. Since these are implicit assumptions made about men and society in general, but applied to particular situations, they become unquestioned determinants of whether an individual will see a particular event as part of a problem or not, whether he will see a set of phenomena as constituting a social problem or not, whether he will believe that "this problem shows how sick the whole society is," whether he believes the problem can be solved within the general structure of society, whether he believes the "only way to solve the problem is to revolutionize the whole rotten society," whether he believes it is impossible to solve the problem, and so on.

In commonsense discourse about social problems, individuals will commonly argue that the truth is just the opposite of what

[10] See "The Impact of the Social Sciences," *op. cit.*

we have been saying; that is, they believe the facts *prove* their conclusions and that these are rationally beyond dispute. For example, the man who sees himself as a radical or Marxist commonly argues that the problems of pollution prove that this is a completely corrupt society, all of our social problems show that capitalism is an evil system, Vietnam proves that America is the greatest threat to all nations today, and so on. On the other hand, the man who sees himself as a patriot or loyal American commonly argues that when you look at the whole balance sheet, you see that America is the last hope of the world, America is solving its problems of race and poverty better than any other society has ever done, and so on. We have seen these kinds of arguments in our earlier considerations of the conflicts resulting from the problematic meanings of social problems, and we have tried to show that even when individuals use the same facts, they can arrive at opposite conclusions about social problems, especially when they try to aggregate these or when they are concerned with the question of what can be done practically to solve the problems. Analyses of their arguments and their own justifications of their conclusions indicates that they have not used the facts to arrive at their conclusions but rather have used their conclusions to arrive at their facts. We have tried to show why this is to some degree necessary (though certainly the degree can be greatly reduced), that is, that the facts, explanations, conclusions and evaluations are to some degree *reflexively* related to each other, or mutually dependent on each other.

Recognizing this partially reflexive nature of the conclusions and the bases of the conclusions is of fundamental importance in understanding many of the phenomena observed in considerations of social problems. We shall see its most important implication in the next section, but we should examine two of its other implications here—those of *problem hysteria* and the idea of the *rotten core*.

It has long been recognized by historians that public concern with social problems, either in a given area or in general, tends to wax and wane and that great concern tends to be concentrated in certain peak periods. In these peak periods of concern we find all of the properties of social hysteria analyzed by the students of collective behavior. While there is commonly a slow build-up in the concern over social problems, with concern spreading slowly from one problem area to another, there is also a sudden coalescence of social problems and a sharp rise in social concern with problems during which an extremely wide spectrum of national life suddenly comes to be seen as problem ridden. During these periods of peak concern, areas of life which had previously been of little concern to the public, even if officials and experts had been trying to arouse its concern over these areas, suddenly become the focus of dire warnings, prophetic visions, apocalyptic forebodings, anguished criticisms, and feverish activities aimed at preventing the feared cataclysmic events. But this fever-pitched concern is followed by a reasonably sharp decline in concern with problems, coupled with increasing counterattacks on the "crackpots." Sporadic outbreaks of anxious concern may continue for some time, but the public as a whole becomes increasingly apathetic about social problems, even then the officials and experts insist that the worst problems that so recently excited its interest have not been solved.

Probably the most famous and perhaps the most extreme instance in American history of this sudden peaking of public concern over social problems was during the last part of the nineteenth century and the first decade or more of this century, which is commonly called the "Progressive Era" or the "Era of Muckraking." [11] During this era, the public gradually became more and more concerned with social problems of corruption, immorality, and pollution in many different realms of life. At its peak, a large proportion of Americans seems to have been

[11] There are many works on the progressive era, but certainly one of the best is Richard Hofstadter's *The Age of Reform.*

convinced that the robber barons were despoiling America, crucifying the common man on a cross of gold, seizing control of the government, and destroying the foundations of all morality; that all government bureaucrats were corrupt and tyrannical; that "drink" was destroying the nation physiologically and morally; and that the earth itself was being destroyed by urban and industrial life. Out of this came many lasting reforms, such as the antitrust laws and conservation, and some not-so-lasting measures, such as prohibition. While some groups, such as the conservation groups, received some lasting impetus from the era, the great mass of the public went back to an overwhelming unconcern with social problems. Most of the old socially defined problems of the muckrakers continued to exist: the powers of big business and government corruption were never more extreme than those revealed by the investigations of the utilities in the 1920s; never was there more drinking, and illegal drinking at that; the automobile had now become a source of grave problems to all efforts at conservation. But never had the general public been more unconcerned with its old self-defined problems than in the 1920s. The depression years brought some reversal to this trend, but the overriding concern was the economic problem, and other problems seem to have elicited little concern in the light of that. And the 1930s were followed by the 1940s' concern with international problems and by the apathetic, silent generation of the 1950s. But, no sooner had the social analysts proclaimed the end of ideology and the complete victory of public apathy in the affluent society than the American public began to "discover" the great social problems of the 1960s. A second progressive era was born.

Probably the first basic social problem to be rediscovered by Americans in this second progressive era was race. Rather than seeing race as obviously the one great social problem of American society, most Americans in the 1950s outside of the South, where the Supreme Court decisions were arousing considerable concern, gave relatively little thought to racial problems. Indeed, a large percentage seemed to consider those problems solved until they were "rediscovered" in the bus boycotts and restaurant sit-ins in the South. In the early 1960s, the social problems of race and civil rights were increasingly defined in the light of, or in relation to, the also newly rediscovered problems of poverty, which in turn were seen in the context of education problems. By the middle 1960s, assassinations and Vietnam had helped to fuel the *spreading* anger and despair of college students and others on the "liberal" side; urban riots and violence in the streets had fueled the spreading anger on the "conservative" side. Problems were now seen everywhere, in almost every realm of American life and at almost all levels. In the late 1960s, the problems of pollution were rediscovered, and quite suddenly large proportions of Americans believed we were heading toward the inevitable extinction of all life on earth—an inevitable sinking into the slime of industrial pollution. Suddenly, many forms of food were found to be partially or wholly contaminated; radiation poisoning was everywhere; every new oil spill or oil pipeline halfway around the world was destroying the delicate balance of nature by which all living things were believed to be ineluctably linked to others by invisible bonds; every woman who produced more than two children was perpetrating a population explosion that would someday destroy us all. In a final climax, the problems of pollution were insuperably linked to all those of affluence, science, technology, and capitalistic production. All of the problems came together and each promised its own form of the inevitable apocalypse, as Joseph Gusfield has called it:

> Among alternative visions of the end of the world created by technical progress and affluence is that of thermal "suicide"—where excessive use of energy has so raised the temperature of the waters as to lead to a melting of the

polar cap. In other versions of the apocalyptic the "green-house" effect of changes in the atmosphere or the impact of the expenditure of increases of CO_2 (Carbon dioxide) into the air make the human environment uninhabitable. Still other forms of the same vision are the decline in health arising from air pollution or water pollution resulting in part from "over-population" and in part from the pollution which pesticides and other polluting chemicals introduce into the food supply." [12]

At their peaks, these eras of *problem hysteria* seem to release the darkest forebodings and free-floating anxieties of some people. Even in our day of sensate culture, all of the ancient forms and ideas of medieval religious hysteria and the dances of death regain their power to excite men's fears and express their dreads. The "secret vapors" that poison man's life, the "chain of evil" unwittingly precipitated by man's inevitable folly, and the "devils" summoned up by man's own sorcery and attempts to play God over nature—all reappear and are mingled with the modern symbols of technology; the evils and the devils wear a modern garb, but their true forms are easily distinguished by the true believer. All of these ancient ideas and symbols of evil, death, and decay are used by such popular writers as Rachel Carson in *Silent Spring* to summon modern men to action:

> Only within the moment of time represented by the present century has one species—man—acquired significant power to alter the nature of his world.
> During the past quarter century this power has not only increased to one of disturbing magnitude but it has changed in character. The most alarming of all man's assaults upon the environment is the contamination of air, earth, rivers,

[12] Joseph Gusfield, "Ecology: The New Apocalypse" (unpublished paper).

and sea with dangerous and even lethal materials. This pollution is for the most part irrecoverable; the chain of evil it initiates not only in the world that must support life but in living tissues is for the most part irreversible. In this now universal contamination of the environment, chemicals are the sinister and little-recognized partners of radiation in changing the very nature of the world—the very nature of its life. Strontium 90, released through nuclear explosions into the air, comes to earth in rain or drifts down as fallout, lodges in soil, enters into the grass or corn or wheat grown there, and in time takes up its abode in the bones of a human being, there to remain until his death. Similarly, chemicals sprayed on croplands or forests or gardens lie long in soil, entering into living organisms, passing from one to another in a chain of poisoning and death. Or they pass mysteriously by underground streams until they emerge and, through the alchemy of air and sunlight, combine into new forms that kill vegetation, sicken cattle, and work unknown harm on those who drink from once-pure wells. As Albert Schweitzer has said, "Man can hardly even recognize the devils of his own creation." [13]

In addition to problem hysteria, at their peak these eras are characterized by a certain universal applicability of the dominant social problems. That is, the problems of greatest concern to people are seen to be necessarily linked to all other problems and prove how serious these are. There is an implicit assumption that the problems prove that society is rotten at its core. These dominant problems are thus seen to support all demands for revolutionary restorations of man's natural state, man's primal goodness, society's basic humanity or whatever else the particular individual feels has been most important in life. In the second era of progressivism, the dominant problem of technology and

---

[13] Rachael Carson, *Silent Spring* (Greenwich, Conn.: Fawcett Publications, 1967), pp. 16–17.

pollution was used by the "radical" social critics as proof that the whole society was corrupt and that only revolutionary changes could restore man to his proper state:

> Today the situation [of environmental decay] is changing drastically and at a tempo that portends a catastrophe for the entire world of life. What is not clearly understood in many popular discussions of the present ecological crisis is that the very nature of the issues has changed, that the decay of the environment is directly tied to the decay of the existing social structure. It is not simply certain malpractices or a given spectrum of poisonous agents that is at stake, but rather the very structure of modern agriculture, industry and the city. Consequently, environmental decay and ecological catastrophe cannot be averted merely by increased programs like "pollution control" which deal with sources rather than systems. To be commensurable to the problem, the solution must entail farreaching revolutionary changes in society and in man's relation to man . . . .
>
> It is supremely ironic that coercion, so clearly implicit in the neo-Malthusian outlook, has acquired a respected place in the public debate on ecology—for the roots of the ecological crisis lie precisely in the coercive basis of modern society. The notion that man must dominate nature emerges directly from the domination of man by man. The patriarchal family may have planted the seed of domination in the nuclear relations of humanity; the classical split between spirit and reality—indeed, mind and labor—may have nourished it; the anti-naturalistic bias of Christianity may have tended to its growth; but it was not until organic community relations, be they tribal, feudal or peasant in form, dissolved into market relationships that the planet itself was reduced to a resource for the exploitation . . . .
>
> It is necessary to overcome not only bourgeois society but also the long legacy of propertied society: the patriarchal family, the city, the state—indeed, the historic splits

that separated mind from sensuousness, individual from society, town from country, work from play, man from nature. The spirit of spontaneity and diversity that permeates the ecological outlook toward the nature world must now be directed toward revolutionary change and utopian reconstruction in the social world. Propertied society, domination, hierarchy and the state, in all their forms, are utterly incompatible with the survival of the biosphere. Either ecology action is revolutionary action or it is nothing at all. Any attempt to reform a social order that by its very nature pits humanity against all the forces of life is a gross deception and serves merely as a safety valve for established institutions." [14]

As the author of this statement recognized, the specific ideas about the rotten core and the proposals for revolutionary restoration vary greatly. Some see the problem as capitalistic exploitation, others as sexual irresponsibility producing a population explosion that pollutes the earth, and others as sexism. But they all assume that there is a dominant problem at the core that causes or affects all other problems and most aspects of life.

Both problem hysteria and the idea of the rotten core, with its attendant demands for revolutionary restoration, become increasingly plausible and widespread in an era of growing concern with social problems, largely because at some point the background assumptions about society and persons, and thus about (strong) social problems, change. The members of society come to distrust, rather than trust, to despair rather than to have confidence. Rather than assuming a happy outcome, or an indifferent one, their thinking about society comes to be based on the presumption of a dreaded outcome. The result is that

[14] Murray Bookchin, "Toward an Ecological Solution," *Ramparts* (May, 1970), pp. 9–12.

problems appear everywhere where before there were no problems and all the problems reinforce each other and "prove" that
something is wrong at the core of society.

The Mass Media and Information on Social Problems

In a face-to-face situation the individuals involved can
simply argue over the meanings of things and each can then
decide for himself who is right, even if he sometimes chooses
for reasons of tact or self-interest not to reveal these decisions.
But individuals in a massive, complex society such as ours do
not depend only on such face-to-face arguments to define the
situation, that is, to define the nature of the social problems or
their solutions. In fact, even the face-to-face arguments depend
heavily on extrasituational factors. Most importantly, these
arguments depend on information and theoretical ideas concerning persons and the whole society for much of their substance
and effectiveness. Each member of our society generally makes
use of some kind of information provided to him by other
individuals whom he cannot see or know to decide the present
state of reality about the social world (American society) relevant
to him; for today, unlike an earlier period in our society when
each community lived to a large extent independently of the rest
of our society, each individual feels that his life is very dependent
on what happens throughout the rest of his society—and, to a
lesser degree, what happens throughout the world. The sources
of this *social information* are primarily the *mass media,* though
we should use this category broadly to include even scholarly
books, since, as we have seen in our considerations of pollution,
there is a reasonably efficient *trickle-down communication sys-*

tem in our society today by which even very esoteric scholarly social analyses eventually get into the media aimed at the widest possible audiences. This makes the structure of the media and the control over their messages fundamentally important in determining the social definitions of our problems and the best strategies for solving them.

In terms of sheer quantity, there can be relatively little doubt that there are a few dominant *hierarchies of communicability* in the mass media. That is, the people who actually construct the messages and especially the people (editors, publishers, station producers, and managers) who then decide what will be communicated over the media (as news) *see certain sources of messages as more relevant, more newsworthy, than others.* The exact hierarchy of communicability varies somewhat for the different types of media, especially between the media most oriented toward massive audiences and those most oriented toward specialized audiences. But for the great majority of media, especially those with the massive audiences, there is an *official bias* in media communications. That is, a message that comes from a public official or public agency is far more likely to be seen as a relevant message for the media—as news. The public officials are at the top of the hierarchy of communicability for the media aimed at the *least-common-denominator audience.* For these same media, the officials of private organizations come next on the hierarchy, with the officials of larger organizations ranking higher than those of smaller organizations, and those of very large private organizations outranking even public officials of smaller and less influential minicipalities and states. Though hierarchical rankings certainly vary with the situations faced, in most situations what the president of General Motors says is considered more newsworthy than what most state governors say, since GM is more powerful in our society than most state governments. Messages from professional experts concerning their professional area of competency seem to come next in line, though they are moving up in the hierarchy as our society becomes more dominated by technology. Statements about problems by individuals without some kind of organizational position or function and without expert status generally become newsworthy only by doing something that makes them the object of official messages. For example, a burglar becomes news when the police issue news items about him; he himself does not generate the news messages, and it is the allegations of officials, not his own statements, which are published. When television news reports did let one very articulate convicted kidnapper tell it his way in 1969, there was an immediate and strong public outcry against the news reporting. Again, when there is an oil spill, the problem is defined in the mass media by statements made by the Secretary of the Interior, or by more local officials, or by geological or petroleum experts. A look at almost any mass-media reports on such things will reveal, for example, that the spill is described by official spokesmen for the oil companies, the shippers, the Coast Guard, and the government. The men who were actually on the scene, saw the oil, and possibly tried to estimate its dimensions are almost never quoted.

There seem to be at least two major reasons for the prevalence of this hierarchy of communicability in the mass media. First, there is a very practical reason from the standpoint of the media. Because of time constraints and cost constraints, they must generate a large amount of news quickly and on schedule. This makes it difficult for them to do much on-the-spot reporting about anything, and certainly about the complicated and far flung issues involved in most social problems. They must generally rely on people on the scene or people concerned with the problem as part of their job. But most of the people who do the work on problems as a job are subject to controls by the officials who are their employers and who also in some cases have legal authority over the relevant information (as in the case of crime statistics, labor statistics, welfare records, etc.). The officials themselves work to maintain maximum control over such information because of the effects it has on their power and their public image. They establish organizational rules against subordinates' divulging such information and appoint official spokesmen and public information officers to control the information that gets to the public through the mass media.

In addition to this, the hierarchy of communicability is further supported by the *hierarchy of plausibility* that is so commonly shared by Americans. As Howard Becker has argued, the statements of those who are officials and those who are successful leaders of any kind are, by that fact alone, commonly considered more *plausible,* more likely to be true.[15] This assumption seems to be based on the commonsense beliefs that social power is necessary to get anything done in our society and that social power in our society is ultimately based on the relative numbers (or percentages) of people who support various values, ideas, programs, and individuals. In its simplest form, this *democratic assumption* in our commonsense social thought means that numbers count and one has to count the votes for anything and anybody to see how important it is. While this view may be an oversimplification, it gets at a crucial truth about power and, thus, importance in a mass democracy. For example, we can see this profound concern with the numbers of supporters for anything in the great attention Americans pay to *polling,* which has become an unofficial form of voting in the mass democracies and which is based entirely on the assumption of one-man-one-vote. It is seen most sharply in the importance of political polls in determining who will be taken as a "serious" political candidate, as we can see from the now infamous *war of pollsters* that precedes each political convention. The conflicts between the Rockefeller and Nixon pollsters in 1968 has thus far been the most newsworthy. As long as anyone believes that the public or private official is in fact the *leader* of a large number of people,

[15] Howard Becker, "Whose Side Are We On?", *Social Problems,* 14 (1967), pp. 239-247.

that is, a social power, it makes sense in terms of this democratic assumption to be concerned with his definition of social problems and what can be done about them.

Very importantly, the hierarchy of communicability becomes all the more important and all the more hierarchical as the society becomes more massive and complex. This is so simply because there are more problems competing for roughly the same amount of time anyone has to consider them. The vast majority of individuals, therefore, have time only for the most important—that is, most powerful—definitions of any problematic situation. *Some of the basic forces lying behind the sense of problems—massive numbers and complexity—lead to an increasing concentration on official and expert definitions of the problems and of the ways to solve them as communicated through the mass media.*

The mass media, then, become very important in increasing the power of officials and experts to define the social problems for the general public. But they do this not only by making the officials and the experts the primary sources of information and theories about social problems, but, perhaps even more importantly, by exercising their influence on public thinking about social problems. Because the media provide the information and are the *only* source of that information about problems that is shared by almost everyone, *they have come increasingly to put a frame around social communications about social problems.* That is, because their information and ideas are the only ones shared by the vast majority of people, their ideas and information increasingly becomes basic determinants of the background assumptions about problems that people either make or, at the least, must contend with in constructing their own meanings of problems and solutions for other people. If one is going to do anything that is practically effective about the problems, one must convince other people, and if one is going to convince them, one must at least contend with the only ideas and information shared by everyone—those known to be communicated by the mass media.

This, of course, does not mean that the media have some secret power over people's minds, nor that the "media is the message." There are plenty of instances of whole peoples' rejecting the messages of the mass media because these did not complement their everyday experience of things; in our own society all of the news broadcasts over national television about the effects of segregation do not magically change the minds of the millions of people who still believe in it. Indeed, these kinds of messages have generated powerful social movements against the media and criticisms from all directions of the political spectrum. President Eisenhower and Vice-President Agnew have been only the most outspoken critics of the news media. Almost all major politicians have tried to increase their own power over the media or to increase the news about the things they wanted publicized. But these very countermovements against the media are based on the assumption that they are very powerful in their influence on social thought when they constitute the only source of ideas and information shared by nearly everyone. This media influence over the background assumptions politicians must make about the thoughts of the public when they are making public statements or formulating public policy concerning social problems is so great that we can truthfully speak of the mass media as having a *publicity effect* on public thought about problems: that is, the very fact of having been communicated through the mass media makes something important in itself.[16] The men who run the media choose to communicate something because it has met their commonsense tests of importance, but the media communication of it makes it more important than people once saw it or, if they did not previously see it as important, they now have to

---

[16] I have discussed the publicity effect in detail in Chapter 6 of *American Social Order, Op. Cit.*

do so, even if only to argue that it wasn't the kind of thing that's important enough to be put on television. Indeed, the publicity effect can be very powerful even when the reports of an official statement are later "disproven" by another official and reported in some media. This is strongly suggested, or example, by events involving attacks by the Congressional House Internal Security Committee on John Ciardi as a "radical," which he and almost everyone else subsequently denied, but in media of less common-denominator scope. As Norman Cousins argued:

> Two weeks ago, Edward J. Patten, member of Congress from New Jersey, announced in the House that he had undertaken an investigation of the charge against John Ciardi, who lives in his district. Congressman Patten reported that "there is not one single bit of evidence to justify Ciardi's name on the list."
>
> Apart from an inconspicuous item in the Perth Amboy (N.J.) *News/Tribune,* Congressman Patten's statement has received no public attention of which we are aware. The original accusation was blared forth on television, radio, and the front page of newspapers. Is equal time a nicety reserved only for politicians engaged in political controversy? Is a man's reputation and standing of less consequence than a politician's right to strike back? In any definition of un-Americanism, can we exclude the propensity of the communications media for highlighting defamatory charges and then ignoring or minimizing errors in those charges?
>
> So far, there has been no HISC apology to Mr. Ciardi. What is even more serious, of course, is the fact that Congressman Patten was able to speak for just one man on the list. Who will speak for the others? [17]

The publicity effect of the media is augmented by increases in the homogeneity of the sources and of the messages com-

[17] Norman Cousins, "Radicals and Mr. Ciardi," *Saturday Review* (Dec. 12, 1970), p. 24.

municated by the media. Since the increased size of government and private organizations has led to an increasing centrality of messages from the officials, and since the media have been rapidly conglomerized or oligopolized both in their business control and in the messages they carry with most messages emanating from only two or three major wire services, there is good reason to believe that the publicity effect on messages about social problems has increased greatly in recent years. In fact, their influence on social definitions of social problems has become so clear that some people have argued that such problems as "the energy crisis" are nothing but "media scares."

This fact, however, does not give us any reason to expect that the media influence will decrease the public's concern with social problems, as many of the more radical social critics have charged. Indeed, there is good reason to believe that the mass media operate in such a way as to produce the opposite effect. In a complex and mass society, especially one experiencing a knowledge explosion and a mass culture boom, there is intense competition for the attention of the public; each person has only so much time to give his attention to any messages and the number of messages is rapidly increasing, so messages are in ever greater competition for roughly the same amount of attention. Audience segregation does occur and this decreases such competition, but the most massive media have aimed increasingly at a least-common-denominator audience. As a result, there is a growing tendency to try to get mass attention for one's messages by using sensationalism. But today's sensationalism is different from that of any earlier day. The fear of libel suits and the greater sophistication of the audience makes yellow journalism of the old kind less effective with the most massive audiences. There are still attempts by the mass media in our second era of progressivism to capture public attention by doing exposes of corrupt officials that are strikingly similar to those done by *McClure's Magazine* in the first era of progressivism, but the fear of libel suits and probably the lower frequency of such corruption makes it very difficult and expensive to do this kind of reporting. It is easier and just as effective in a techno-logical society to concentrate one's efforts on the latest attacks on social problems. There are always some people, including officials and experts, in a pluralistic society who will make strong statements about this problem or that problem, this form of "impending doom" or that "absolute injustice."

Indeed, even in the most precise sciences there is always someone who will disagree with anything, so it is not surprising in the highly problematic realm of social problems to find that there are always some officials or some Nobel-prize winning scientists who will decry a new horrifying social problem or propose some new panacea for all our ills. Moreover, there are people who, understanding this aspect of the media, have devised means for demonstrating their grievances in ways that will get public attention when communicated by the media. In fact, the most skilled demonstrators, such as Abbie Hoffman, have care-fully described in publications how they go about constructing messages for the media so that the media will broadcast them and they will, thereby, become the background for public thought and action about the purported problems.

Rather than silencing public thoughts and fears about social problems, the media seem to have become important stimulants to public thinking and fears about problems; they search out those who give the most dramatic demonstration of some kind of problem and make it a common property of public thinking by broadcasting it. Indeed, it now seems reasonably clear that the media are not only involved like everyone else in constructing the specific meanings of social problems, but that they are also involved in purposefully trying to create, or "find", new social problems so that they can scoop their competitors and attract more public attention. In an age when almost everyone is totally dependent on the media for the highly problematic information and ideas he must use in constructing his own ideas about social problems, the media become newsmakers in roughly the same way Daniel Boorstin long ago argued they do in other more objective realms of life by creating events, which he called "pseudo-events":

It is the [news] report that gives the event its force in the minds of potential customers. The power to make a reportable event is thus the power to make experience. One is reminded of Napoleon's apocryphal reply to his general, who objected that circumstances were unfavorable to a proposed campaign: "Bah, I make circumstances!" The modern public relations counsel—and he is, of course, only one of many twentieth-century creators of pseudo-events—has come close to fulfilling Napoleon's idle boast. "The counsel on public relations," Mr. Bernays explains, "not only knows what news value is, but knowing it, he is in a position to *make news happen*. He is a creator of events. . . ."

A pseudo-event, then, is a happening that possesses the following characteristics:

(1) It is not spontaneous, but comes about because someone has planned, planted, or incited it. Typically, it is not a train wreck or an earthquake, but an interview.

(2) It is planted primarily (not always exclusively) for the immediate purpose of being reported or reproduced. Therefore, its occurrence is arranged for the convenience of the reporting or reproducing media. Its success is measured by how widely it is reported. Time relations in it are commonly fictitious or factitious; the announcement is given out in advance "for future release" and written as if the event had occurred in the past. The question, "Is it real?" is less important than, "Is it newsworthy?"

(3) Its relation to the underlying reality of the situation is ambiguous. Its interest arises largely from this very ambiguity. Concerning a pseudo-event the question, "What does it mean?" has a new dimension. While the news interest in a train wreck is in *what* happened and in the

real consequences, the interest in an interview is always, in a sense, in *whether* it really happened and in what might have been the motives. Did the statement really mean what it said? Without some of this ambiguity a pseudo-event cannot be very interesting.

(4) Usually it is intended to be a self-fulfilling prophecy. The hotel's thirtieth-anniversary celebration, by saying that the hotel is a distinguished institution, actually makes it one.[18]

Because problems are so highly dependent on internal states and so little dependent on externally perceived conditions, it is far easier for entrepreneurial reporters and columnists to use the media to create pseudo-events about social problems than about other realms of life. While a careful study remains to be done, it seems probable that the great majority of these attempts to create social problems are complete failures. Generally a magazine or newscaster will attempt to create a problem by coining a phrase for it, such as the "beat generation" or the "hooked generation," and marshalling all possible "evidence" to show what a terrible and growing problem it is. When the public fails to pay much attention, the "terrible problem" is allowed to die a sudden death by editorial pencil. But the more convinced the public becomes that something is wrong at the core and the more problem hysteria there is, the more frequently these *instant social problems* will be seized upon by an anxious and concerned public, thereby increasing the incentive for the social problems entrepreneurs to create more. There are, of course, countervailing forces, which we shall soon discuss, that prevent this process from spiraling upward to complete morbidity and paranoia.

Besides creating and focusing attention on problems and

[18] Daniel Boorstin, *The Image* (New York: Atheneum, 1961), pp. 103-104.

providing the only generally shared background of information and meanings of problems, the media are also of great importance in constructing public social problems by providing the *sense of immediate personal participation and threat that is so important in generating a sense of the problem and, especially, the sense of need for action to solve the problem.* Because most things that are defined as social problems in our society are not directly experienced by most people, they commonly do not pay much attention to messages about problems *unless they feel the immediacy of the problem* and, often, unless they feel somehow personally threatened by the problem. For example, for years people may pay no attention to scare news about mercury pollution of the oceans, but the official announcement that the mercury poisoning may be in their cabinets or on their table right now generates an immediate sense of personal involvement and threat that convinces them that we are faced with a serious social problem and that something, almost anything, must be done to solve the problem at once. This is even more true of social solutions. As we have seen earlier, the meanings of solutions for problems and the actions associated with them are the most problematic in the whole realm of social problems phenomena, simply because all the difficulties involved in defining the problems are implicated as well as the additional difficulties associated with the ideas about the solutions themselves and those difficulties inspired by the conflicting interests involved in attempts at solutions. Because of this, the sense of immediate involvement and, especially, of immediate personal threat are generally vital for producing any public support for attempts to solve problems. (Obviously, those problems that remain at the expert or official level can commonly be constructed by the officials or experts simply because of their professional commitments to deal with such things and because of the rewards that come to such professionals for being creative at their work. However, as we shall see in the next section, the larger ones of these problems almost inevitably get into the public arena, so the sense of personal involvement and threat becomes vital once again.)

There are many famous examples of the way in which the media produce a sense of immediate participation and a feeling that something must be done about the problem that is now so tangible. Quite a number of these come from the emotional area of race relations in the 1950s and 1960s. For example, in the following statement Crane Brinton describes how people were emotionally aroused by the sight of a black girl being verbally abused by whites during an attempt to integrate the southern schools:

> In September 1957 there appeared in most American news-papers a news photograph that showed a Negro girl in Little Rock, Arkansas, after a vain attempt to enter a white high school, leaving the premises with a group of whites trailing and abusing her. The face of one white girl was contorted in a shocking way; the Negro girl looked dignified and self-controlled. Commentators in the North were unanimous that the expression of the Negro girl symbolized the good and the expression of the white girl the bad; and commentators in the South were at least much disturbed by the picture, for they could not help making the same specific classifications of good and bad that their Northern colleagues did. My point here, however, is not so much the fact that in a certain sense moral goodness and moral badness were in this striking photograph made real, concrete, even "objective" or "universal." My point is, rather, that, dismissing for the moment the great philosophical problems lurking here, it is clear that no one could look at that photograph in quite the way he could look at a diagram of the occultation of Saturn by the moon that might well have appeared in the same issue of his newspaper or news weekly as did the photograph from Little Rock. Even the diagram of the occultation of Saturn might conceivably have stirred the

emotions of an occasional reader, for it might have acted as a trigger to release a chain of thought-feeling about the vastness and impersonality of the astronomer's universe and the smallness and helplessness of man, a chain for which much in popular contemporary culture supplies the materials. But the picture of the good Negro girl and the bad white girl (some editorial writers preferred to call the white girl "evidently neurotic," a fact again good grist for the historian of morals) roused very strong emotions indeed, emotions best described as those of moral indignation.[19]

While he does not directly relate this emotion to the social problems of segregation and racial conflict, these are the socially defined problems that such pictures and descriptions "brought home" to most Northern Americans during the long series of civil rights demonstrations. The organizers of the demonstrations commonly understood both how to arouse such feelings and the need to do so if they were to make most people see what it's really like and stimulate them to action to solve the problems. As Brinton pointed out next, this picture not only aroused the feelings of indignation but thereby produced a sense of the need for action to end this kind of thing:

One very obvious difference in the two cases cited above throws light on the special conditions under which moral emotions are commonly felt. The newspaper reader knew and felt at once when he saw the faces of the two girls that "something should be done about it," that he himself might do something about it, write a letter to the editor, to his congressman, join something, pay dues, demonstrate, at the very least express an opinion. To no sane reader did the thought occur that he could do anything at all about the occultation of Saturn; in that form, the thought probably

[19] Crane Brinton, *A History of Western Morals* (New York: Harcourt, Brace, 1965), Introduction.

did not even occur to the reader who happened to be a devotee of the newspaper's daily column on astrology.[20]

There are many other pictures that aroused the same immediate sense of participating in the problems and of the need to do something about them. The cover picture in *Life* magazine of a small black boy in Newark lying in a puddle of his own blood during the rioting there immediately communicated a sense of horror about what had happened there and a general feeling that the nation must do something to stop this. The cover picture in *Newsweek* magazine of the young girl screaming over the body of one of the students killed by the national guard at Kent State not only produced massive reactions and demands for action, but the picture itself became of major concern to people around the country and led to many wire-service stories about the girl, her feelings at the time, her family, and the outcome of her being in the picture.

Most members of the media and other people in our society understand very well the power of the media to produce a sense of immediate personal involvement, personal threat, and the need for action to solve the problem. As a consequence, we commonly find them using the media purposefully to create these. For example, when the police in New York City wanted to defeat a referendum measure subjecting all police actions to review by a civilian police review board, they communicated the importance of crime problems and of having police power to solve the problems by using television films of (acted) obvious criminal types and their deeds to show people what the problem is really like, how widespread it is, and how independent police power is in stopping the problem. (The measure was defeated.) Howard Becker's analysis of the news stories given to media all around the country at the same time by the Federal Bureau of Narcotics to help pass federal laws against marihuana shows a

[20] *Ibid.*

use of the principle of the immediate sense of threat: each story about the marihuana user emphasized his violent attack on other people, especially strangers who could be members of the reading public.[21] This same approach is used in all of the radio and television advertisements that continue today against drugs. The announcers try to show that "it is not just kids in the slums; it is your kids and you who are threatened; so you must act now to stop the menace." The same principle was used by the television producers, directors, and cameramen to "show" people the problems of poverty in the black ghettos, in Appalachia, in the camps of migrant farm labourers, in the black belt of the South, and around the world. The cameras would focus on the shacks, the ruined plumbing, the scrawny bodies. The dolorous voice would reveal the sense of inner despair that was being "seen" on the screen. They did not often focus on laughing children playing in the woods or adults enjoying their evening talks with friends, though sometimes these are shown as the small pleasures that allow a temporary escape from the deadening poverty that haunts the days of the poor. While these kinds of television reports were sometimes done as background documentaries, they were most commonly done with the supporting social definitions of officials and experts. The common format was to have a senator—generally a would-be presidential candidate—or an expert visit the hovels of the people while the cameras followed, then to have him express his sense of shock over these social problems, which he (generally) did not know were so intense or widespread, and call for a national effort to end the problems of poverty. These attempts to elicit the sense of immediate involvement and the need for action to solve the problems seem to have been quite important in creating and maintaining support for the very expensive federal projects aimed at solving poverty problems in the 1960s.

[21] Howard Becker, *Outsiders, Op. Cit.*

Since "seeing is believing" and "a single picture is worth a thousand words," it is probably true that television has greatly increased the public's sense of participation in those events and experiences that members of the media are trying to define as social problems. This may even be one significant reason for the rise of a second progressive era and for the sense of urgency and despair that has characterized so much of the social communications about our social problems in this era of television. But, while this may be a special effect of one major media or an accentuation of the more general effects of the media, there are certain properties of the media in general that are of great importance in determining the media's effects on the social definitions of problems and solutions.

All of the *mass media are necessarily highly selective in their presentations of ideas and information about social problems.* This is true even of the news documentaries of television, which purport to be unbiased, highly objective presentations of slices of reality. The documentary is supposed to let the viewer see how it is for himself so that he will "see" the truth. But, in fact, even the most total coverage in a documentary of any problem presents only an hour or two of pictures of a small number of places, people, and events. Documentary makers are selective first in deciding what subject to cover, such as choosing to cover a social problem rather than birthday parties or some other happy events. They are selective as well in choosing which few events out of millions to present from that realm of life and they are selective in choosing a given perspective for cameras, a given tone for voices, and so on. Even then the selectivity is not finished, for they must then select one hour of film from the hundreds they shot; the rest is cut, so that most of the "on-scene reality" is left on the floor of the editor's room.

This necessary selectivity means that *all media reports on social problems, even those one can see with one's own eyes, are necessarily determined by the preconceived (commonsense theoretical) ideas about problems of those who make the decisions about media coverage and presentation.* As the publicity effect has increased and the centrality or homogeneity of messages has been increased by oligopolistic controls and by the concentration of the media within a few square miles of Manhattan, the media have come increasingly to communicate the preconceived ideas about *problems of a relatively few members of society.* In addition, as the media have come to concentrate more on constructing problems, both because of the nature of the media themselves and because of the saleability of social problems constructions during a progressive era, the media have increasingly communicated the preconceptions of a relatively few people about the *proportion of social problems in society.* Because an increasing amount of media reporting has been in the form of "eye-ball accounts," which are more involving and convincing, the presentations of these theoretical ideas of the relatively few people in control of the media have probably been increasingly convincing to people. While there has been a great controversy over the whole issue in recent years, there is some evidence from studies of journalists, such as those by Paul Weaver,[22] that a solid majority of journalists define themselves politically as liberals. If this is so, and if they hold ideas about social problems that are as consistent as the journalists themselves assume is true of liberals, then the greater preoccupation of liberal commonsense theories with social problems may account in some small part for the rise and persistence of the second progressive era. In any event, there is no doubt that the messages about social problems that originate in the giant broadcasting corporations and news services based in Manhattan are strikingly different from those

[22] Paul Weaver, "Messages and Media," in Jack D. Douglas, ed., *Introduction to Sociology: Situations and Structures* (New York: Free Press, 1972).

that originate in local stations and newspapers, even in giant cities such as Los Angeles, but especially in areas such as the Bible Belt.

In addition to the necessarily selective and possibly biased presentations of messages about problems that are created by those who produce the news stories and programs, *the very fact that an individual or an action is going to be presented as news about a social problem becomes an important determinant of what will be observable by the newsmen themselves and, thence, by the public.* Because human beings are always so concerned with presenting their self-images and their life situations in a specific way in any given situation in order to determine the responses of other people to them, and because they believe that being in the newspaper or on television provides them with the means to do so, any situation observed or filmed by newsmen will greatly affect the kinds of things people being filmed will say and do. For example, if newsmen present themselves to an individual as newsmen who have come with many bright lights, complex cameras, and a camera crew of six to a dozen to interview him for national television about his problems of poverty in Appalachia and if they do not ask him anything about the pleasures of fishing in the local creek, then the tendency for the individual to talk about his sufferings and problems is somewhat overwhelming. If the platoon of cameramen is joined by one senator, two congressmen, a governor, and a platoon of aides who are nationally committed to passing legislation that will provide more money for the individual and his children, the tendency to concentrate on the problems and the sufferings is even greater. In fact, there are few poor people in such a situation who could manage to *think* anything about their everyday lives, far less manage to say anything except "Yes, I think you're right about that, Senator." There are also few people who would care to disagree in that situation. The importance of these situations for the poor and obscure of this world is obvious when it is remembered that there literally are camel drivers on the other side of the world who have become famous because they had one talk about their problems for a few minutes with a vice-president in front of television cameras. Any social scientist knows that there is hardly any situation in which the methods of observation would be more biasing of the results than this, yet this is precisely the situation in which the "true realities of social problems" are most commonly created for millions of Americans to see with their own eyes, and this is the kind of information on social problems most people use to construct their social meanings of social problems.

In general, because of the highly problematic nature of social problems, the lack of direct experience of the relevant phenomena, and the apparently growing publicity effect of the media, we have every reason to believe that the nature of the mass media themselves is becoming a basic determinant of the social meanings of social problems. Assuming this is so, we can see that the more media information people have about social problems, the less objective their understandings about problems and their responses to them will be. Media-filtered or created information about problems, then, is far more subject to the "intelligence pathologies" that social scientists such as Herman Kahn and Anthony Wiener have long maintained result from the growing separation of actors from firsthand experience and the growing centralization of information in our society:

. . . centralized "command and control" or other administrative systems tend to filter the information that goes to the top and thus give a very incomplete or dangerous picture of reality, and yet they may be used as substitutes—often poor and dangerous substitutes—for other modes of information. Modern management techniques, in government, industry, and the military, produce enormous advantages. Yet there may be serious losses in terms of seeing, feeling, hearing, and otherwise absorbing the full situation, of being "on the scene," or talking directly with the people involved in not using sufficiently the more "normal" and traditional human organizational and information networks. Even if one does not actually degrade one's information by excessive reliance on the automated system but retains the more direct techniques, the enormously detailed and orderly information that one gets from the new system may lead to unjustified confidence that one understands what is happening, possibly resulting in overcontrol or miscontrol. In any case, the more impressive and "scientific" system may out-compete the other sources of information and thus result in as much mis-informed control as if the other systems did not exist. . . .[23]

The Necessarily Political Definition of Social Problems and Social Solutions

We have seen that the social meanings of social problems are necessarily problematic in our pluralistic society, that con-flicts inevitably grow out of these problems, that these social meanings are necessarily grounded in the practical thought of everyday life, and that the reflexive nature of this thought makes it impossible for the members of society to totally rationalize their definitions of problems and solutions. These properties of the commonsense meanings of social problems lead us to con-clude that *a crucial part of the processes by which social problems are defined in society are necessarily political.*[24] This unavoidably political nature of social problems is their most important property.

[23] Herman Kahn and Anthony Wiener, "Faustian Powers and Human Choices," *Op. Cit.* Also see Harold Wilensky, *Organizational Intelligence* (New York: Basic Books, 1967).

[24] Much of this discussion of the political definition of social problems draws upon my discussion of politics in *American Social Order: Social Rules in a Pluralistic Society* (New York: The Free Press, 1971).

Unfortunately, the term "politics" has a number of different meanings. First, politics is sometimes used to mean any socially oriented value commitments or any statement that is partially based on such value commitments. This is often the way people are using the term when they say such things as "any argument that the poor have equal opportunity is just so much politics." In this sense, any values that might have implications for how the individual acts in society come to be politics. This most general meaning of politics is based on the most common dimension of the meaning of politics, that is, dealing with practical social concerns. But it only confuses the issues to identify value commitments that are involved in political action with the political action itself. Second, there are a large number of commonsense uses of politics which involve the idea that politics is somehow concerned with the art of the possible. These meanings of the term are somewhat more restricted in that they refer only to those social involvements that are concerned with affecting the course of events *in concert with others,* but they are still too general and confuse politics with any form of social organization. Third, politics is often used in the sense of any *practical activity aimed at influencing others to achieve certain goals.* In this sense, politics comes to be a general form of manipulative activity, but without any clear idea that it involves power or that the manipulation is sinister. Fourth, and probably at the core of the commonsense idea of politics, politics is used in the sense *of any activity which intentionally involves the use of (physical or material) power to influence others or to achieve scarce goals for which there is some kind of competition.*

The last two dimensions of the commonsense meanings of politics are subsumed under the earlier two, which are too global to be of value in our analysis. Moreover, these latter two dimensions constitute the core meanings (denotations) of the commonsense term. The best strategy for our purposes, then, seems to be to combine the two meanings to provide the explicit meaning of the term. We can then examine the ways in which the problematic nature of social problems necessitates the use of each of the basic dimensions in constructing the social definitions of social problems.

Our basic proposition about the necessarily political nature of the social definitions of social problems can now be restated more precisely: *the necessarily problematic meanings of social problems makes it necessary for the commonsense actors of society to use (1) practical activities intended to influence others to seek certain goals (this is the rhetorical imperative); and (2) the international application of physical or material power to influence others in the competition for scarce goals (this is the power imperative).* By simple extension we can also expect that the more problematic the meanings of any social problem, the more political action will have to be used to get its meaning shared.

Certainly the argument that social problems are necessarily political does not mean that all reason and facts are really irrelevant or that it's all a matter of manipulation and power. For one thing, we have never argued that social problems are totally problematic in our society. While there may be some that are, the great majority of social definitions of social problems do contain, either actually or potentially, either explicitly or implicity, some values, or ideas, or feelings that are shared by the parties involved in the definition process. As we saw at the end of Chapters 4 and 5, rather than being totally problematic, almost all of the meanings of social problems are only partially and relatively problematic. Second, while we have argued repeatedly that social problems cannot be totally rationalized, if for no other reason than their necessarily situational and reflexive nature, we have never argued that rational argument is incapable of reducing the problematic meanings and the conflicts that grow out of this. The members of society do share certain *interpretive rules,* especially the rules of rationality. The application of these rules is itself necessarily problematic, since their meanings must be constructed for each situation the members face, but the fact that they are highly shared makes arguments over definitions of problems less problematic than they would otherwise be. Third, the members of our society also generally share certain fundamental *procedural rules,* especially those of the democratic process (rule by the majority), "fair play" (especially giving everybody a chance to be heard), civil rights (especially free speech and protecting minority positions from the overwhelming weight of the majorities), and judicial procedures (especially rule by law). These procedural rules make it possible to carry on the arguments over social problems in a less problematic and conflictful manner than would be the case if we did not have them.

The crucial point of the argument is simply that problems and conflicts necessarily remain and that these can only be *bridged for practical purposes,* not completely eliminated, *by political activity.* Almost any political activity that is going to be effective in defining social problems and carrying out practical policies aimed at solving them will build on all of the shared meanings that do exist and will utilize the shared rules of rationality, interpretation, and procedure in carrying on the arguments over social problems and their solutions. Any political activity that is thought to be contrary to these shared meanings or to go against the shared rules will probably be seen as illegitimate or absurd, so it is not likely to work. But, while political activity must build on these shared meanings and rules to be effective, it must also go beyond them to be effective.

In fact, the first political imperative, the rhetorical imperative, is specifically concerned with bridging the problematic meanings of problems and solutions by constructing unifying meanings among the different constructions of definitions of problems and solutions. Where he finds disagreement and conflict, the politician tries to search out and emphasize the agreements. Where he finds concrete arguments and conflicts, he tries to put them in the context of more general values, ideas, and feelings that are shared: "We must always remember that we are all Americans, sharing a common ideal and facing common problems." Where he finds general values, ideas, and feelings in conflict, he must focus the attention of the contending parties on the concrete issues in which they may have common interests: "We may disagree on the big questions, but we can work together to solve the practical problems that face us today." This is the function of rhetoric, of convincing people to do something by the use of symbols and feelings in practical affairs. The skilled politician uses his cultural wisdom of the political values, religious beliefs, bright hopes, and dark fears of all the different groups of society to *construct consensus sufficient to achieve the practical goals he has set himself*. This does not mean that he always tries to build universal consensus or total agreement. Commonly the degree of consensus required to achieve practical goals in a pluralistic society can best be achieved by openly attacking some parts of the society: "The robber barons are our common enemy." "Respectable citizens of all persuasion must stand together against the forces of anarchy." "We are united against the hippies." Unity is thus built by opposing the common enemy.

The particular rhetoric used must, of course, be adapted to the particular groups and situational purposes involved. The mayor who calls for community support for a beautification program to preserve the "glory of our heritage" has a different problem from that of the president who wishes to launch a "war on poverty," and a war on poverty must be treated in different terms than an anti-pollution crusade. At the national level, however, politicians have come increasingly to rely upon certain *least-common denominator national goals* as sources of rhetorical support for almost any policy. These are goals of such general appeal and interest to everyone, such as health, wealth, and national security, that they can be used rhetorically to build support for any project that comes under their broad aegis. The only problem may be in fitting a project under the aegis, but then, so many things are seen to be related to those goals that the difficulty is not so great. There are also certain *sacred-cow goals,* such as education, that serve this purpose very well. These are goals that people believe in for many different reasons, even when these reasons are shown repeatedly to be either nonsensical or self-fulfilling. Higher education, for example, is believed by most Americans to be of vital economic importance to the nation and to the individuals. While some of it obviously is, most of it can hardly be shown to help the nation economically or to advance the individual's economic interests. Most people would make more money being plumbers than by getting a college education. Nonetheless, there is an almost universal belief in the economic value of higher education; it is a "sacred cow" (though certain doubts have been raised in some minds by the violent demonstrations at most of the major universities).

While these rhetorical constructions seem quite necessary in building agreements about social problems and solutions, they can only go so far. There almost always remain problems and conflicts, especially when there have been great difficulties to start with in defining any problem. These problems are commonly bridged in part by the use of *compromise strategies.* In our pluralistic society there have always been so many clear, distinct, and fundamental conflicts over problems and their solutions that it has been necessary to develop political strategies capable of resolving them. In fact, the conflicts have been so persistent and fundamental that they seem to have constituted a basic reason for the adoption of a democratic form of government. No one group or coalition of groups was able to gain sufficient power to entirely exert its will over the other groups. At the national level this led to the adoption of a confederate system at first, by which each colony kept to itself all powers except those that seemed absolutely necessary in any given situation to solve common problems. When this failed, the federal system was adopted, but this greater unity was counter-balanced with numerous checks and balances that were intended to guarantee the rights of the different groups. Our democratic form of government was founded on the situational necessity of compromising interests. The same can be seen to be the case with so many other aspects of American society, in spite of the absolutism of our social beliefs and values. Alan Grimes, for example, has argued that the same is true of our freedom of religion and the separation of state and religion: "The rise of religious freedom has been in large measure the unintended result of our early history, prompted by accident, conditioned by necessity. It has been at once the triumph of our experience over our initial ideology, and the triumph of diversity over uniformity. It has marked the settling for the second-best alternative—religious equality—where no religion was able to achieve that perfect freedom which comes with perfect power." [25]

Whereas rhetoric can be used to bridge the problems and conflicts involved over definitions of problems, compromises are used primarily to bridge the problems and conflicts involved over the solutions. There is a steady increase in the degree of open conflict as members of our society pass from definitions of nonproblem conditions, to weak problems, to strong problems, to solutions of problems. At each stage the direct implications for definitions of concrete situations and for concrete, practical solutions increase. This increasingly focuses the problematic aspects of values, beliefs, and feelings. It also increasingly focuses the differences of material interests. At the stage of defining whether something is a shared problem at all—that stage involved in passing from nonproblem to weak social problem—the discussions are pretty abstract, with few direct implications for taxation

[25] Alan P. Grimes, *Equality in America* (New York: Oxford University Press, 1964), pp. 3-4.

or controls, so discussions can be more academic. To pass to the stage of defining a problem as caused by society—that of a strong problem—brings in the problems of defining causes and makes the implications for practical action more direct. The argument gets more intense. At the stage of the solution, where policies must be made and society reoriented to produce solutions, the conflicts reach their maximum. As long as the argument is over whether a problem exists and is weak or strong, each man can hold his own views—it doesn't cost him anything. It is at the level of solutions that all of the conflicting interests are focused. It is here that the conflicts over definitions tend to be most intense and open, though in many cases, of course, they become even more intense at the stage of executing the decisions.

Much of the art of politics in American society consists in finding some compromise that will be acceptable to the many conflicting, powerful interests involved. Since the conflicts cut in such different directions, the compromise solutions to social problems often wind up as crazy-quilt compromises, with something for each party tacked on or some aspect being tacked on for extraneous political reasons that defy reason. As we saw in Chapter 2, this is what Daniel Moynihan argues happened to the OEO program when the provision requiring participation of the poor people in the local planning and execution of programs was made part of it by unknown members of the bureaucracy.

A strategy of compromise, which might even better be described as a strategy of evading a compromise until it seems possible to get enough agreement to strike one, is the *crisis strategy* that characterizes so much of our handling of social problems. As we have noted before, there is a general tendency for political leaders to use a *foxhole* strategy toward social problems; that is, they lie low when a problem looms on the horizon in the hope that it will go away, that the people pushing this definition of things as a problem will stop. Part of this behavior is probably due to simple laziness or lack of time, part of it to disagreement with the definition. But there is a further justification for the foxhole strategy. In a pluralistic society with such disagreements over social problems and with conflicting views of what a politician should do or not do about the proposed problems, leaders often find it prudent to wait and see if a proposed problem is likely to gain the public support necessary to lead people first to define it as an official problem and then to attempt compromise solutions for it. If a leader tries to get a problem defined as such or propose a solution before there is public support, he is risking a failure in leadership which will cost him political capital, making it harder for him to win in the next struggle to define problems or solutions. The result very commonly is that politicians wait, even when in full agreement that there is indeed a great problem that should be dealt with by the government. All too commonly, this means that the problem continues to grow until it reaches crisis proportions and the people suddenly clamor for action. The leader can now safely lead in defining the problem and its solutions. The problem is that the social conditions that constitute the problem may by then be so complex and ingrained that it is very difficult to do anything about them, especially because the anxiety and clamorous conflicts that burst forth once the problem is seen as a crisis by the people may also become impediments to striking any workable compromises.

Not all compromise strategies are so seemingly unguided by reason or so haphazard. Indeed, some of them are of crucial value in making it possible to get anything done about problems in a pluralistic society and in preventing the growth of open conflicts that could destroy the society through civil war. One of these is the *strategy of incrementalism,* found in almost all American social planning. This strategy involves approaching any problems in piecemeal fashion and only slowly building up any program to handle the problems. Commonly. Congress and the president will first pass a bill that states the problem and what is to be done, and only later fund the project. The funding almost always involves a "getting the foot in the door" allocation at first and progressively larger allocations later as the program is "proven" to be successful, even though the data used to do the proving is commonly supplied by those responsible for making the program a success, which often leads to "pseudotests." This strategy minimizes opposition at first, unless those against it foresee the use of this progressive strategy and decide they must fight or fail on the first bill. The strategy also works in part because it builds up a constituency of experts who will support it in the media and in Congress since they make a living out of it as well as a constituency of people who are vocally more against giving up benefits than they were in favor of getting new ones. Most of these strategies were apparent in the anti-poverty programs and in the programs against discrimination in employment.

An important compromise strategy found in many different approaches to problems is that of *spreading the burden and the benefits.* This is simply to reduce the cost to any single group and bring in as many as one can to support a program. It has been used in most attempts to handle economic problems. The Kennedy and Johnson administrations, for example, decided to attack the whole problem of unemployment by increasing economic activity through an across-the-board, deficit-financed tax cut. The alternative is generally to deal with what are called structural factors, such as specific retraining and specific tax benefits to spur specific investments. This was tried too but only as a complement to the general strategy of increasing the gross national product (a least-common-denominator goal) through a tax cut for everyone. This same kind of strategy is generally followed in dealing with the opposite problem of inflation. Everyone must suffer a little bit through gradual deflation produced by tight-money policies. The alternative is to deal with "structural causes of inflation," such as bottle-necks in production and wage-price spirals in such key industries as construction. Since structural unemployment and inflation have proven increasingly resistant to such broad-gauged solutions in almost all Western societies since the second world war, economists and other social scientists have come increasingly to favor more specific, direct attacks on the structural factors; but this concentration of the costs, even if only for the short run, immediately arouses intense opposition from the very powerful groups directly affected, such as richer tax payers and organized labor. Political leaders thus far have relied generally on compromise strategies, and those who haven't probably wish they had. Since the problems remain so great and since the educational efforts of experts and politicians seem to be convincing more and more people through the mass media that we need this more structural approach, in time they will probably be able to build a large enough coalition to force a better compromise on the special interest groups affected, better for the vast majority of people and probably in the long run for the special interest groups themselves.

Regardless of how successful the rhetorical and compromise bridges are, the problematic meanings and the resultant conflicts are inevitably so great in many situations that power, including the use of physical force, must be used to resolve the conflicts. Because there is no way of totally rationalizing our disagreements over social problems, either through common sense or through sociological analysis and knowledge, we are doomed to eternal conflicts over social problems and to the use of power to repress those conflicts that become too great to be solved through compromise. Our greatest hope is that we can use our commonsense and sociological understanding of social problems and solutions objectively enough to be able to minimize our conflicts and, hopefully, prevent their becoming great enough at any time to destroy us. If we cannot attain through our reason some utopian world of total rationality and peace, we can at least realistically hope to progress toward a far greater rationalization of our problems than we have thus far.

SUGGESTED READINGS

Freedom and Tyranny: Social Problems in a Technological Society (New York: Alfred A. Knopf, 1970), collection of essays edited by Jack D. Douglas, is concerned in general with the forms of control that are arising in our technological society, especially those that are tyrannical in nature; that is, that do not involve controls over the controllers by the controlled. One of the most important forms of potentially tyrannical controls in our technological society is that of "expert controls" such as we find so often in the definition of social problems. Parts IV and V on expert knowledge and control are especially relevant.

Americans have become very concerned about the influence of the mass media on their thinking about such things as social problems. Much of this concern, however, has been focused on the effects of the nature of the media themselves on the messages communicated (as we find in the works of Marshall McLuhan) and on the individual political biases of writers and commentators. While there may be such influences on the messages about social problems, they seem small compared to the affects on the messages of the *social organization of the media*. It is these organizational effects on the messages that Daniel Boorstin has concentrated in a highly readable and important book, *The Image* (New York: Atheneum Publishers, 1961). Specifically, he has focused mainly on the ways in which the social situations of the media become the creators of the messages, for example, the ways in which the need for publicity in a mass society make appearances on the media so vitally important to public figures. The need of the media to compete for scarce attention is another important effect on the messages communicated, especially in the area of social problems where it can lead to an increasingly shrill approach to problems.

In a highly complex society, in which massive governmental organizations make the most important decisions about what the social problems are and what should be done about them, the nature of the organizations becomes a vital determinant of the information used by them to make these key decisions about social problems. *Organizational Intelligence* (New York: Basic Books, 1967) by Harold Wilensky is concerned with the ways in which organizations create and use information in our society. Specifically, it is concerned with the ways in which the structures of the organizations are involved in the determination of the information created and the ways it is used. Much of the work is devoted to describing and explaining the information patholo- gies" in a complex, massive society. While there is little direct concern with social problems, the book is a valuable source of ideas about the construction of social problems.

Propaganda commonly has a perjorative meaning in our society. Propaganda is seen as information that is somehow necessarily untrue or biased. In this sense, propaganda is seen as something to be avoided, something perpetuated upon us by our enemies. Jacques Ellul believes, however, that propaganda is a vital part of all mass democracies and that, indeed, social order would not be possible in such societies without propaganda. The very meaning of propaganda must be modified in the light of his analysis in *Propaganda* (New York: Alfred A. Knopf, 1965). Propaganda comes to be seen as the highly simplified near truths that are so nearly universal in our mass media and that seem to be demanded by the massiveness of them. The creation and manipulation of the meanings of social problems would clearly be one of the crucial ways in which propaganda is used to order the society's efforts. This work by Ellul is probably even more important than his work *The Technological Society* (see Suggested Readings in Chapter 1) and will help to revive the whole sociological study of the mass media.

Radical Chic and Mau-Mauing the Flak Catchers (New York: Bantam Books, 1971) is a hilarious but serious work on the definition of social problems, though its author, Tom Wolfe, probably never thought of it that way. "Mau-mauing the Flak Catchers" is especially relevant to the definition of social prob- lems in our society. It is concerned with the criteria used, in fact if not in theory, by government officials running the OEO to find out what the problems were and who was suffering from them. Since the officials didn't know what was going on in the teeming cities beyond the air-conditioned offices, they tended strongly to respond to the greatest, most immediate pressure. The greatest, most immediate pressure came from the tiny minorities of ghetto residents (or those who could present themselves that way) who understood that. They "mau-maued" the government agents, the "flak-catchers," with various rhetorical threats which convinced the officials that these must indeed be the poor whose problems they were supposed to solve. This is a brilliant, but unofficial, look at the way officials actually defined many of the problems of poverty.

Whereas Polanyi, Ellul, and Marcuse (see Suggested Readings for Chapters 1 and 2), are all concerned in various ways with what they see as long-run trends in our society producing basic social problems, *The Crisis in Confidence* (New York: Bantam Books, 1969) by Arthur Schlesinger, Jr., is concerned with recent, more situational events that have led Americans to become more concerned with social problems. He tries to show that many problems have come together at the same time to produce a real crisis of national confidence, that is, a crisis in the belief that we can deal with our problems. This is probably the best available description and analysis of the kind of "social problems hysteria" we have analyzed in this chapter.

chapter 7

Conclusion:
Social Problems in the
Technological Society

We started our work on social problems by arguing that if
the scientific-technological revolution that is now sweeping the
earth follows the precedent of the industrial revolution, we can
expect the rapid social change and growth in complexity brought
on by it to produce vast dislocations and human suffering which
increasingly will be seen as the social problems of the technological society. The traditional absolutist sociology of social
problems would have led us to proceed from this to analyze the
rates of technological development, the expected rates of social
change, the likely dislocations, and the best policy alternatives
for dealing with these—for "solving these obvious social problems in the technological society." This would certainly have
been a difficult enough task for anyone and might have left us
feeling more secure in knowing that the problems we face are
definite—indeed, absolute—and that their solutions will prove
easy enough once "rational men of good will can stop the
irrational politicians from destroying our society and our earth."
But we quickly recognized this traditional perspective on social
problems as being fundamentally inadequate for dealing with
social problems in our pluralistic society. It was not completely

wrong by any means and many problems on which there is a
real social consensus can still probably be dealt with effectively
in this simplistic manner. But we argued that the complexities
of social phenomena associated with social problems were
actually far greater than the traditional sociologists had thought.
As a result, the task we set ourselves was a more complex one,
but one directed at the whole social reality of social problems.

We were forewarned of the nature of these complexities by
our observations that once Americans had "solved" what they
once saw as their greatest social problems, once they had overcome poverty to become the wealthiest and most powerful nation
in the history of the world, once they had overcome ignorance
and scientific backwardness to become the most highly educated
society and the center of almost every branch of science and
technology, they suddenly "discovered" that they had worse
problems than ever before. Suddenly, where before they had
seen affluence, they now saw grinding poverty; where before they
saw the fat of the land, they now saw hunger and nutritional
starvation; where before they had seen the fear of unemployment
and the evils of the soup kitchen, they now saw the shame of
welfare; where before they had seen the soulless government
shirking its responsibilities of aiding the poor, they now saw the
dangers of deadening, impersonal, bureaucratic tyranny; where
before they had seen the problems of ignorance resulting from
an inability to pay for education, they now saw the evils of
education factories forcing everyone to obtain a degree; where
before they had seen the great discomforts associated with travel
on dirt roads and endless detours, they now saw the ugliness of
concrete ribbons of super highways girding the land; where
before they had seen the depravity of slum tenements, they now
saw the deadening effects of bright new public housing projects;
where before they had seen bright hopes of dignity and independence in Henry Ford's promise to make a car available to every
working man, they now saw the horrors of pollution in the

fulfillment of that promise and attacked Ford for helping to produce death by green-house effect; where before they had seen modern man's odyssey of space exploration, they now saw a "moondoggle" and a diversion of funds from urgent social problems. Each of the promised solutions, each of the bright hopes that had borne so many generations through the anguish and toil involved in building a new nation, suddenly seemed empty to so many millions, and to these many millions yesterday's "solutions," once achieved, became the social problems of today. For many millions of others, yesterday's minor problems became today's horrifying problems. America had entered a second progressive era and things seemed as bad off—or worse— to Americans today as they had to Americans at the turn of the century.

Earlier sociologists might have been tempted to see it all as a simple matter of social actions having unanticipated consequencies for society. Many of those who demand something more than reconceptualizations in their explanations might be tempted to see the whole thing as a morality play in which Americans had gained the world, or two-thirds of its production, only to lose their souls. Others might prefer to see these developments as a simple result of man's inability to find happiness in this world, perhaps because of the vicissitudes of fortune, or the insatiable nature of man's restless will, or an evil fate that hangs over us all. And the existentialists might see it as an expression of man's ceaseless search for external escapes from his dread of the inevitability of death; no matter how our external conditions change, they are still largely an arena into which we project our dread, so one problem solved will merely be replaced by another, unless we can somehow solve the ultimate problem of death.

While such explanations might provide us with some insight into what we have observed and might prove quite morally satisfying to some of us, they do not provide us with any very systematic, detailed understanding. We have tried to show that this general experience of American society over the past century is simply one aspect of the whole realm of complex factors left out of consideration by the absolutist sociologies of social problems.

This added level of complexity consists of the subjective elements of social problems, the social meanings of social problems imputed by the members of society to external events. We have found that these meanings vary quite independently, though by no means entirely, from variations in what the members of society actually see to be the external events. It is what they make of the perceived events, the ideas they use to think about them, the criteria they use to judge them, the commonsense theories they use to analyze their causal relations, and the preconceived ideas they hold about the whole society and the prospects of human action to solve problems that become the crucial determinants of social problems and social solutions. The analysis of concrete communications about social problems and solutions by members of our pluralistic society then showed us how necessarily problematic these meanings of problems and solutions are. While they do share certain ideas, values, and feelings (meanings in general) that, in concert with common national experiences, can produce agreements about social problems and solutions, we also found that these agreements must normally be constructed by actors, especially by politicians, who are intentionally trying to produce such agreements about the definitions of social problems; and we found that there are certain factors, such as the mass media and compromise political strategies, that today are of crucial importance in these attempts to construct the meanings of social problems.

At the same time that we greatly increased the complexity of the analyses of social problems, this new complexity added a crucial realm of social reality whose existence before had been implicitly denied by the absolutist assumptions about the meanings of problems and solutions. We were now able to see things in the world which before were not supposed to exist or were supposed to be merely the confusions, doubts, uncertainties, and absurdities of commonsense thinking about social problems. By adding these complexities we transform our understanding of social problems in American society and give ourselves more realistic hope that sociology can fulfill its promise of providing objective knowledge about social problems that can be used by a conflict-torn society to find its own self-defined solutions to social problems, rather than providing a pseudoscience of social problems that can be used by bureaucratic experts to impose their "solutions" to problems through a technological tyranny.

The analysis of the social meanings of social problems in our pluralistic technological society leads us directly to certain general implications for all of our practical efforts to deal with our problems. First, the analysis of the meanings of social problems and of commonsense arguments over social problems today is an important contribution in itself, in that it offers the members of society a self-corrective means for reducing *some* of the elements of their arguments that, in terms of their commonsense views of rationality, they themselves would see as irrational. While the general semanticist's view of all the world's problems as direct outgrowths of linguistic (conceptual) mis-understandings is ridiculous, understanding the nature of our own conceptual analyses is sometimes of crucial importance in managing our social conflicts so as to avoid uses of force which we should see as unnecessary or unjustified if we understood the nature of the arguments better. There are many examples of this in our everyday lives, and there are many people who have been killed because someone misunderstood, or simply misheard, what they said. Moreover, while it may not convince the "true believers," Ernst Cassirer's analysis of the mythical, conceptual nature of the modern idea of the state in *The Myth of The State* will lead any man striving to be rational (in a commonsense manner) to seriously question any proposal of warfare for the glory of the nation or for anything else that presumes the existence of a transcendent but real state. Again, Sartre's analysis of the nature of the concepts of race in *Anti-Semite and Jew* may not eradicate racism in the world, but it provides a valuable corrective, in very commonsensical terms, for any social policy based on such ideas and shows some conceptual reasons why it is so difficult to change basic patterns of racial conflicts. Analyses of the social meanings of social problems promise even greater correctives for our practical efforts to deal with problems.

Understanding the necessarily problematic nature of social problems becomes in itself a partial corrective for absolutist approaches to social problems and the violence that often stems from such absolutism. It does not provide us with any magic means of making violent men change their paths, but it does tend to unmask the arguments of absolutism, as Peter Berger has argued sociology does in general. By revealing the assumptions lying behind their arguments and showing how independent they are of the external events, these analyses help us all to judge the rationality or irrationality of such appeals.

By unmasking such absolutist definitions of social problems and by showing the ways in which the basic pluralism of American society contributes to the development of problems, thus making compromise political strategies essential elements in defining them and determining policies aimed at solving them, our analysis leads us to see the importance of devising these new compromise strategies. It leads us to see that any solution we might propose to the members of our society will have a far greater chance of being accepted if it is in some way a compromise solution. It leads us to see the general necessity of using *incremental* (or piecemeal) *strategies* for dealing with problems, as opposed to using the more sweeping, *transformational strategies* that many structural analyses might have led us to prefer. (Structural approaches to problems of the sort proposed by C. Wright Mills commonly see problems as related to the social structure or the social system that functions as a whole, so that any solution to the problem would often be seen as depending on general structural changes.) Understanding the pluralistic moral meanings of social problems, such as those we have seen to be involved in the conflicts over poverty, also leads us to see the need to find compromise strategies for dealing with social problems that allow us to go around such moral differences as much as possible. We often find, for example, that the poor or their self-appointed spokesmen insist that "we must reorient all of our government policies toward ending all poverty in this country immediately—because that's the only moral thing we can do." Since various commonsense theories of man and society lead many millions of Americans, perhaps a majority, to consider the poor to be responsible for their own poverty, this kind of moralistic argument often does nothing more than generate moralistic counterarguments—"Get the poor off the welfare rolls and on the payrolls." Not only does our analysis of problems enable us to see the need to directly analyze the various common-sense theories that lie behind these conflicts, but it also leads us to see the value of taking a *social investment perspective* toward planning solutions. Rather than trying to force people to help the poor because it's their moral obligation to do so, we can emphasize what seems to be true, that investing in the education and general welfare of any group of people in our society will pay off many times more than investments made in them through future tax revenues and general social development.

In addition, our analysis has many fundamental implications for understanding the social problems that are peculiar to the technological society that is being created in the United States and disseminated throughout the world. Technology is created largely to solve the problems of our lives, yet the social problems in the technological society seem inevitably to become greater. This is probably due partly to the association of the technological society with certain human experiences that are closely related to our common physical form and therefore very apt to lead to the construction of consensus social problems. Massive pollution and atomic weapons that can only be developed by the technological society pose direct and indirect threats to our physical existence and well-being, so they tend to become fundamental social problems. Because the technological society lives by change and makes change a basic value, there are inevitably more dislocations that are not predictable to the average man and thereby threaten such things as the job on which he depends for his livelihood, so structural unemployment is apt to be a long-standing problem of the technological society. But in addition to these, there seem to be certain things about the technological society that lead to a commonly shared sense of increasing social problems that are largely independent of any directly or indirectly perceived threats to our physical being. The rapid change in itself seems difficult for men to accept as a normal condition of life, so there may indeed be some kind of "future shock" that comes from such change. This may be accentuated by the complex interdependencies of the technological society that transcend the understanding of the average man, increase his sense of the *problems of social order,* and, possibly, even create a fear that the whole complex thing simply can't work. This sense of the problems of complexities and the dread associated with it seems to be implicit in the widespread speculation today about how fragile is the web of urban living, how easily broken. This dread of our complex interdependencies, heightened by our feeling that we cannot trust other groups in such a pluralistic society to always do what is sensible for everyone's good, can be seen in Max Lerner's discussions of the effects of a small action like a police strike: "always there is the spectre of a city left unguarded against violence and death, abandoned by the very men who have sworn to be its guardians. In the end, there is the nightmare breakdown of order that happened in the police strike in Montreal . . . " [1] The technological society may free us from the problems most directly related to physical needs, but it thereby makes us free to worry about the problems created by itself.

Indeed, there is the distinct possibility that the general sense of the problematic nature of life may inevitably grow greater as the technological society develops. We have seen that social problems can grow simply because people change their criteria of satisfaction or of what constitutes a problem. For example, we now have many people who believe that our medical problems have become a disaster, not because medicine does not save more lives or decrease suffering, both of which it does vastly better than medicine or anything else ever did before, but simply because the very success of medicine has encouraged a change in our criteria of adequate medical care that leads us to see a growing problem of inadequate medical care. This may happen on a very general scale in the technological society both because of the underlying belief that life can be made better through progress, a belief important in producing the technological society in the first place, and because the "miracles" of technology encourage the belief that anything is possible if we will just devote ourselves to technology and if the selfish politicians will just devote the necessary funds for it. In addition, the consumer-based society that is so tied up with the development of our technological society and which seems to have gained a foothold even in such different, but increasingly technological, societies as the Soviet Union encourages the growth of desires and expectations independently of any common physical needs. But, once again, the sociological analysis of such developments may help either to stem them or to prevent their having disastrous consequences.

However great such contributions of the sociology of social problems to our practical efforts to deal with problems, they will not allow us to transcend all the limitations that may result from

---

[1] *Los Angeles Times* (January 24, 1971), Section F, p. 6.

the nature of commonsense thinking about problems, and they can make no promise of leading us to a brave new world in which all our basic social problems will be solved. On the contrary, our analysis leads us to expect that we shall always have social problems with us, with new ones replacing those that are defined as solved. All we can hope to do with scientific analyses of society is provide progressively objective understandings of the meanings of social problems and of the social situations in which they arise and, hopefully, progressively rational implications for practical action drawn in part from those analyses. Our science lends no support to those who prophecy technological bliss or who propose to be sociological kings or technocrats. On the contrary, it makes us see the dangers of technological tyranny that lie in all such promises and desires.

There are no panaceas and few certainties in our understandings of social problems. Ultimately, our success in handling social problems, and our very existence, depends on the practical wisdom we bring to the political arena in which we must forge our common destiny. Reason and science are powerful allies on the side of everyone in these struggles and I believe they are necessary allies if we are to avoid catastrophies in the technological society. But they provide no miracles and no magic solutions. We still must create our way as we go, facing the vast uncertainties common to all men's lives, but borne on by the hope that we, like most men before us, can find our way.

Index